ERASMUS AND HIS AGE

ERASMUS AND HIS AGE

Selected Letters of Desiderius Erasmus

Edited by
Hans J. Hillerbrand

Translated by
Marcus A. Haworth, S.J.

HARPER TORCHBOOKS ⸸
Harper & Row, Publishers
New York, Evanston, and London

First HARPER TORCHBOOK edition published 1970

LIBRARY OF CONGRESS CATALOG CARD NUMBER: 71-119064

CONTENTS

ACKNOWLEDGMENTS

To record here my indebtedness to the Allen edition of Erasmus' letters is to say that without its rich and detailed annotations this collection would not have been possible. Of that great work more will be said in the Introduction.

I am grateful to Professor Roland H. Bainton, of Yale University, and to Professor Ernest W. Nelson, of Duke University, for reading the manuscript. It is surely better for their many helpful suggestions, especially with regard to letters worthy of inclusion. I should like to think that Erasmus would have approved of the project—and possibly even the selections. A word of appreciation is also in order to Professor Marcus A. Haworth, S.J., St. Louis University. His translation succeeds admirably in bridging the gap between the sixteenth and twentieth centuries. I have confined myself to only a few alterations of his translation. A few of the letters I translated myself. Annabelle Learned served as an uncommonly competent and conscientious copyeditor, Mr. Tom Emswiller as an eagle-eyed proofreader. Professor Haworth and I stand in their debt.

I should like to dedicate this little volume to my son Stephan, suggesting thereby that the wisdom of these letters transcends the time of their writing.

H.J.H.

TRANSLATOR'S PREFACE

Erasmus knew well the perils of a translator. In his early attempts at translating Greek verse into Latin he was rather rigid, but he gradually adopted a freer approach, though always aiming at fidelity to the original. Later, when doing a Latin version of Scripture, he complained: "In a translation it is impossible to express more than one meaning" (EE 2807.39–40). For that very reason it is no little challenge to render into English the elegance and subtle charm, the irony and wit of Erasmus' own Latin style. I have attempted to produce a readable translation without sacrificing fidelity. The result is admittedly uneven. But in any case it has been great fun doing this work. Putting into modern English garb the sly and caustic remarks aimed at his own contemporaries, but which also have a relevance for modern society and the modern Church, has been, incidentally, a very enlightening experience for me.

It has also been a pleasure to collaborate on this edition with Professor Hans J. Hillerbrand, a recognized scholar in the field of sixteenth-century church history. He has selected the letters to be translated, edited them, and done the editorial comments.

In the fall term of 1965 a group of eleven graduate students at Saint Louis University gave me considerable assistance by doing rough drafts of about three-quarters of the letters here translated. In fulfillment of the promise then made, I here express my sincere thanks to the following: Carol Bodlovic Nisbet, James H. Ebbesmeyer, Richard J. Hebein, Robert K. McIntosh, S.J., Leonard A. Martin, S.J., Thomas J. Melancon, S.J., Theo C. Smid, William J. Sneck, S.J., John J. Wiesner, S.J., Thomas J. Wiesner, and Sister M. Richelle Williams, S.S.N.D.

I also wish to express my gratitude to the St. Thomas More Project at Yale University and the Yale University Press for permission to use the following translations which I had done originally for the Project: EE 222.1–78; 412.1–2, 22–31; 785.21–36; 1162.12–84, 134–170. I am likewise grateful to Miss Rosemary A. Boylan and Miss Jane S. Koch for their care in typing the final copy of the translations—and for their delightful remarks about the personality of Erasmus.

MARCUS A. HAWORTH, S.J.

Saint Louis University

"I send you, therefore, an abridgment of my whole life. It is an Iliad of woes, for nothing was ever created more unfortunate than I. But perhaps some will feign even more ills."

Erasmus to Conrad Goclen
April 2, 1524

INTRODUCTION

Erasmus of Rotterdam, the great humanist, was a most prolific correspondent, a fact to which the 3,141 letters found in the eleven volumes of the *Erasmi Epistolae*[1] bear vivid testimony. He himself must have been quite aware of his immense epistolary output: "I have written and am still writing so many letters that two carts would hardly be able to hold them," he noted on one occasion, while in the Preface to his *Opus Epistolarum* he remarked that for none of his lucubrations did he care less than for his letters.[2] In terms of sheer volume his correspondence constitutes a formidable part of his literary corpus, and one wonders how he found time to engage so extensively in letter writing, especially since most of his letters were composed with considerable care. For reconstructing Erasmus' life, these letters, especially the early ones, are of singular importance. At the same time, they present random reflections on the time and

1. The reference is to P. S. Allen, H. M. Allen, H. W. Garrod, eds., *Opus Epistolarum Des. Erasmi Roterodami,* 12 vols. (Oxford, 1906–1958). Hereafter quoted either as *Allen* or EE. A splendid introduction to the epistolary tradition in the sixteenth century is found in *Thomas More: Neue Briefe. Mit einer Einführung in die epistolagraphische Tradition* (Münster, 1966).
2. Allen, I, 36–37; VIII, 249.

comment on politics and the arts no less than on religion. His letters thus form an indispensable source both for his life and for his time. Collectively they may well constitute one of the most important documents of the sixteenth century. None other than J. A. Froude remarked in his book on Erasmus that to understand the sixteenth century one should look at it "through the eyes of Erasmus."[3]

Any study of the Erasmian epistolary corpus must recognize that the term "letter," as employed here, refers to several different categories of communication. Some letters are actually prefatory dedications and statements that accompanied Erasmus' various publications, both his own and his editions of the writings of others. These prefatory letters, in the form of communications to friends, acquaintances, and benefactors, contain Erasmus' reflections on the work or the author at hand. They are brief scholarly essays or treatises, and only occasionally are there personal comments that shed some light on Erasmus' thought and movements. The use of the term letter is appropriate only on account of the epistolary form in which they are clad and Erasmus' own wish that they be included among his letters.

A second type of letter consists of actual communications to associates or acquaintances. They deal with a variety of concerns: they offer comments on the contemporary scene and on eminent figures, discuss a scholarly question, or make inquiries about scholarly matters. This is Erasmus' "professional correspondence," the kind inevitable in the case of public figures and scholars. We need to remember that, despite a very lively scholarly activity, no formal medium of discussion and exchange among scholars was then available. In a way, private correspondence had to perform the function of modern scholarly journals. Erasmus used his letters for such a purpose on numerous occasions. Exchange of ideas by way of correspondence was virtually the only method by which the European community of scholars could keep in scholarly contact.

A final group of letters comprises communications to close friends. These contain Erasmus' personal reflections, information about his activities and thoughts. More than either the first or the second group

3. J. A. Froude, *Life and Letters of Erasmus* (New York, 1912), 420.

of letters, they are personal statements, at times revealing, but mostly strangely guarded; Erasmus always seemed to write as if someone were looking over his shoulder. As a rule he saw his letters as elegant exercises and not as penetrating historical sources. It is surely telling that he provided for the publication of some of them during his lifetime and, in so doing, carefully selected those he thought proper for public consumption. "Not everything that is written is intended to be given to the world."[4] One suspects that he never fully freed himself from the fear that someone might get hold of his letters and thereby learn his innermost thoughts. Writing to Beatus Rhenanus, he expressed the hope that the publication of certain letters would "do as little harm" to his name as possible,[5] noting at the same time that changes made by the printer might be costly—but would prove an advantage if he could maintain his honor.[6]

The irony of the matter is that even though Erasmus sought not to show his innermost being, his letters reveal much about him. His very hesitation to speak discloses a characteristic side of his personality, and thus his letters (both those whose publication he approved and those he meant to keep from the eyes of the public) do draw aside the veil after all. Johan Huizinga's splendid psychological portrait of him would be nothing without the letters.[7]

What manner of man stood behind this correspondence? Erasmus' birth year is uncertain. Probably it was 1469, though it may have been 1466; the enigma seems characteristic of the mystery surrounding the great humanist.[8] Erasmus suffered as the illegitimate child of a cleric, but during his youth enjoyed the blessing of the *Devotio moderna,* the lay movement of The Netherlands concerned about the

4. Allen, IX, 287. One must note that Erasmus was not the only one who published his letters; Budé, Sadoleto, or Bembo might also be mentioned.

5. Allen, IV, 500.

6. Note here Erasmus' own frank statement, Allen, IV, 501.

7. An early study of Erasmus based on his letters is by John Hortin, *Life of Erasmus,* 2 vols. (London, 1758–1762).

8. See here the note by F. M. Nichols, ed., in *The Epistles of Erasmus* (London, 1904), I, 474, as well as the lengthy essay by E.-W. Kohls, "Das Geburtsjahr des Erasmus," *Theologische Zeitschr.* 22 (1966), together with the rejoinder by R. R. Post, "Nochmals Erasmus' Geburtsjahr," and Kohls's response, "Noch einmal das Geburtsjahr des Erasmus," in the same volume of that journal.

devoted exercise of spirituality. He tried his best to forget the former and always remained indebted to the latter. His intellectual prowess early caught the attention of his elders and he received unusually thorough schooling with the Brethren of the Common Life, who at the same time exposed him to their world of spiritual Christianity. In 1488 he entered the Augustinian monastery at Steyn, an action he lived to regret. He was ordained to the priesthood in 1492, but in the following year received permission to leave the monastery in order to accompany the Bishop of Cambrai to Rome. As matters turned out, the Bishop never reached the Eternal City, and Erasmus never returned to the monastery. He studied at Paris, where he came into contact with a young English nobleman, Lord Mountjoy, whom he subsequently accompanied to England. There he met Thomas More and John Colet, the eminent English humanists, who exerted a lasting influence on him. He encountered the Neoplatonism of his English friends, which in turn had been nurtured by the thought of Pico della Mirandola: here was a harmonious system that sought to give its due to both biblical religion and classical antiquity, with a view to delineating the cosmic stature of man.

This world of thought produced in Erasmus a deepened (and different) appreciation of religion. This is not to say, as has sometimes been suggested, that prior to his first English sojourn Erasmus was not concerned about religion, for indeed he was. But his encounter with Colet and More precipitated a more comprehensive understanding. "I cannot tell you with what eagerness I turned to the study of sacred letters, so that I consider everything a nuisance which keeps me from them."[9] The first literary outgrowth of this new concern was his famous "Handbook of the Christian Soldier," the *Enchiridion militis Christiani*. Thomas More had also persuaded him of the importance of the Greek language. Upon his return to the Continent he commenced the study of it, a difficult undertaking, for he did not have funds for either books or a tutor. Still, the publication of the *Adagia*, a collection of Greek and Roman proverbs, in 1501 demonstrated his new linguistic accomplishment.

Afterward came an impressive literary production: "The Praise of Folly," the "Colloquies," the "Complaint of Peace," as well as a host

9. Allen, I, 181.

of editions—beginning with the Greek New Testament (together with Erasmus' own Latin translation) in 1516, followed even that same year by an edition of Jerome; afterward came Cyprian (1519), Arnobius (1522), Hilary (1523), Irenaeus (1526), Ambrose (1527), Augustine (1529), Chrysostom (1530)—and finally, in the year of his death, Origen. In addition, Erasmus edited the writings of classical authors—Cicero (1520), Seneca (1515), Suetonius (1518), Ptolemy (1533), to name but a few.[10] Then there was a work not strictly an edition, the *Paraphraseon* of the New Testament, a commentary or "paraphrase" of the biblical text. This project occupied him for almost a full decade and may well be called one of the most significant efforts from his pen.[11]

These publications, their erudition and insight, established Erasmus as a figure of European renown. Honors were showered upon him, and various stipends improved his economic situation. He was friend of kings and popes, of statesmen and scholars. His opinion was sought, his friendship coveted, his insights admired. And he was moved by this universal expression of esteem—not only because of what it said about him, but also because it supported his program, that of a humanist revival of true learning. Though by temperament pessimistic and suspicious, he gloried in the anticipation of the future. A golden age appeared about to be ushered in.

It did not come. Quite the contrary, turbulence cast a shadow over the last years of Erasmus' life. A new name, that of Martin Luther, appeared on the horizon, and a new program of reform began to dominate the scene. For a while it seemed as if Erasmus had found a comrade in arms in his quest for the restoration of true spirituality. But then he discovered what he thought to be the true nature of Luther's program and resolutely divorced himself from it. He refrained from taking an open stand for several years, though there was no dearth of encouragement to do so from the sidelines. When he finally did, in 1524, with the publication of his "Diatribe on Free Will," he precipitated a vehement theological controversy with

10. Erasmus' own list of his writings is found in a letter to Hector Boece, Allen, I, 35 ff. A convenient list also occurs in P. S. Allen, *Erasmus* (Oxford, 1934), xi.

11. R. Padberg, *Personaler Humanismus* (Paderborn, 1964), 78; see also R. H. Bainton, "The Paraphrases of Erasmus," *Archiv. f. Reformationsgeschichte* 57 (1966).

Luther and at the same time brought about the return of many humanists to the Catholic fold. But despite this clash, he remained too liberal for most Catholics, who continued to be suspicious of his profession of orthodoxy. He stood between the two ecclesiastical factions—despised by most Protestants and condemned by many Catholics. "I am a heretic to both sides," he remarked astutely.[12]

In 1521, after years of peripatetic wandering, Erasmus settled in Basel; but when that city became Protestant toward the end of the decade, he chose to leave for Catholic Freiburg, less than a hundred miles to the north. There he continued to pursue his scholarly studies, edited the writings of several Church Fathers, and published several tracts, such as "The Proper Pronunciation of Latin and Greek" (1528), "On Restoring Concord in the Church" (1533), and the *Ecclesiastes* (1535). The latter was a handbook on how to preach: to the end of his life Erasmus believed in man's educability (even preachers').

In 1535 he returned to Basel on the invitation of his publisher, Froben. To be sure, the city was still Protestant, but the sharpness of the initial period of storm and stress was gone. Yet to live there was for him not exactly a pleasant experience. The ecclesiastical statues had been destroyed, the images burned, the Mass abolished, and the authority of the pope repudiated. He found comfort in his studies. Death came to him on July 12, 1536, and he who during a long and prolific career had written only in Latin spoke his last words in his native Dutch: "Lieve God"—"Dear God." Erasmus found his final resting place in the Basel Minster, his epitaph graced by a picture of the pagan god Terminus,[13] symbolic of the dual concerns he had pursued in his lifetime: Christianity and classical antiquity.

Erasmus' had been a scholar's life, not without its own modest excitement, but unmarked by any kind of dramatic involvement in the larger affairs of man—as characterized, for example, the life of his friend Thomas More. And yet this scholar-humanist was one of the great men of the sixteenth century, indeed of Western civilization. Had he done nothing more than make available the works of

12. As quoted in M. Mann Phillips, *Erasmus and the Northern Renaissance* (London, 1949), 186.
13. See Letter 2018, p. 215.

the sages of the past, his name would be worthy of honor. Erasmus did not have an antiquarian's concern in his voluminous editorial work. He meant to direct his contemporaries to the "sources," of both classical and Christian antiquity, for he was persuaded that these were indispensable for the proper understanding of man and the world. His editions were part of his concern for reform. This was what mattered: he propounded a program of intellectual and spiritual renewal. One may think of him in many ways—as writer of graceful Latin prose, as skillful social observer and critic, as a pedagogue of shrewd insights. Yet his real significance surely lies in his broader program: the attainment of true humanity. Since he did not find such humanity in the attitudes of his time, he became a reformer; since he believed it to be most eminently expressed in true religion, he became a theologian.

He saw no real differences between the best of antiquity and authentic Christianity, since he found the notions of Scripture echoed in the best of classical antiquity. The goal, as noted above, was the achievement of true humanity (*humanitas*)—not in a shallow, moralistic sense, but in the sense of realizing man's divinely envisioned stature. Scholars have had differing opinions as to whether Erasmus thought the truth of classical antiquity and of revealed religion one and the same.[14] One may surely say that he did not consider the two incompatible. The uniqueness of Jesus of Nazareth did not for him obscure the insights of the wisest of the pagan sages. Accordingly, he was able in his "Colloquies" not only to exclaim "Holy Socrates, pray for us!" but could also write that "perhaps the spirit of Christ is poured out further than we are accustomed to interpret."[15] He was able to suggest that the classical dualism of body and spirit corresponds to the biblical tension between the "old" and the "new" Adam, and to note that the classical concept of "reason" applies to the scriptural notion of the "spirit."

Erasmus was much concerned about man's own involvement in this quest for authentic humanity. "We must imitate Prometheus,

---

14. See the brief survey of G. Kisch, *Erasmus und die Jurisprudenz seiner Zeit* (Basel, 1960), 457–461.

15. *Erasmi Opera Omnia emendatiora et auctiora* (Lugduni-Batavorum, 1703), I, 682 A, as quoted in R. Pfeiffer, *Humanitas Erasmiana* (Leipzig, 1931), 8.

who dared to seek life for his earthen object from the stars, but only after having done everything that he humanly could."[16] True humanity was the only way to true divinity—and it could only be achieved if man effectively made use of his human potential. Toward the end of his tract on free will, Erasmus used the illustration of the little child who desires an apple. Though it is the child's father who points out the apple and takes him by the hand, the child himself must strive, walk, and do his share. In similar vein, man must strive to exercise the noblest and the best in himself.

All this left little room for a doctrinally oriented understanding of the Christian faith. Accordingly, Erasmus' notion of the Christian religion was simple: he espoused a moral precept propounded by Jesus and cared little about details of dogma beyond certain basic affirmations, as for example those of the Apostles' Creed. The controversy engendered by the Protestant reformers was distasteful to him. Metaphysical speculation, such as the scholastics undertook ad infinitum et nauseam, had little to do with authentic "humanity" and the true *philosophia Christi*. The improvement of life was more important than doctrine, morality more than subtlety of theology. As long as the Protestant reformers appeared to reflect this goal, Erasmus was in sympathy with them, though from the very beginning of the controversy he expressed his disgust over the *tumultus* that ensued. True learning was bound to be disrupted by this uproar: "If only this unprofitable quarrel about dogmas had not disturbed tranquillity," he wrote about the Reformation.[17]

Many of his contemporaries denounced his point of view, none more vehemently than Martin Luther, who was persuaded that Erasmus was "an enemy of all religion and especially an enemy and opponent of Christ . . . a perfect picture and image of Epicurus and Lucian." And in a mood not quite so vehement he compared himself with Erasmus: "Verba sine re: Erasmus; res sine verbis: Lutherus" ("Words without substance: Erasmus; substance without words: Luther"). Posterity, while rarely echoing Luther's drastic pronouncement, has generally cited Erasmus' weaknesses and shortcomings, especially with regard to his religious orientation: for

16. *Erasmi Opera*, X, 1742 B.
17. See the many references cited in K. H. Oelrich, *Der späte Erasmus und die Reformation* (Münster, 1961), 53 ff.

Catholics he was not orthodox enough, while for Protestants he seemed not sufficiently serious about religion. Above all, however, he has been chided for his effort to stand between (or, rather, above) the religious factions.[18] Johan Huizinga called his "refusal or inability ever to draw ultimate conclusions" a "tragic defeat."[19]

What shall one say? It is true that though he remained Catholic, Erasmus did not take sides in the ecclesiastical controversy. He followed his own path, for he was persuaded that both factions indulged in false emphases, stressing esoteric points of theology rather than fundamentals. Since he abhorred turbulence and strife he preferred to stay with the Catholic Church, at least, as he told Luther, until he had found something better. Not that he did not find fault with it. There was much he wanted changed: theology should not be scholastic, but simple; ceremonies should be considered nonessential; the clergy should be allowed to marry; rules and regulations should be eased. But he was willing to wait and be patient, trusting in education, in the increasing enlightenment of man and the gradual dispelling thereby of darkness and ignorance.

There may well have been a bit of cowardice in Erasmus' refusal to take sides in the great religious controversy that swept Europe—perhaps even an excessive concern for his own health and well-being, for his "poor little body" as he often called it. Numerous letters testify to his chronic desire not to be misunderstood, or to set the record straight. In the last analysis, however, this was a disposition which flowed, as Margaret Mann Phillips has aptly noted, from the very heart of his ecclesiastical program. Erasmus was persuaded that this program could only be realized through tranquillity, and accordingly his charge against Luther was that his writings seemed to produce turmoil.[20] Such perturbation, no matter how profoundly oriented, was bound to lead to decline and decay.

The learned members of society thus carried a special responsibility, since to them was entrusted the charge to bring about that connection between the *bonae litterae* and the *sacrae litterae* to which

18. See, for example, the essay by H. Bornkamm, "Erasmus und Luther," *Luther-Jahrbuch* 25 (1958), 3 ff.

19. J. Huizinga, *Erasmus and the Age of Reformation* (New York, 1957), 147.

20. Allen, IV, 391.

Erasmus aspired. As far as he was concerned, the solution of Luther's controversy was to be found "through books among learned men."[21] Perhaps his major weakness was not his unwillingness or inability to take sides, but a view of life and man which made him overlook the fact that some men (in the sixteenth century at least) held to their religion with zeal. Erasmus was an aesthete of the mind, an intellectual, an academician. He went about his program of renewal on the basis of such assumptions, disregarding the elementary emotions engendered by the religious controversy. It was natural that he should ponder the question of "who had contributed more to our religion—the blood of martyrs or the pens of learned men."[22] And even though he did not choose to provide an answer, the direction of his thinking seems clear enough.

Personally, he was profoundly grieved by the Reformation controversy and on a number of occasions stated that he would willingly give his life to allay the dissension. But this is more the desperate expression of his desire to restore peace and tranquillity than a seasoned reflection on the real solution, which had to come through the pen, through the proper study of the sacred and human letters, through *sancta eruditio* (holy studies).

Erasmus called himself *Roterodamus*, "of Rotterdam," but in actuality he was a man of the world—"of Christendom," as the title of Roland Bainton's recent biography has aptly put it. His home was nowhere and yet everywhere: his very horse was said to have seen more European universities than most academics. He moved restlessly from place to place, from country to country, from university to university. Still, his peregrinations were never without their clear purpose. His life was a persistent and dogged pursuit of a comprehensive program of intellectual and spiritual reform and renewal. Though the Protestant Reformation—and the Catholic reaction to it—dominated the sixteenth century, there can be little doubt of Erasmus' influence. It extended far and wide: it was found among those who aspired to the restoration of classical antiquity, who despaired of the bitter and violent strife over theological doctrines that divided brother from brother, son from parent. It also was found

21. Allen, IV, 46.
22. *Erasmi Opera*, X, 1724 F.

among those who believed in man, his divine glory, his educability. Those who in subsequent centuries share these notions deserve to be called Erasmus' disciples. In our time, no less than in his own, he has many.

Erasmus took a special interest in his letters. Indeed, one might suggest that he was generally concerned about the art of letter writing, as his tract "On How to Write Letters" (*De Conscribendis Epistolis*) tellingly indicated. The earliest were mainly exercises in grace and skill of composition and showed him greatly concerned with improving his style.[23] In the preface to the edition of his letters published in 1521, itself in the form of a letter to Beatus Rhenanus, the humanist, he noted the pains he had taken to improve his epistolary skill and concluded with the mild understatement: "As a letter writer I may possibly appear not completely incompetent."[24] Erasmus soon became aware of the importance of his correspondence and sought to make sure that his letters were carefully collected and preserved.[25] In 1515 a modest collection of letters was published, of which one of the most important was a letter to Pope Leo X.[26] Within a year followed a somewhat larger collection under the title *Epistolae aliquot illustrium virorum ad Erasmum et huius ad illos*.[27] As the title indicates, the letters were to and from eminent personages—for example, Pope Leo X and Henry VIII; they had all been written within the preceding two years. Another collection of letters appeared at Louvain in 1517 and was reprinted the following year in Basel by Froben, who, also in 1518, brought out a larger collection, edited by Beatus Rhenanus.[28] A still more extensive collection of letters was published by Froben in 1519, and another in 1521.[29] This last edition included Erasmus' lengthy letter to Rhe-

23. Nichols, I, xix.
24. Allen, IV, 500. Note also the comment in Allen, IV, 499.
25. There is a question of authenticity, discussed by Nichols, I, xlvi.
26. *Erasmi Rot. Epistola ad Leonem X* (Basel: Froben, 1525).
27. Louvain: Theod. Martinus, 1516.
28. *Aliquot Epistolae Sane quam elegantes Erasmi Roterodami et ad hunc aliorium* . . . (Louvain: Theod. Martinus, 1517), and *Auctarium Selectarum aliquot Epistolarum Erasmi Rot. ad eruditos et eorum ad illum* (Basel, 1518).
29. *Farrago nova epistolarum Des. Erasmi Roterodami; Epistolae D. Erasmi Roterodami ad diversos.*

nanus, which commented on the nature of letters and expressed his hesitation over the publication of his own. The next major edition came in 1529, with the *Opus Epistolarum Des. Erasmi Roterodami*.[30] This was the most extensive collection up to that time, noteworthy for the insertion of dates and places in letters that in earlier editions had appeared without such information.

Of several editions of letters after Erasmus' lifetime three must be noted: the so-called London edition, published in 1642 under the title *Epistolarum B. Erasmi Roterodami libri xxxi*,[31] the famous *Opera Omnia* published by Le Clerc in 1703, which included in its third volume the Erasmian correspondence; and the definitive modern edition. In contrast to previous arrangements, Le Clerc's is chronological, though the absence of dates on many of Erasmus' letters, especially the earlier ones, made this a precarious undertaking. Accordingly, the editor had to establish two appendixes: "letters which could not be arranged in their proper place"[32] (mainly letters from the years 1514–1518 not previously published and found in a manuscript in the Library of Deventer) and a special category for several undated letters, arranged alphabetically according to the names of the correspondents.

The modern scholarly publication of Erasmus' letters is a monument to painstaking and competent scholarship. It comprises eleven volumes and was the result of the dedication of one man: Percy Stafford Allen, who began his work in 1893 at the age of twenty-four and continued it until his death in 1933, always greatly aided by his wife.[33] Allen was *vir unius libri*, a man of one book: the Erasmian correspondence, over which he labored for forty years. The first volume of the *Erasmi Epistolae* was published in 1906, and by the time of Allen's death the number of published volumes had increased to seven. Four more volumes of letters, together with an index volume, were to complete the edition. Alongside this scholarly edition of Erasmus' correspondence, F. M. Nichols' English translation of select early letters must be noted. This appeared in three volumes

30. Basel: Froben, 1529.
31. The edition also contained letters of Melanchthon, Thomas More, and Ludovicus Vives.
32. "Appendix epistolarum quae loco suo reponi non potuerunt."
33. A biographical appreciation (in Latin) is included in Allen, VIII, v–xx.

(the last published posthumously) and had as its primary purpose "to enable English readers of every country to follow the author through the earlier years of his life."[34]

The fact that a large number of Erasmus' letters were published during his lifetime is of great significance for establishing their authenticity. Only letters not then published—and this means primarily those written before 1515—stand in need of verification. Needless to say, the actual publication of certain letters during Erasmus' lifetime does not mean that their published version corresponds to the form in which they were originally composed. Editorial changes made by the author are manifest throughout.[35]

The proper chronological arrangement of the letters is not easy. Those that come from the first three decades of his life are undated. And even after Erasmus began to supply a date together with a place, he did not indicate the year; probably he did not begin to add the year until 1515.[36] The Allen edition provides chronological identifications throughout. They have been used in the present collection, although they have, in certain instances, been challenged.[37]

As far as the present edition is concerned, the enormous quantity of Erasmus' correspondence and the obvious necessity of a rigorous process of selection meant the choice of either printing a few letters in their entirety or offering pertinent sections of a greater number. Either alternative entailed both advantages and disadvantages. In the first instance it meant the reproduction of the entire train of thought with its various changes of subject (important because for Erasmus

34. Nichols, I, v.

35. Note here, for example, Erasmus' own comment, Allen, IV, 499, "Farraginem recognovi, quaedam expunxi quibus animadverteram quorundam offensos animos, nimui profecto teneros atque irritabiles; quaedam mitiora reddidi" ("I have revised the *Farrago* [an earlier edition of letters], deleted some passages by which the tender and irritable minds of some had been offended, and softened the meaning of others").

36. Nichols, I, lxvi. A minor complication consists in the matter of the actual beginning of a new year, since January 1 was then not universally accepted. Accordingly, some dates in the present collection reflect this uncertainty by noting both years.

37. Note, for example, the demurrer of V. de Caprareis, "Per la datazione dei due Lettere di Erasmo," *Rivista Storica Italiana* 64 (1952), 222 ff. He suggests that the dates of EE 30 and 37, as supplied by Allen, should be reversed.

letters were works of art), though the restriction to very few selections. In the second instance, it meant the risk of short snippets, with a much wider purview. For better or worse, the decision was made in favor of the latter. Omissions from the original, where noted, are signaled in the usual manner. However, to avoid a wearisome recurrence of ellipsis dots, the address and sometimes material from the opening or closing of a letter are omitted without indication, as also occasionally at the beginnings of paragraphs.

The letters were selected with a view to acquainting the reader with the many facets of Erasmus' personality: scholar, humanist, theologian, friend, and person. They show him commenting on friend and foe, writing letters of recommendation, complaining about his ill health, reflecting on the state of learning and religion. Erasmus analyzes, complains, prophesies, rejoices. Since the last two decades of his life were overshadowed by Luther and the Protestant Reformation, it is natural that these themes come to the fore again and again. The order is chronological, with two exceptions: at the beginning are an autobiographical letter and another one containing reflections on letter writing.

The brief bibliography included in this volume is to direct the interested reader to pertinent Erasmus literature.

H. J. HILLERBRAND

Duke University

ERASMUS ON LETTER WRITING

TO BEATUS RHENANUS[1]

EE 1206 (86–141)   Louvain, May 27, 1520

As a writer of letters I may perhaps seem not particularly inept.
But many things have deterred me from that kind of writing. In the
first place, if letters lack feeling and do not represent a man's real life,
they do not deserve to be so called, as, for example, the letters of
Seneca to Lucilius, or those of Plato. And among the letters of
Cyprian, Basil, Jerome, and Augustine, evidently in imitation of the
apostles, there are few which should properly be called books rather
than letters. And again, the letters left in the name of Brutus,
Phalaris, and Seneca can hardly be regarded as anything but declamations. Real letters, on the other hand, which represent as in a
picture the character, fate, and feelings of the writer and reveal at
the same time the general and particular conditions of the time, such
as the letters of Cicero and Pliny, or among recent writers those of

1. On Rhenanus, see letter 3135, p. 289.

Aeneas Pius,[2] entail considerably more danger than writing recent history. . . .

Therefore, if anything of this sort is to be published, I would not want anyone to do it in his own lifetime, but to entrust it to a Tiro, who is said to have shown more zeal than judgment in editing his master's memoirs. Whether you praise or blame a particular person, you cannot avoid giving offense. Moreover, there are people who cannot bear to be praised in books, either because they disdain to be mentioned by anyone who so chooses or because they fear to be suspected of having succumbed to flattery. In light of this, I am greatly surprised that St. Bernard should have published his letters, in which there are so many names marked in ink. Today, if anyone mentions a Dominican or a Carmelite monk without a lengthy and flattering preface, even with the name suppressed, it is thought to be a capital crime. There is also the complication that, as the state of human affairs is rather changeable, our greatest friends sometimes turn into our greatest enemies, and vice versa, so that one may regret both the praise bestowed on the one and the disparagement cast on the other. Finally, the reputation of the writer is likely to suffer because most people evaluate the character of a man from a single letter—and sometimes we write after drinking a glass of wine, sometimes when we are sleepy, occasionally when we are worn out or even sick or while our mind is on some other matter, sometimes when we are not in the best of humor. Frequently we adapt our words to the level and judgment of the person to whom we are writing. No wonder then that an inexperienced person may suspect us of inconsistency, when the differences he observes are to be attributed to variations in age and of feeling, to differences among recipients and of circumstances.

Such reasons might well deter any other person, however distinguished, from publishing his letters. In my own case something in particular dissuaded me from such a course. My fate has not always been humble, but has constantly remained depressed. The style of my life has not been such that I would be able to avoid any sort of accusation—nor would I want to do so. There is no reason, therefore,

2. Aeneas Sylvius Piccolomini, subsequently Pope Pius II (1458–1464), a widely read and learned man inspired by Italian humanism. His voluminous writings, poems, reports, and letters afford a detailed view of his personality.

for me to wish that traces of these should be preserved. The same argument might even affect those to whom we write, since they would not want the gossip, confided in a letter to a friend, betrayed to everybody; and after all, there are those persons who, born under the curse of the Graces, place an evil meaning on everything. It happens again and again that a word, which uttered at dinner or among friends has its own charm, gives rise to stark tragedy when repeated out of context.

I.
Youth and
Apprenticeship:
1486–1495

The letters from this period are mainly stylistic exercises from a time when Erasmus, through personal experience, studies, and first writings, began to lay the foundation for his subsequent scholarly activities.

TO LAMBERTUS GRUNNIUS[1]

EE 447 (69–73; 78–120;
249–286; 325–344; 351–
387; 448–479; 486–501;
536–544; 553–579; 613–
620; 660–679)[2]

[London, August 1516]

1. This letter accompanied Erasmus' appeal to the Roman curia, probably in 1516. The case described is his own and thus affords an excellent biographical introduction to his early life. The appeal had to do with permission to wear secular dress and, despite his illegitimate birth, to receive ecclesiastical benefices. The name Grunnius may be fictitious.

2. These references refer in each instance to the number of the letter in the Allen edition. The numbers in parentheses refer to the linear designation of the letters in that same edition.

There are two brothers, Florence and—the older of the two—
Anthony. In early boyhood they lost their mother. Their father, who
died some time later, left them a very small inheritance. It would
have been enough for them to finish their studies, had it not been
diminished by the greed of relatives who were present at their
father's deathbed. Of the ready cash not a single penny was ever
found. . . .

Their guardians made up their minds to have the boys educated in
a monastery, thinking it was an extraordinary act of devotion to look
out for the boys' livelihood. They were encouraged in this inclination
by a certain guardian of a Franciscan house, a haughty man with a
great reputation for piety, who in this matter had particular influence
on the guardian of the boys, who had been their elementary teacher.
Now this man was commonly regarded as pious and good, in the
sense that he had not developed a bad reputation by gambling,
wenching, living extravagantly, drinking, or by any other vice. He
was a man who lived for himself, in an extremely frugal manner; his
sense of judgment was no better than that of the common folk. The
only learning of which he approved was the disorganized bit of
knowledge which he himself had acquired. For instance, at thirteen
years of age Florence wrote him a polished letter. In reply, he was
sternly told if he were to send such a letter again to add a commentary; his own manner of writing, the fellow explained, had always
been clear and "to the point"—that was the exact phrase he used. He
apparently had the conviction, like many others I have known, that
he was offering to God a most pleasing victim whenever he dedicated
one of his students to the monastic life. He often boasted about the
number of young men he gained each year for Francis or Dominic or
Benedict or Augustine or Bridget.

When the boys were ready to attend a university, they were well
enough grounded in grammar and had learned, for the most part, the
dialectic of Peter of Spain.[3] Even so, this guardian of theirs was
afraid they would imbibe something of the spirit of the world and
would refuse to submit to the yoke; therefore he arranged to have
them sent to a boarding school conducted by the Brethren of the
Common Life,[4] who are building their nests all over the world and

3. Author of many works on logic, later Pope John XXI (d. 1277).
4. Actually *Fratres Collationarii*, a reference to the emphasis on the part of
the Brethren on *collationes*, or "addresses."

making a business out of training boys. Their prime objective is this: if they observe a lad with a generous and enthusiastic disposition—and such lads are usually highly intelligent—they employ blows and threats, harsh words and various other tactics to break and subdue their spirit—they call it "taming"—and thus to mold it for the monastic life. For this reason they are naturally very much loved by the Dominicans and Franciscans, who maintain that their orders would quickly die out were it not for the nurseries run by these men. Those are the reserves from which they draw their recruits. Some of these fellows are not at all bad. But they suffer from a lack of excellent advisers and they live in the dark shadows of their own lives amid their own practices and rituals. They never compare themselves with others, only with themselves, and they are forced to spend a good part of the day in the performance of prayers and duties to which they are assigned. Consequently I do not see how they could give boys a liberal education. At any rate, the facts speak for themselves: no other schools produce young men with such a boorish education and of such inferior character.

So the brothers wasted two years or more under such teachers. It was certainly a waste of time for the younger one, since he had more learning than his teachers, at least in those subjects which they professed to teach. . . .

Meantime that stupid guardian was determined to accomplish his design; in order to bring the play to its final scene, he produced a variety of characters with different backgrounds—both men and women, monks and half-monks, male and female relatives, young men and old men, acquaintances and strangers. Among them were such natural fools as might have strolled around the town as jesters with foolscaps and bells, had they not been wearing a distinctive religious garb. There were others too, who I suspect erred more out of superstition than bad will. But what difference does it make to a dying man whether he is the victim of stupidity or perversity? And then all the battering rams that came crashing against the boy's [Florence's] resolute spirit! One painted a lovely picture of monastic peace; he selected all the best points (in this way one can praise even the quartan fever), adding a huge number of lies and suppressing the other side of the story. Someone else melodramatically exaggerated the perils of this world, as if monks lived outside the world. As monks often do, he represented them as being aboard a sturdy ship, while all other men are tossing about in the waves, destined to perish unless the monks reach out to help them with a pole or a rope. Another drew a terrifying picture of the torments of the damned, as if there were no road leading from monasteries down to hell. Another tried to frighten him with wild moralizing anecdotes, of which those fellows have a goodly supply. . . . A person happened to visit a group of monks, who strongly urged him to remain with them; but he was persistent in his decision to leave, and on his way the poor wretch encountered a lion who tore him to pieces. They also told stories of marvelous visions, which were just as silly as those told by little old ladies about phantoms and ghosts. Some tried to win him over by tales of a quite different sort; for instance, about the monk with whom Christ conversed several hours every day, or about Catherine of Siena, who as a girl had such an intimate relationship with Christ her spouse, or rather her lover, that they used to stroll back and forth together in her room and on occasion even finish the canonical hours together. These men placed particular emphasis on the communion of good works, implying that they themselves had a superabundance of such works. They did not seem to realize that sometimes they were more in need of the Lord's mercy than were the laity, and that the whole body of Christ shares in the communion of good works.

To avoid going into further detail on this part of my story, every type of artillery was employed against the simple lad, who was stranded by the treachery of his brother and finally broken in health. The siege was carried on with all the precision, concentration, and attention used in storming a prosperous city; so important was it for these consummate Pharisees to bury a young man alive. . . .

Florence was welcomed with an even more furious bombardment from the others. They had been preparing more formidable artillery. The barrage included remarks on such points as the utter hopelessness of his financial situation, the wrath of his friends, and finally the danger of starvation (the most painful form of death), if he failed to renounce the world. That is the way these fellows talk; they use the contemptuous words "the world" when referring to those whom Christ redeemed from the world. They maintain that monks alone possess what is the common property of all Christians. These men harassed him for some time; but they failed to shake him. Then he

returned to Cantelius[5] to have a talk with him. For some time that
fellow had been making every effort to get hold of someone who
could act as his tutor, in secret and without charge. Florence was
inclined toward forming friendships and was easygoing in obliging
his friends. Since there was no end to the deafening bombardment
and no hope in sight, he went off to a college, not the one which his
guardian had intended for him, but one where he happened to discover his old foster-brother. This college was such a filthy and unhealthy place that it was hardly fit for raising cattle, let alone for one
with a delicate disposition. But he was at that age when one has not
as yet learned to pay attention to food and climate and physical
surroundings. However, his intention in going there was not to
enter the religious life, but only to escape for the present from
those deafening shouts, until time itself should suggest something
better. . . .

The boy was delighted to have companions his own age. They sang
songs, played games, matched verses. Florence was not compelled to
observe the fast; he was not roused out of bed at night to join in the
chant; nobody admonished him, nobody scolded him. Everybody was
friendly and cheerful.

Thus several months flew by without any serious reflection. But
when the time drew near to lay aside his secular garb and don the
religious habit, Florence came to his senses and began to sing the
same old song. He sent for his guardians and began his plea for
freedom. Then came the same old dire threats. Again it was pointed
out to him how utterly hopeless was his financial situation if he did
not persevere in the course he had so well begun. Nor did Cantelius
fail to play his part vigorously; for it would be no advantage to him to
lose a tutor who gave him lessons at night and free of charge. Now, is
this not a case of sheer force employed against a boy who was un-
sophisticated, naïve, and thoughtless? Well, to avoid further detail, in
spite of the objections Florence raised, the habit was forced upon
him, although they knew that his mind was unchanged. After that,
they again continued to cajole him with endearments and to allow
him indulgences.

5. The reference is to Cornelius of Woerden, who appears in EE 296, but
about whom little is known.

Once again almost a whole year flew by without serious reflection. By now he had discovered that neither his mind nor his frail body was suited for this kind of life. His mind enjoyed only intellectual pursuits, which in that place were neither respected nor practiced. While piety was not distasteful to him, he felt very little attraction in chanting the office and the ceremonies which occupied almost the entire life of these men. Besides, people who are thrust into such communities are often slow intellectually—are half-wits, boors, and more in love with their belly than with learning. If anyone shows unusual talent and a capacity for learning, these people make it their business to squelch it and prevent it from blooming. Yet these such men claim tyrannical power for themselves, and as a rule the one with the most influence among them is the man who is most stupid and most perverse, provided he has strong muscles. Just imagine what a cross it must be for a person born for culture to spend a lifetime in such company. Nor is there any hope for freedom, except to be put in charge of a convent of nuns, and that is the most wretched kind of slavery. For, apart from constantly caring for a flock of women, one has to attend daily long-drawn-out feasts, not without risk to one's chastity. . . .

No matter how much Florence gained control over his mind, still no man can fashion his own body. And so in the meanwhile the young man did what inmates of a prison are accustomed to do; he consoled himself in study, as much as he was allowed—for this had to be done secretly, whereas drunkenness was openly permitted. With literary pursuits he diverted his thoughts from the monotony of his captivity until an unexpected event, like a *deus ex machina,* gave him hope of deliverance. A certain very influential bishop summoned him to his household. Then, after advancing to orders, he attended a renowned university. If this had not happened, his brilliant nature would have become corrupt through idleness, luxury, and drinking parties. It is not that he wants to find fault with his associates, but his natural disposition was not suited for that sort of thing. Indeed, often what is life for some men is death for others. This young man is so bashful and modest that he will not make any hostile remark about his old associates; sometimes, though, a bashful silence speaks louder than words.

Not a single one of these steps was taken by Florence except with the permission, and even at the command, of his local bishop, and with the permission of his local superior and of the superior-general, and finally with the approval of the entire community. Even though he felt free in his conscience and knew that he was not bound by a vow taken under duress, he did make a concession not only to his natural modesty, which was so immoderate as often to cause him trouble, but also to the invincible scruples of ignorant and superstitious men; and so he refrained from changing his religious garb, though his bishop had invited him to do so.

Some time later he had the opportunity to pursue his studies abroad. There he followed the French custom of wearing a linen shawl over his religious habit, thinking that this was a not uncommon local custom. But it almost resulted in his losing his life on two occasions. The physicians of that area who treat persons suffering from the plague wear a white linen shawl over the left shoulder, which hangs down in front and behind, so as to be easily recognized (and avoided) by people approaching them from front or rear. Even so, if these physicians should walk down a crowded street, they would be stoned by the pedestrians. The people have such a terrible dread of death that they become wild even at the smell of incense, which is ordinarily burned at funerals. . . .

One day he was going to visit some friends who were fellow countrymen of his. Suddenly a crowd of people gathered around with sticks and stones, wildly shouting and urging one another on, "Kill the dog, kill the dog!" Some priest came by, who smiled and whispered to him in Latin, "Those asses, those asses." Soon after, while the crowd was still in an uproar, a very well dressed young man in a purple cloak stepped out of a house. Florence ran over to him, like a suppliant to an altar, for he was utterly unfamiliar with the language spoken by the crowd. He wondered what they wanted to do. "You can be sure of this," the stranger told him, "if you don't get rid of that linen thing, some day you are going to be stoned. I am warning you; take my advice." Florence did not get rid of the shawl, but he did hide it under his habit. Good God! What a ferocious commotion over nothing at all!

Stupid people who regard the habit as the essence of religious life will be shocked at this; though I do not mean to say that the habit should be tossed aside for no reason at all. The Carthusians frequently change to the garb of a merchant to travel more safely on their way to a synod. Canons, when pursuing their studies or making a long trip, either change to another garb or conceal their regular dress, without the permission of anyone and without being reprimanded. . . .

For business reasons Florence had to move from one place to another and to wear many modes of dress—as many as the many-footed polypus has feet! For a style that is respectable in one place is considered outlandish in another. Besides, he was a guest and had to deal constantly with men of distinction, who are not satisfied with any old attire. At length it seemed best to his friends that, inasmuch as he had a free conscience, he should also have his freedom completely restored to him by papal authority and thereby be relieved of every scruple. They were afraid that the constant putting on and taking off of his religious garb would beget even graver scandal for idle gossipers. . . .

Here I will not discuss the question of monastic vows, whose importance is considerably exaggerated by some people. For this kind of obligation—I almost said slavery—is not to be found in the Old or the New Testament. Furthermore, since on the authority of Christ the Sabbath was established for man and not man for the Sabbath, it is even more reasonable that regulations such as these should yield whenever they become a hindrance to man's well-being, especially that of his soul. In fact, in the passage referred to the Lord is speaking of the welfare of the body; it is a matter of hunger and the healing of a man on the Sabbath. On the other hand, the real Pharisees are those people who will pull an ox or an ass from a ditch in violation of God's Sabbath and then allow a fellow man to perish because of their own Sabbath regulations.

Nor will I mention here the huge flock of monasteries where the practice of virtue has so declined that, by comparison, brothels are more temperate and chaste. Nor will I cite the many monasteries where, apart from ceremonies and external appearance, no religious fervor exists. Yet the latter class seem almost worse than the former, for while lacking the spirit of Christ they strangely pride themselves on their pharisaic ceremonial observances. They place the whole of Christian piety in externals, and because of these they daily beat boys to death. The monks themselves, though—paradoxically—go through those ceremonies quite bored; and they would never go through them if they did not believe that this kind of show impresses the common people. Moreover, how remarkably few communities there are where the religious life is lived sincerely according to the rule of piety; and even in these, if, as in opening up a silenus, you were to look more closely and apply the test of true piety, how dreadfully few genuine monks would you find! The cleverness of Satan's tricks, the complexity of the human heart, crafty duplicity—these are the means whereby even older men with all their experience are often deceived! And yet they expect a young boy to understand all this within the course of a few months, and then they call this the profession. . . .

I shall not speak of all the man-made regulations, all the different types of religious garb, and all the prayers and ceremonies; the most insignificant of all these, namely, one's clothing, is the most important in the eyes of these persons. The man who gets drunk every day in his religious habit, who is a slave to his palate and his belly, who wenches openly and secretly (not to mention other more filthy things), who wastes the Church's revenues on debauchery, and who is addicted to fortune-telling and other forms of magic—such a man is a good monk and is chosen abbot. But one who, for any reason whatever, has laid aside his religious habit, they curse as an apostate. . . .

It is not my purpose to campaign against religious orders. I will grant that this or that mode of life may be suitable or even necessary for this or that person, and that a lifelong commitment may be approved. The more sacred and more difficult a profession is, the more cautiously and slowly it should be made, and at a later age of life; before the fortieth year, I would think, is soon enough. Other vows are not binding unless it can be established that the person was of sound mind and balanced disposition, was not terrorized, and was free from any other jarring anxieties. But is such the case when enticements and threats and deceptions and intimidations are employed to ensnare a young boy in spite of all his protests? Are we speaking here of the effects of fear upon an adult of strong character, or rather of the effects of deception and terrorism upon a simple, inexperienced adolescent? And furthermore, many boys are very naïve because of their age and temperament. But on this point no distinction is made, as long as the lad shows the signs of puberty. The

vow is binding—so binding that by virtue of it the bride is cast off
before she is known. What laws!

Therefore since Florence, in spite of his constant resistance and
protests, was thrust into this life as a result of all those tactics, and
since the only action on his part was the wearing of the religious
habit while keeping his conscience free, he is in my opinion not
bound by any vow—no more than if he had made a solemn promise
to pirates under threat of death to perform some evil action. I have no
doubt but that the Pope, in his kindness, will feel highly indignant at
the outrageous conduct of those kidnapers and will also be highly
favorable to Florence's case. . . .

TO SERVATIUS ROGER[1]

EE 7 (1–52)   [Steyn, *ca.* 1487]

My love for you, my dearest Servatius, has always been and still is
so strong that you are dearer to me than my eyes, my life, indeed my
very own self. What can it be that makes you so cold to me all this
while? Not only have you no affection for the one who cares most for
you, but you scarcely give him a thought. Are you so churlish as to
love those who hate you and hate those who love you? There has
never been anyone so uncivil, so perverse, or so stubborn as not to
manifest some sort of human feeling at least toward his friends. Are
you the only person who is not affected by advice, not swayed by
entreaties, not softened by a lover's tears? Are you so cruel-hearted as
to be incapable of feeling pity? I have tried to win you with every

1. The recipient was a monk whom Erasmus had met at the monastery at
Steyn and who subsequently became prior there, dying in 1540. Erasmus, who
had lately entered the monastery, was desperately lonely. He felt himself
attracted to Servatius Roger but was rebuffed, for the monastic rule forbade
intimacies "lest they lead to carnal affections." Since letter writing was deemed
a literary exercise (with which he was greatly preoccupied), Erasmus poured
out his sentiment in this form. It is important to note that when he wrote the
letter, the first extant from his pen, he was probably not more than eighteen
years of age. It is difficult to say whether it was mainly a stylistic exercise or
whether, in contrast to his later habits, he was speaking very directly of his
own feelings.

kind of persuasion, with pleas, with tears too. But no, you are harder
than the hardest rock; the more attention given you, the more
obdurate you become and the more unyielding. With perfect right I
can complain about you in those words of Vergil: "He has not been
moved to tears nor shown pity for his lover."[2] How am I to explain
your attitude, Servatius? Is it hardness? Or obstinacy? Or pride? Or
haughtiness? Or perhaps you are being pigheaded the way girls often
are, and are gleeful over my anguish; the gloom of your friend makes
you happy and his tears make you smile. Is that the case with you? I
could very well apply to you those lines of Terence:

> Unhappy me! If only
> You had as much love for me as I do for you,
> So that either this would cause you equal pain
> Or I would give no thought to what you've done.[3]

Tell me, what fault have I committed against you, what crime or
what offense, that you should feel such an aversion and such hostility
toward me? I cannot imagine what I have done wrong. Maybe in
your eyes my one fault has been my extraordinary love for you. Being
so hard on one who loves you, how would you treat one who hates
you, I wonder? Your name is always on my lips, you are always in my
heart. You are my only hope, you are my other self, you are the
solace of my life. When you are absent, nothing is sweet to me; when
you are present, nothing is bitter. When I see you happy, I forget my
troubles. When something goes wrong for you, I swear by heaven I
feel it more deeply than you yourself!

Has this behavior of mine only merited your disdain? And yet
right now, Servatius, I can tell how you are going to answer my
question, just as you have so often done in the past. You will say,
"What on earth do you expect? What do you want from me? Surely,
you don't think I hate you, do you? What then do you mean?" Do
you really want to know? I am not asking for expensive gifts; only
that you feel toward me as I do toward you. Then you will make me
happy. But if you feel such an aversion for me that you cannot be

---

2. The citation is from Vergil, *Aeneid* 4.370.
3. The quotation is from Terence, *Eunuchus* 91–4.

won over by any appeal, then be honest and tell me so. Why keep toying with me? Why keep me on tenterhooks? At times you pretend to be my friend; then again you hide your feelings. And meanwhile I am suffering every pang of the heart. So, my dearest friend, if there is any chance left for me to plead with you, I beg and beseech you with all my heart: please disclose your true feelings without any deception, so that you no longer torment me by your cruel vacillations.

But why do I pour forth these vain complaints?

Already I know that you will refuse to listen. Why do I keep trying with fruitless toil to farm the seashore, to wash the color out of a brick? Why roll this stone any further? If you are determined to keep our relationship as it is—to prefer hatred to love—then hate on as you like; for my part, however, I shall never be able to stop loving you. I will, to be sure, do so with more restraint, so as not to torture myself uselessly, since no relief comes from your direction.

TO CORNELIUS GERARD[1]

EE 20 (89–106)   Steyn, May 15, [1489?]

I am very well aware that Augustine and Jerome held different views; in fact, they had arguments over them. And these two men were outstanding for their learning and were honored for the sanctity of their lives. Nor would I consider this the only case of disagreement. One can quote several other instances. Aristotle, Plato, Chrysippus, Epicurus, and Zeno each had his own teachings, which were quite different from those of the rest. Nor should we suspect that any feeling of rivalry or jealousy came between these men because of their disagreements.

I have my own guides to follow. If you happen to have different ones, that would not bother me. For poetry I prefer Vergil, Horace, Ovid, Juvenal, Statius, Martial, Claudian, Persius, Lucan, Tibullus,

1. The recipient was an Augustinian monk, author of several historical and theological works, among them a tract, De Patientia, and the Alphabetum Redemptorum. The letter indicates Erasmus' early interest in classical antiquity, which grew out of his intellectual loneliness in the monastery. Gerard was then at a neighboring monastery.

and Propertius; in prose, Cicero, Quintilian, Sallust, and Terence. Furthermore, for remarks on niceties of style I have more confidence in Lorenzo Valla than in anyone else.[2] He has no rival for mental acumen or retentive memory. Whatever has not been committed to writing by these men, I confess I dare not bring into use. Now, if you prefer some others, I would not find any fault with you.

TO CORNELIUS GERARD[3]

EE 29 (39-48) [Steyn], 1489

But I, my dear Cornelius, hate nothing so much as civil war, and therefore I consider even a very unfair peace settlement preferable. And so if you also prefer peace to war, you will find me quite obliging, provided you accept the terms which my diplomatic corps will offer you. There are three in particular, and they are not very difficult. Thus you cannot rightly complain that those conditions are either too numerous or unfair. Now just settle down and listen. First, if you are guilty of any abusive language, you are to make amends by employing laudatory language. You will now call Lorenzo the Quintessence of Eloquence and the Attic Muse instead of a croaking crow. Second, you will learn his *Elegantiae* so well that you have it at your fingertips.[4] Finally, you are to make available to me your abundant store of manuscripts, over which you brood like some Hesperian dragon. Are you laughing, and do you think I am joking? Well, laugh all you like, but take care not to think I meant the whole thing as a joke. I would not want my remarks about your sending me the manuscripts to be taken as a joke.

2. An Italian humanist (1406–1457), known for his proof that the "Donation of Constantine" (the notion that the Emperor Constantine had "donated" his realm to the papacy) was a forgery and for his notes on the New Testament, which Erasmus subsequently published. See Letter 182, p. 48. See also Fr. Gaeta, *Lorenzo Valla; filologia e storia nell' umanesimo italiano* (Napoli, 1955).

3. See Letter 20, p. 16. This letter again shows Erasmus' early interest in classical antiquity and his desire, through the medium of epistolary exercises, to share that interest (here especially in Lorenzo Valla) with friends.

4. Valla's *Elegantiarum latinae linguae libri* (1442) was the basic work on humanist Latinity.

II.

Further Studies and First Travels: 1495–1509

Paris, Tournehem (a castle near Calais), Louvain, Paris, London, and Italy were the next stations along Erasmus' way, as he penetrated more deeply into the "sources" of classical and Christian antiquity. He began to establish himself as writer and became a figure of European renown.

TO NICHOLAS WERNER[1]

EE 48 (5–24)   Paris, September 13, [1496]

Very recently a young priest came to me. He is very wealthy and, as he told me, had refused the offer of a bishopric because he realized his own lack of education. Even so, within a year he is to be asked

---

1. Prior at Steyn, d. 1504. Werner had arranged for Erasmus to leave the monastery in order to join the Bishop of Cambrai. The letter allows a glimpse of Erasmus' life in Paris and indicates his intention to pursue serious academic studies.

again to take the position—by the king—although, even apart from a bishopric, his annual income is more than two thousand scudi. When he heard of my learning he began to shower me with extraordinary signs of affection, attention, and reverence. For a while he even lived with us. He offered me a hundred scudi if I would be willing to teach him for a year, and a benefice within a few months. He offered to lend me three hundred scudi in case I needed them to obtain the position, until I could repay him with money from the benefice. With that offer I could have put under obligation to me all the English of this town, since they are all from the first families; and through them the whole of England, if I had wished to. I turned down a very great amount of money and an even greater prospect. I spurned their entreaties and the tears which they added to the entreaties. I am telling you the facts; I am not adding to the story. The English know that I think nothing of the wealth of all England. It was not without thought that I refused these offers then, and continue to refuse them. No reward can draw me away from sacred studies. I have not come here to teach or to make a fortune, but to learn. I shall get a doctorate in theology, if the gods so will.

TO CHRISTIAN NORTHOFF[1]

EE 56 (28-65)   Paris, [Spring 1497?]

Learn from the first the very best things. It is most foolish to learn what has to be unlearned. Whatever doctors usually prescribe for an ailing stomach, consider that same advice worth following in the case of your intellectual life. Be careful not to ruin your mental powers by eating harmful or immoderate amounts of food—for by both it is harmed. I am neither able, nor do I think it worth while, to work through Ebrardus, Catholicus, Brachilogus, or others of that sort.[2]

1. Erasmus spent the years between 1495 and 1499 at the University of Paris. In order to support himself he gave lessons to Christian and Heinrich Northoff, sons of a prosperous Lübeck merchant.
   The letter, addressed to one of his pupils, offers advice on reading, studying, the proper planning for a day. It shows Erasmus' ability to discern the needs and temperament of his correspondents.
2. The books mentioned are reference works.

Leave this kind of uncultured writing to those who think it worth all the hard work. In the beginning, what counts is not the amount but the quality of the things you learn. Develop a technique to help you learn, not only more correctly, but also more easily. In an artist, it is the technique of his art that is responsible for his ability to create so great a work not only more correctly and more quickly, but also with more ease. We read that it was the practice of Pliny the Elder and Pope Pius,[3] men held in high esteem, to divide the day up so as to have a special time for each task. In the beginning, and this is important, listen with attention and even eagerness to the teacher's explanations. Do not be content simply to keep up with the teacher; occasionally strive to get a few steps ahead of him. Commit all his words to memory and the important ones to writing, that most faithful guardian of words. On the other hand beware of trusting in them as did that foolish rich man in Seneca's anecdote, who so deluded himself as to believe he could recall whatever any one of his servants remembered. Do not make the mistake of possessing learned books, while you remain unlearned yourself. Do not let the things you hear go in one ear and out the other; go over them, either by yourself or with others. Not content with that, remember to devote some time to quiet meditation, which is, as the Emperor Aurelius wrote, the one thing especially profitable for both the intellect and the memory. Discussion too, being an exercise of the wits, is especially good for flexing and challenging and developing the muscles of the mind. Do not be ashamed to ask questions if you do not know, or to be corrected if you make a mistake.

Avoid working late at night and studying at unsuitable times. These habits exhaust the mind and seriously affect one's health. Dawn, the friend of the Muses, is the best time to study. After dinner either relax, take a walk, or take part in light conversation. Even among these relaxing activities one is able to learn something. Eat as much as will satisfy the demands of your health, but not the demands of pleasure. Take a short stroll before supper, and then again after supper. Before retiring read something that is especially good and worth remembering, which you will think about when you

3. Pius II (1458–1464), Enea Silvio de' Piccolomini, was a humanistically oriented pope.

fall asleep, and which you will recall upon rising. Always keep this saying of Pliny in mind: "All time is lost which is not devoted to intellectual things." Remember that nothing is more fleeting than youth, and once it is gone, it never returns.

Here I am, offering you encouragement. Follow it—or, if you can, follow something better.

TO THOMAS GREY[1]

EE 64 (21–91)   Paris, [August, 1497]

Once upon a time there was a man named Epimenides, the same who wrote that all Cretans are liars; though a Cretan himself, on that occasion he was not telling a lie. It was not enough for him just to live to a ripe old age; in fact, long after his death his skin was found covered with writing. There are those who maintain that it is preserved presently at Paris in that ultra-sacred temple of Scotistic theology, the Sorbonne, and that it is no less valued than was the Sacred Parchment among the Cretans long ago or the Sibylline Books among the Romans. For it is said that they seek from it oracular responses whenever they are in want of syllogisms. No one is permitted to view it unless he has had the title of professor for fifteen full years. If anyone so much as dares to direct his profane eyes toward it, he straightway becomes blinder than a mole. As proof that this is not just a fairy tale, there is a very ancient Greek phrase, "the hide of Epimenides," by which they meant something abstruse, something not to be revealed to the common herd. Epimenides published books on theology, being especially distinguished in the theological profession, although he was also considered a prophet and

1. The recipient of this letter was also a pupil of Erasmus' at Paris, for whom he developed a great affection. Erasmus seeks to characterize in this letter the kind of (useless and futile) scholastic theology taught at the Sorbonne in Paris, which he himself had to study to qualify for an academic degree. The letter also conveys his ability to differentiate between this false theology and the genuine, as well as his flair for making fun of something he disliked.

a poet. In these works he devised such knotty syllogisms that even he
was unable to untie them, and piled up mysteries which he himself
would never have understood had he not been a prophet.

One day, it is said, he went out of the city to take a stroll as there
was nothing at home with which he was pleased. Eventually, he
entered a deep cave; perhaps he was bothered by the heat and the
coolness attracted him, or perhaps he was tired and wanted a place to
rest. Or perhaps the reason was that he had lost his way (as happens
even to theologians) and was afraid that night would overtake him in
the open fields and he would encounter some wild animal. Probably,
however, he simply sought a place suitable for reflection. There, as
he was biting his nails and puzzling much over instances, quiddities,
and formalities, sleep overcame him. You would not believe me, I
know, if I told you that he did not get up until the evening of the
next day, though of course drunkards sleep longer than that. But as a
matter of fact, this theological slumber lasted, as authors unanimously
affirm, for forty-seven years; they also say that there is some mysterious meaning in the fact that his sleep lasted that length of time and
neither more nor less. Oh, you will say, the man was dead. But to me
it seems a special blessing for Epimenides to regain consciousness
even at so late a date. After all, many of the theologians of our time
never do wake up, and when they are drugged with mandrake they
think they are wide awake.

But back to the awakening of Epimenides.

He woke up and rubbed his drowsy eyes, not quite sure whether
he was awake or just dreaming, and left the cave. Then he noticed
that the whole landscape was different. During the lapse of all those
years the rivers had shifted their courses; here the woods were cut
down, there new ones had sprung up; hills rose where once there
were level fields, and there were level stretches where hills had been.
Even the entrance to the cave was different, overgrown with moss
and brambles. So the fellow began to doubt who he was. He went
into town, and there also everything was new. He did not recognize
the buildings, the streets, the money, not even the people. Their style
of dress, their customs, their language were different. Such is the
mutability of human things. Everybody he met he accosted, "Hey
you, don't you recognize me, Epimenides?" But the other person,

thinking he was being mocked, would answer, "Go to the devil!" or "Watch out for strangers." In that way the fool passed some months walking about until he fell in with some of his former drinking companions, who were by now quite old. Somehow or other they recognized him.

Well now, my dear Thomas, what do you suppose Epimenides dreamed of during all those years? What else but those supersubtleties which the modern descendants of Scotus love to parade. I would almost swear that in Scotus we have the reincarnation of Epimenides. Why, if you were to see Erasmus sitting in the midst of those holy Scotists all agog,[2] while Gryllard lectures from his lofty throne[3]—if you were to see his forehead wrinkled, his eyes wide open, his whole countenance intent, you would conclude it was somebody else. It is said that the mysteries of this science can never be grasped by one who has ever had anything to do with the Muses or the Graces. You must forget anything acquired by contact with good learning; you must get rid of any drink you have had from Helicon. I try with all my might never to use good Latin, never to utter an elegant or witty phrase, and apparently I am making progress. There is hope that eventually they will recognize Erasmus.

What is the purpose of all this? So that you will not hereafter expect from Erasmus anything that savors of his former studies or way of life, remember who my associates and my classmates are. Look for someone else to be your boon companion. However, so that you will not misunderstand, dearest Grey, I would not want you to interpret my remarks as being directed against theology itself, for which as you know I have always had the highest esteem. I have only been amusing myself by poking fun at some of those pseudotheologians of our time. There is nothing more rotten than their brains, nothing more barbaric than their tongues, nothing more stupid than their wit, nothing more thorny than their teaching, nothing more crude than their conduct, nothing more counterfeit than their lives, nothing more virulent than their language, nothing blacker than their hearts.

2. To qualify for the academic degree Erasmus had to attend lectures on the philosophy of Duns Scotus.
3. One of Erasmus' teachers.

TO WILLIAM HERMAN[1]

EE 83 (85–126)   Paris, December 14, [1498]

So do you want to know what sort of life Erasmus is living here? It is only right for you to know all about me. Erasmus is alive—in fact, I am quite sure that he is living. But the life he is living is absolutely wretched, wearied with every kind of sorrow. He is the victim of so much deceitfulness, so often disappointed by the failure of friends, tossed back and forth by countless disasters, and yet his life is blameless. I know I shall scarcely be able to make you believe this. You're still thinking of the old Erasmus, and my independent spirit, and whatever brillance was mine. But, if I could speak to you in person you would be easily convinced. Therefore, if you want to form a true picture of Erasmus, do not imagine him as being silly or carousing or indulging in love but as one crushed by misfortune, plunged in grief, and loathsome even to himself, one who has no desire to live and yet no right to die. To put it briefly, he is absolutely wretched, not through his own fault, but through the injustice of fortune. Still, what difference does it make which it is; he is absolutely wretched. However, he is still very fond of you and deeply interested in you.

May heaven change these troubles of mine for the better or end them by an early death! I swear, never has my own reputation been more important to me than yours, nor my renown more welcome than yours, nor my own life dearer to me than yours has been. If I am hated by the rest of men, I am not surprised, for who would not be perfectly justified in hating such a wretched human being? But how could I have been afraid that I was losing even your affection because of my unhappy state, for you are the only person I always felt I could trust, one whom I esteemed so much and by whom I thought I was loved not in some ordinary way but in that grand old fashion of days gone by. But if I see that I am hateful to such a

---

1. A fellow monk and friend of Erasmus at Steyn, where he shared Erasmus' interest in classical antiquity. This letter is a lengthy catalogue of Erasmus' own misfortunes and wretchedness, perhaps an attempt to convey to the recipient that his academic pursuits in Paris were not altogether delightful.

person, and hateful for the reason that I am utterly wretched, what reason have I to want to go on living?

O my dear William, my former and, I would hope, my constant solace, grief almost forces me to cry out with tears. If I had dishonored our friendship by some serious outrage, even then instead of righteous anger you would have owed your unhappy friend some pity and compassion. But as the case now stands, it is one whose affection for you could never be shaken by any adversity or change of circumstances that you can attack with abusive language and insults—as if there were a lack of men striving tooth and nail to destroy me, men wanting to dispatch me by fire and sword. What pleasant memory of Steyn has not been gradually forgotten amid all these misfortunes? You yourself have seen me act on occasion like a carefree youngster, and most of the time you just smiled. You know what feelings I am expressing. Whom could I ever have loved more tenderly? But now, strange to say, how coldhearted I have become. All those lesser loves of mine have been forgotten; you are the only one to remain dear to my heart. So dear have you been that the interruption of communication between us has served to increase my love for you, not to snuff it out. And is it possible that a friend so resolutely devoted to you, one whom you could not envy when he was happy, can be hated by you when he is utterly wretched? I know that this is the way most people behave, but how unfortunate if learning cannot rescue you from the ways of common folk.

TO JOHN FALCON[1]

EE 87 (16–27)   Tournehem, February 3,
                                                   [1499]

I shall conclude my letter with a few words of advice. Prudence is wasted if one does not show prudence in his own regard. Admire learning and commend it, but pursue money-making. Avoid displeas-

1. Nothing is known about the recipient. This letter surely shows Erasmus' ability to be ironic and to give tongue-in-cheek advice. Perhaps the counsel offered conformed to the temperament of John Falcon. Tournehem was a castle near Calais.

ing yourself, for such action beclouds your radiant charm. Above all
else, take care of your own skin. Prefer your own convenience to
everything else, and cultivate friendship for your own sake. In apply-
ing yourself to learning, be stinting. Love passionately, study moder-
ately; be lavish with words, but tight-fisted with money.

There is more advice you ought to receive, but I must bid farewell
to My Lady in courtly fashion, and tomorrow I am off for the Low
Countries. I am leaving my better set of clothes at home. Do you
know why? Because I am afraid your sisters would tear it to shreds.
. . . I shall not expect a letter from you, as I shall probably arrive
before this letter does. Just live for yourself and take good care of
yourself and continue to love only yourself.

TO ADOLPH OF VEERE[1]

EE 93 (91–106)   Paris, [March?] 1498/9

If you do this [i.e., continue to practice composition], I am confident that your family, your country, and all your friends will experience great renown and advancement from your writings, and in turn
your writings will receive all the same advantages from your good
fortune. I shall add this final thought which I hope you will take
deeply to heart: that you be thoroughly convinced that nothing so
befits men of noble birth as genuine piety. I have good reason for this
advice. For I have discovered that there are many persons in high
places who have felt without fear and have said without shame that
the teachings of Christ are not for the princes of this world, but
should be left to priests and monks. Turn a deaf ear to the bewitch-
ing but deadly advice of such persons, and listen rather to your
mother and to Batt.[2] And as you are now beginning to absorb the

1. In an early printed version, this letter received the designation *Exhortatio
ad virtutem* ("exhortation to virtue"). The recipient, Adolph of Veere (1490–
1540), was later admiral of Flanders. To understand the letter one must keep
in mind that it was a word of advice to a boy, this time concerning not matters
of external daily routine, as in EE 56, but the genuine practice of piety.

2. James Batt (*ca.* 1464–1502) was a close friend of Erasmus and a tutor to
the Veere family.

spirit of Christ from your elementary readings, I am sending you some prayers which were requested by your mother and which Batt urged me to write.[3] They are intended for you, and therefore I have adapted the language somewhat to your age. If you say them regularly, you will not only grow in the habit of prayer, but you will disdain those little magic formulas so popular at court as being very stupid and also very superstitious.

TO FAUSTUS ANDRELINUS[4]

EE 103 (6–25)   England, [Summer] 1499

I too have made some progress in England. In fact, the Erasmus you knew has now become an almost proficient sportsman, a fairly good equestrian, and a courtier with some skill at bowing graciously and smiling pleasantly; yet all this is quite unnatural for me. As for my own affairs, they are advancing well enough. And you too, if you have good sense, will rush over here. How can a man with your intelligence enjoy going to seed amid all that French scum? Perhaps you are held back by your gout. Well, your gout be damned—though not you! And yet if you were thoroughly acquainted with the endowments of Britain, Faustus, you would indeed come running here with wings on your feet. And if your gout tried to prevent you, you would pray to become a Daedalus.

Just to mention one of the many advantages here: the girls look like goddesses, so charming and gracious you would readily prefer them to the Muses of your poetry. Besides, they have a custom which has never been adequately lauded. No matter where you go everybody welcomes you with a kiss. When you leave, they kiss you goodby. When you return, they smack you. People come to visit you and greet you with a smack. When they leave you, a round of kisses.

3. See Allen, I, 232.
4. An Italian poet and humanist (ca. 1462–1518), poet laureate to the King of France. Erasmus' letter reflects his readiness to adjust to the temperament of his correspondents. Andrelinus had written a great deal of amorous poetry, and writing from England Erasmus singles out the impression his correspondent will surely enjoy: the English practice of kissing.

Whenever people meet, there are kisses in abundance. In fact, wherever you go, the place is overflowing with kisses. And what kisses,
Faustus! Once you have tasted their tenderness and fragrance, you
would indeed desire to travel about in England not just for ten years,
as Solon did, but for the rest of your life. As for the rest of my story,
we shall joke about that together, for I shall see you, I hope, shortly.

TO PRINCE HENRY[1]

EE 104 (32–67)   [Greenwich?, Autumn] 1499

I am aware that very many princes of our own day neither enjoy
literature nor do they understand it. Such men regard it equally silly,
in fact disgraceful, for a nobleman either to have a knowledge of
letters or to be praised by men of letters; as if these men were worthy
of comparison with Alexander or Caesar or any of the ancients at all
in importance or wisdom or renown for noble deeds. They think it is
silly to be praised by a poet, because they have stopped doing anything deserving of praise. And yet they do not shrink from the
adulation of their parasites; if they have any intelligence they know
they are being mocked by them, and if they do not realize that, they
are absolutely stupid.

In any case, I consider such men even more obtuse than Midas,
who was disfigured by ass's ears, not because he had no esteem for
poetry but because he preferred cloddish verses to polished songs.
Therefore Midas lacked not so much a good intention as good
judgment; our modern princes lack both. I realize that your noble
nature violently shrinks from the stupidity of such men, and for that
reason, even now in your boyhood years, the ideal toward which you
are striving is that of the ancients rather than that of your contemporaries. Therefore I have no hesitation in dedicating to you this
panegyric, such as it is. If it seems (as indeed it is) a work quite

1. Dedicated to the future King Henry VIII, this letter forms the preface to
Prosopopoeia Britanniae majoris ("Prosopopoeia of Great Britain"). Here
Erasmus discusses the propriety of dedications and praise from a poet to a
person of eminence. See also Letter 272, p. 63.

unworthy of a person of your high rank, then recall how the outstanding King Artaxerxes accepted with a cheerful smile a drink of
water from a farmer who generously offered it to him as he rode up
on his horse. And recall, too, how another king of the same name—or
so I believe—was just as grateful for an apple given him by a poor
man as for the most resplendent gifts; obviously he realized that it is
no less regal to accept small gifts graciously than to bestow great ones
magnanimously. Besides, are not even the gods themselves, who need
the services of no man, so delighted with humble gifts that, though
ignoring the hecatomb of the wealthy,[2] they are appeased by a crumb
from a peasant or a pinch of incense from a pauper? Surely they
measure our offerings by the spirit of the giver rather than by the cost
of the gift.

TO JOHN COLET[1]

EE 107 (37–57)   Oxford, [October 1499]

To forestall any complaint from you that merchandise of unknown
value has been foisted upon you as a result of a fraudulent recommendation, and so that you can make a free choice before you love,
here is a description of myself. It is a better description than anyone
else can give, for I know myself better than anyone else does. You
will find me a man of little or no means, a stranger to ambition,
always ready to add new friends; one with little acquaintance with
learning, yet having an ardent admiration for it; one with deep
respect for the good in others, but fully conscious of his own lack of
it; one who yields to others in learning, but to no one in loyalty; one
who is simple, open, and free, with no pretense or false modesty, a
man of few words, diffident but honest, to put it briefly, one who has

2. A sacrifice of a hundred oxen.
1. An eminent English humanist (ca. 1466–1519). One of Erasmus' trusted
friends, he became dean of St. Paul's, where he founded a school in 1510. See
E. W. Hunt, Dean Colet and His Theology (London, 1956). Other letters to
Colet are Nos. 108, 181, 227, 237, 260.
This is a letter of introduction—of Erasmus himself—together with a brief
praise of learned Englishmen, especially Colet!

only his heart to offer. If you can feel affection for such a man and judge him worthy of your friendship, then count Erasmus among your possessions and consider him yours more than anything else you own.

As for England—I find it most pleasant for many reasons, but especially because it has an abundance of the things that give me most pleasure: men well acquainted with good learning. And among these I consider you, without a doubt, easily the first. For such is your learning that, even without the recommendation of noble character, you would deserve the admiration of all men; and such is your holiness of life that, even without the recommendation of your learning, no one could fail to love you, and respect and revere you.

TO JOHN COLET[1]

EE 108 (19–103)   St. Mary's College, Oxford,
                                          [October 1499]

But now a few words in answer to your letter, so that the young man who brought it does not go back empty-handed. As to your remark about being displeased by this new breed of theologians who go to seed amid nothing but distinctions and empty sophistry, that disturbs me too. It is not that I condemn their studies, for I praise every intellectual pursuit; but studies that are concerned only with such matters and not seasoned with any ancient elegant literature seem to me to produce a man who is superficial and quarrelsome; whether they can make him wise, that is for others to decide. They waste their talent with their barren, thorny subtlety. Being lifeless, they cannot invigorate, they cannot inspire. And worst of all, their stammering, ugly, filthy style of expression strips of its beauty that Theology which is the queen of all the sciences and which was so

1. See previous letter. This is the preface to Erasmus' *Disputatiuncula de tedio, pauore, tristicia Jesu,* a dialogue on the nature of Jesus' agony in the Garden of Gethsemane. The letter undertakes to describe the difference between false and true theology, and calls on Colet to support the struggle for the latter.

enriched and adorned by the eloquence of the ancients. A theology which had been explained by geniuses of old they now are confusing with knotty problems, entangling everything while supposedly attempting to disentangle everything. And so one can see that she who was once a queenly sovereign, full of majesty, is now almost speechless, helpless, and in rags. Meanwhile we are being enticed by a sweet, attractive disease—a contentiousness that is never sated. One quarrel springs from another, and with amazing arrogance we wrangle over trifles.

And then, for fear of appearing to have added nothing to the discoveries of the ancient theologians, we have quite brazenly set down definite logical explanations for the revelation of God's mysteries. It would be better to accept by faith the fact of revelation and to leave its explanation to God's omnipotence. Furthermore, out of an eagerness to flaunt our talent we sometimes discuss questions hardly suitable for pious ears, as for instance when we ask whether God could have assumed the form of a devil or an ass. Perhaps it could be tolerated if a person, to exercise his wits, handled such questions with restraint and for a period of time. But we spend our whole lifetime amid such things, like one clinging to the Sirens' rocks, and we even fade away amongst them, and in preference to them we disdain all learning. Furthermore, theology, the supreme branch of learning, is in our day generally studied by men whose dull wit and lack of sense renders them almost incapable of any learning.

Now, these remarks of mine are not directed at learned, competent professors of theology, for whom I have a special respect and reverence, but toward the despicable, supercilious mob of theologians who hold in contempt the learning of all other men—while thinking highly of their own. You have engaged in battle, Colet, with this impregnable breed of men so as to do your utmost to restore that ancient and genuine theology, now overgrown and entangled with thorny subtleties, to its pristine splendor and dignity. In so doing, you have selected, I assure you, a sphere of activity that is glorious in many ways, one that indicates great devotion as regards theology itself, and one that is most beneficial for scholars everywhere, especially here at this flourishing university in Oxford. But to tell the truth, it involves much hard work and also much odium. However, your learning and industry will rise above the difficulty of the work,

while your magnanimity will easily overlook the censure. Among
theologians there are not a few who are willing and able to help you
in your noble efforts. In fact, no one would fail to offer a helping
hand, since every one of the professors at this renowned institution
has listened most attentively to the public lectures you have delivered
on the Pauline Epistles during the past three years. In this matter,
which is more deserving of praise: the modesty of these professors,
who are not embarrassed at being seen listening to a man who is
quite young and without the prestige of a doctorate; or your excep-
tional learning, your eloquence, and moral integrity, which they
judge worthy of this high honor?

I am amazed, however, not so much at your undertaking a
burdensome task for which you have the capacity, but at your
inviting a worthless person like me to be your partner in so noble a
service. For you are urging, in fact demanding with almost violent
language, that I do a commentary on ancient Moses or eloquent
Isaiah as you have done on Paul, and thereby try to fire the intellectual interests of this university, which, according to your words,
become frosty during the winter months. But I, who have learned to
reside within myself, know very well how poorly equipped I am, and
so do not claim for myself the amount of learning requisite for undertaking such a great project, nor do I think I have enough strength of
soul to bear up under the spite of all those fellows who valiantly
guard their own preserve. Such a task requires not a raw recruit but
an experienced general. Do not call me shameless for refusing; I
would be completely shameless if I did not. My dear Colet, you are
not very prudent in trying to squeeze blood out of a turnip. . . .
Really, what impression shall I make, teaching something I have not
learned myself? How shall I, all trembling and shivering, fire the cold
indifference of others? I would consider it the height of rashness to
put my abilities to the test with such an important matter; I would be
trying to fly before I could run. Now you may object that you had
looked forward to this and complain of being deceived in your hopes.
In that case you must blame yourself, not me. I have not played you
false; for I have not promised anything of the sort, nor have I even
suggested it. You simply deceived yourself in refusing to believe me
when I spoke the truth about myself. On the other hand, I did not

come here to teach poetry and rhetoric. Those studies ceased to be attractive to me as soon as they ceased to be necessary. I am rejecting them because they are beneath my ambitions, and I am rejecting that previous offer because it is above my abilities. In the first case your rebuke is undeserved, dear Colet, inasmuch as I have never indicated that secular learning was my profession. In the second case, your pleas are fruitless, because I know that I am not at all capable of it. And even if I should happen to be most capable, I could not do it. For I am soon going back to Paris.

TO JAMES BATT[1]

EE 123 (11–26)   Paris, [March 1500]

I am completely engaged in literary work, planning to compile a collection of ancient adages; of course, it will be a hurried production.[2] I can see there will be several thousands of adages available, but I intend to publish only two, or at the most, three hundred. I shall dedicate them to your pupil, Adolph. I still have my doubts whether I can find a printer; you know that my funds amount to less than nothing.

I am puzzled at your failure to send a message with Francis' brother. Keep a sharp lookout for my package—Galba, as you know, is an Englishman—and when you get it, make sure you forward it to me. It contains a black coat with black and gray lining, a woolen cloak that I bought from you, and a pair of violet-colored stockings. Also, Augustine's *Enchiridion* written on parchment, Paul's Epistles, and some other things, too.

The study of Greek has just about undone me. I do not have the time for it, and I do not have the money to purchase either books or

1. A schoolteacher at Bergen who had helped Erasmus to pursue academic studies at Paris. See Letter 93, p. 26. Other letters to Batt are Nos. 138, 139. This letter comments on Erasmus' current scholarly efforts. It also asks the recipient for help in a personal matter.
2. The project referred to is the *Adagia*, a collection of proverbs eventually published at Paris in 1500.

the services of a tutor. And in the midst of all this wild confusion, I hardly have enough to sustain life. Such is my debt to scholarship.

TO JAMES BATT[1]

EE 138 (39–89)   Orleans, December 11, [1500]

I must scrape together funds from some source so that I can put some clothes on my back and buy a complete set of Jerome's works— I have in mind to do a commentary on them—and also buy a set of Plato and get some Greek books and hire a Greek tutor.[2] I think you realize how much all of this matters for my prestige, in fact for my general welfare; and yet I do ask you to take my word for it, since I am speaking from firsthand knowledge. My heart burns with an incredible passion to bring to term all the little productions I have in mind and also to attain some facility in Greek, and then to devote myself completely to sacred learning, which I have long desired to do.

My health, thank heavens, is fair and I hope it continues so. Therefore during the coming year I must strain every nerve to publish the writings which are now in the press, and by doing commentaries on theological literature drive the huge number of my mean critics to hang themselves, as they deserve. For some time now I have made serious threats, but I have been slowed down either by my slothfulness or by some harsh fate or my health. But the day has come at last when I must stir up my courage and strain every nerve so that finally I can boast with Horace that "I have triumphed over Envy, and now I suffer less from its gnawing tooth."[3] I trust that, with the blessing of heaven, the brilliance of my achievement will obscure the spite of the most envious, provided I am granted three more years of life.

1. See Letters 93 and 123, pp. 26 and 33 respectively. In this letter Erasmus comments on his various scholarly projects, speaks rather highly of them and the fame they will bring, and seeks the recipient's support.
2. This is the first reference to Erasmus' proposed edition of St. Jerome.
3. The reference is to Horace, *Carmina*, 2.20.4.

In effect, my whole future depends upon you alone. Therefore, you must lend an equal amount of effort to my endeavors. That is your duty for several reasons: the first indications of a promising future for me came from you; the bond of friendship that has long linked us is the closest that can exist between two mortal men; and finally, as you can see, the perpetuation of your name is intimately bound up with the immortality of my writings, so that if I can use my talent to preserve my works from perishing, the memory of your sincere heart is destined never to perish. Come now, fire that heart of yours which is consecrated to sincerity and the Graces; unseal all those hidden sources of kindliness; and if you have ever thought of doing a friendly service to your dear Erasmus—something you have never ceased doing—then now is the time to bend all your energies to the task.

It is true, I have long committed a grave injustice to our relationship by making such constant demands upon you, when merely a suggestion would have been more than enough. Accordingly, I will not ask you to love me, since your love could not be more ardent; I will not ask you to favor my fortunes, since you rank them above your own; I will not ask you to guarantee a constant devotion to my interests, since you surpass even me in that respect. I ask only one favor. It is a very slight one, but it is most important that you grant it—namely, do not consider all that I am writing to you about my personal affairs as nice phrases, cleverly contrived so as to benefit my own purposes. In times past, we have spent moments together in light talk, and as befitted the circumstances we trifled with the truth. Such things have their proper time, my dear Batt. But in present conditions there is absolutely no time to indulge in clever talk and no reason for me to lie. I sincerely hope that heaven may grant the two of us a happy old age together in mutual love, and to the memory of our very true affection a long, long life among future generations. And with equal sincerity I swear that this letter does not contain a single word that does not reflect my true sentiments. I can share everything safely with you, my very soul; and I ought to share everything freely with you. Therefore, my dear Batt, I plead with you not to look upon these words of mine as humbug, since they are written with even more earnestness than either of us desires.

TO JAMES BATT[1]

EE 139 (25–62)   Orleans, [*ca.* December 12,]
                                                 1500

If you are sincerely interested in the future of your friend
Erasmus, then do as follows. Explain to My Lady[2] in winsome
language that it was because of my natural bashfulness that I could
not bring myself to reveal my poverty, for my stay in Orleans has
proved very expensive, since it meant leaving those who were some
source of income for me. Tell her that the proper place to receive the
doctorate is Italy, and that a person with fastidious tastes cannot go to
Italy without a large amount of money. This is particularly true in
my case, since my reputation for learning, such as it is, does not allow
me to live in shabby circumstances. And point out to My Lady how
much greater fame I am going to bring her by my learning than will
the other theologians whom she is supporting. Their sermons are full
of trite sayings; I am producing works destined to live forever. Their
ignorant nonsense is heard in one or two churches; my books will be
read by students of Latin and of Greek in every nation throughout
the world. Ignorant theologians exist everywhere in great abundance,
while a man like myself is discovered barely once in several centuries.
All this you should tell her, unless you happen to be so extremely
scrupulous as to be reluctant about helping a friend with a few little
white lies. Then point out to her that she will be none the poorer if
with a few gold coins she assists in the restoration of the corrupt text
of Jerome and thereby of true theology, whereas now so much of her
wealth is being shamefully squandered.

After employing your native rhetoric in enlarging upon these
points, give My Lady a description of my character, my future hopes,
my affection for her, and my great bashfulness. Then add that I have
mentioned to you my need for two hundred francs, so that she will

---

1. See Letter 123, p. 33. Erasmus had gone to Orleans to escape the plague
in Paris. He was without regular income and thus depended on the financial
support of various wealthy benefactors. This letter is an instance of his search
for such support. Naturally, his case is made in superlatives—all the way to the
assertion that a man like Erasmus comes only "once in several centuries."

2. The person referred to is Anne of Borsselen, the Lady of Veere, whose
son Batt was tutoring. See Letter 145, p. 39.

advance me next year's pension. That is by no means a lie, my dear Batt. For I do not think it is safe for me to go to Italy with only a hundred francs—in fact, less than that—unless I want to be somebody's slave again. Before I do that, I would rather die. Then too, what difference will it make to her if she gives me the money now or a year from now? But it does make a big difference to me. Then urge her to turn her immediate attention to a benefice for me, so that on my return I will have a place in which to do my scholarly work in peace. And do not urge only that, but further, give her the best possible argument you can devise, so that she will promise me, out of all the applicants, the very first benefice—maybe not an extraordinary one, but at least acceptable and one that I can change when something better comes along. I know very well that there are many applicants for benefices. But tell her that I am the one man who, when compared with all the rest, etc. You know your old habit of telling lavish lies about Erasmus.

TO GREVERADE[1]

EE 141 (1–62)   Paris, December 18, [1500]

This unexpected letter from a total stranger, my good and noble sir, is a bold intrusion. And yet you ought not therefore accuse me of impudence, but rather appreciate my kindly feelings and the confidence resulting therefrom. Besides, you are not really a stranger to me. Many a time Heinrich Northoff,[2] the most honest man alive, has described to me in intimate conversation your disposition and character and interests, and so I feel as if I had a portrait of you before my eyes. If, as we see, the admiration for nobility of character and for learning can be so effective as to link closely together by the bond of love hearts that are poles apart in space, then shall I not employ any and every means to catch the favor of a man who is such a modest and enthusiastic and sincere admirer of good learning, and who lives

1. The recipient of this letter is unknown; possibly the name is incorrect. The letter describes Erasmus' project of an edition of the writings of Jerome and dwells at length on the significance of that Church Father. Once again the object of the communication was pecuniary.
2. Of Lübeck, who together with his brother Christian was a pupil of Erasmus in Paris. See Letter 56, p. 19.

nearby? It is not my intention to enter into a common, ordinary relationship of friendship. The society of scholars is a sacred thing, and it must be made so by a kind of sacred pledge. Let me briefly explain the nature of that pledge.

I have long had an extraordinarily passionate desire to do a commentary on the epistles of St. Jerome; some deity is firing my heart and prompting me to venture upon a project of great importance never before attempted. I am motivated by the piety of that holy man, who is beyond all question the most learned and most eloquent of all Christians. Although his writings deserve to be read and studied by all persons without distinction, only a few read them, fewer still admire them, and very few understand them. My God! Shall Scotus and Albert[3] and even less learned authors be mouthed in all the schools, and shall Jerome, who is the unparalleled champion, exponent, and brilliant light of our religion, and who alone deserves to be taught—shall he be the only one passed over in utter silence? I observe the shameful fact that Jerome is neglected for the very reason he should not be neglected. He is harmed by the eloquence which once did service to religion. Many persons are alienated by his abstruse learning, and yet that should have been the principal reason for recommending him. And so only a few people admire one who is understood by very, very few. Now if such an author were explained by a fitting commentary, I can foresee that the glory of Jerome would dawn again and spread its brilliance far and wide, and that he would be read and studied everywhere—in schools and in lecture halls, in churches and at home, in public and in private.

I have no illusions about the boldness of my project. First of all, what a task it will be to root out the errors that have settled in the text in the course of many centuries! Second, what a vast amount of ancient lore, of Greek learning, and of history is found in Jerome! Then, too, there is his diction and mastery of style! In that respect, he leaves all Christian writers far behind, and even challenges Cicero himself. When I compare the language of Jerome with that of Cicero, I for one feel that something is wanting even in the prince of eloquence, unless my love for that very holy man deceives me. In Jerome one finds such a rich variety, such a depth of meaning, such a

3. Albert "the Great" (ca. 1193–1280), philosopher and theologian.

flow of argument. It is very difficult, but indeed useful, to point out such craftsmanship in the style of eloquent writers. I trust that I shall accomplish that very thing, provided Jerome blesses my work. If so, then those who have heretofore admired the eloquence of Jerome will have to admit that they never realized how eloquent he really was.

Whatever service I can render by sleepless nights and constant research—by my modest learning and by a talent that is not altogether bad—that service will be zealously rendered to Jerome. But just as an important war requires auxiliary forces, so too do I realize that this difficult task requires direction and inspiration. Who would be the most suitable choice for that, no one could tell better than you, because first of all you have always been, as Heinrich frequently told me, ablaze with an extraordinary love for this author, and then secondly, because this is the pledge by which we are to initiate our alliance of friendship. Come, my distinguished sir, offer me your hand and enter with me upon this noble task with a lofty heart. Jerome will give his blessing to the champions of his writings, which cost him so many sleepless nights. And our devoted efforts will not be cheated of their due reward.

TO ANNE OF BORSSELEN[1]

EE 145 (51–136)   Paris, January 27, 1500/1

The thought occurs to me as I write this letter to you (and to whom would I rather disclose my misfortune than to her who alone is able and willing to remedy it?) that this morning's sun dawned upon the anniversary of that day when my supply of funds, intended to support me with my studies, was shipwrecked on the shore of Britain. And from that day, as I recall, right up to the present, fortune has linked together for me a never-ending chain of sorrows. As soon as the British Charybdis had flung me back all naked into our part of

1. Anne of Veere, of Burgundy, was the mother of Adolph of Veere, pupil of James Batt (Letter 93, p. 26). See also Letter 139, p. 36, for an earlier approach to this patron.

Here is another instance of what must have been a painful exercise for Erasmus—securing funds for his livelihood. It is clad in a historical exposition of the support of worthy men and a description of Erasmus' scholarly concerns, namely, to repudiate false learning by further studies in Italy.

the world, I was caught in a savage storm which made the voyage extremely rough. Then I was welcomed by pirates with their sharp blades pressed against my throat. Then came a fever and after that the plague, which however did not seize me, but only made me flee. Add to these the personal problems which the life of mortal man brings daily in great abundance. And yet, so help me God, I do feel embarrassed: first of all at the thought that I, a man, to some degree buttressed by learning and armed with the teachings of philosophy, am panic-stricken while you, formed by nature a woman, born into a family of noble rank through the smiles of fortune and reared amid luxury, you too have something to bear, and you bear it in no womanly fashion. Secondly, I am embarrassed because, in spite of the thunderings of fortune, I am determined that nothing shall cause me to abandon learning or be crushed in spirit as long as your light, constant as the North Star, shines upon me. Learning can never be stolen from us by fortune, and the small amount of money required for my leisure can easily be supplied from your wealth, which is as generous as is your heart. Your ability to do this you owe to your fortune; your willingness to do it I owe to your generous heart. You are only too glad to support my scholarly work, which depends completely upon you and looks to you alone for aid and is dedicated to you alone. The writer Cherylus, though wicked and cruel according to Lucilius, was supported by Alexander the Great. The poverty of Vergil and Horace was relieved by the unstinting generosity of Maecenas. The midnight toils of Pliny were encouraged by the interest of Vespasian. . . . In recent times Lorenzo de' Medici exalted Poliziano, the darling of our age, as if he were his foster son. To put it briefly—for, as the Greeks say, I am trying to count the sands on the seashore—every genius has found a Maecenas.

And it is no objectionable favor that such men have returned to their patrons, whose memory they have immortalized by their writings. In all truth, my dear foster mother, I would never, in my right mind, exchange you, not even for a Maecenas or for an emperor. And so far as compensation is concerned, I shall make every effort, as much as my small talent allows, so that future generations will be well informed about my Maecenas, and will marvel that there emerged from a remote part of the globe a woman who by her beneficence strove to spur on good learning, which had been corrupted through the ignorance of amateurs, ruined through the fault of princes, and slighted through the indifference of men. This woman would not allow Erasmus' smattering of learning to die of want, after it had been deserted by men of grandiose promises, robbed by a tyrant, and beset by all of fortune's calamities. May you continue the work you have begun; my literary works are your foster-child, and she is raising her supplicant hands to you. She is pleading with you, not only in the name of your fortune, which when favorable you scorn—a most praiseworthy act—and when unfavorable you bear with courage; but also in the name of her own fortunes, which have always been violent. Against those fortunes she is taking a firm stand, thanks to the patronage of only one person, yourself. She also pleads with you out of love for that distinguished queen, Theology of old, whom the inspired Psalmist describes, in Jerome's version, as standing at the right hand of the eternal King, not filthy and ragged as she now appears in the schools of sophists, but in a dress of gold and a cape of many colors. My nightly toils are spent on rescuing this queen from her present degradation.

To accomplish this, I have long felt two things are very necessary: to go to Italy, so that my humble learning may derive some prestige from the renown of that country, and to obtain a doctorate. Both reasons are of course absurd. Those who race overseas, as Horace says, do not thereby change their minds, nor would the shelter of a mighty title make me one bit more learned. But the fact is, one must adapt himself to the times. And according to the opinion, not only of the masses, but also of those who occupy preeminent positions in the world of learning, no one is considered learned these days unless he is addressed as "Master," in spite of the prohibition of Christ, the Prince of theologians. In ancient times a person was not regarded as a scholar just because he had purchased the title of Doctor, but those men were called scholars who by publishing books had given clear evidence of their scholarship. However, as I have said, there is no point in staging a good play if everybody is going to boo it. And so I must don the lion's skin in order to be accepted as a competent scholar by those who judge a man by his title and not by his writings, which (as goes without saying) they cannot understand. Certain of these fellows have been trained in a ridiculous type of education, and have doubtless paid a high tuition to learn utter nonsense; they are dull-witted, with hardly any common sense, but by God! what stiff-necked arrogance and consummate pride!

TO NICHOLAS RUISTRE[1]

EE 177 (35–52; 92–104)   Louvain, November 17, 1503

Indeed, all these distinctions of yours, by their very brilliance, might have daunted me. However, I received encouragement from other reports about you: that you are extraordinarily gifted with learning and piety; that you hold in deep affection all those who show any unusual evidence of virtue or learning; that you are lavish in bestowing your kindness upon such persons; and that for centuries there has not been anyone who could equal the enthusiasm and candor, the aggressiveness and indifference to disfavor, with which you have guarded the dignity and fortunes of both Church and intellectual pursuits. For you enjoy devoting your full ability, whether that be the gift of nature or the result of industry, to honoring, assisting, and promoting virtuous and learned men. All this and much more have I learned about you.

For some time I had passionately desired to put you under obligation to me in any way I could, but when a guest of mine encouraged me to do so, it was like spurring on a speeding horse. I grew even bolder when I recalled the old story told by Plutarch of a poor commoner who, for the gift of a large apple,[2] gained the high favor of King Artaxerxes.[3] Vergil acquired the good will of Augustus with a single couplet. There are many other instances of men of high station who have been extremely delighted to receive a trifling gift. Even the gods, as Pliny[4] nicely tells us, will accept an offering of salted grain from those who have no incense. . . .

The whole matter is quite insignificant. But I thought it best to try my luck by starting with a project like this. I did not want to try to run before I could walk, but rather to experiment first with some-

1. Bishop of Arras and Chancellor of the University of Louvain. The letter is the preface to Erasmus' translation of the "Declamations" of Libanius. Here we have much flattery and verbosity in the form of a dedicatory letter, but also at the end Erasmus' brief description of the principles of his work as translator.
2. The offering was not an apple, but water.
3. Plutarch, *Apophthegmata*, 172 B.
4. Pliny, *Historia naturalis*.

thing of little value. I have followed that old rule of Cicero, that in translating one should weigh the sense and not merely count the words. However, being a novice in the art of translating, I have tended to be too literal rather than too free. How successful I have been in this attempt, I leave to the judgment of others. One thing I can vouch for, as a result of my experience; it is very difficult to turn good Greek into good Latin. If I learn that you are not displeased with this debut of mine, then relying upon your good judgment and authority, I shall take heart and enter upon something more ambitious. Then will I be bold enough to send you, not just a few blossoms, but a full harvest gleaned from the fields of literature.

TO JOHN DESMARAIS[1]

EE 180 (39–87)   Antwerp, [February 1504]

To begin with, those who regard panegyrics as sheer flattery are apparently quite unaware of the purpose which men of great wisdom had in mind when they invented this literary form. Their purpose was to hold up to men an ideal of virtue whereby wicked rulers would mend their ways and good ones continue to improve, whereby the ignorant would be instructed, those in error admonished, the indolent spurred on, and even those considered hopeless feel a sense of shame. Is it credible that the great philosopher Callisthenes in speaking the praises of Alexander—or Lysias, or Isocrates, or Pliny, or numberless others when they employed this literary form—had any other object in mind than to encourage men to virtuous conduct, under the guise of praise? Or do you suppose that kings, born and reared as they are, should be presented with the stern doctrines of the Stoics or the yelping of the Cynics? Surely you would either provoke a loud guffaw or irritate them to no end. A man of good breeding is

1. A friend of Erasmus and secretary of the University of Louvain. The letter was included in Erasmus' *Panegyricus,* published in 1504.

One might call it a panegyric on panegyrics! The argument is put forth with much classical allusion. Erasmus' point is to suggest the deeper meaning of panegyrics—not empty flattery or praise, but the praise of people to make them better. A different glimpse of his own perspective on such writing may be had in Letter 181, on p. 45.

more easily led than forced; he is more readily corrected by gentle words than by insults. The most effective method, in fact the only method of encouragement employed by men of wisdom, is to concede the possession, in great part, of those attractive qualities which they are urging a person to acquire. Is it not true that "excellence grows by being praised and that glory is a powerful motivation"?[2]

Does not even the Apostle Paul make frequent use of this device of pious flattery, praising people in order to make them better? Indeed, could one reproach a wicked ruler for his cruelty with greater impunity and greater severity than by lauding him for his clemency? Could one reproach him for his greed, his ferocity, or his lust more effectively than by extolling his generosity, his self-control, or his chaste life—"so that he can catch a glimpse of virtue and grieve at having abandoned it"?[3]

Augustine, it is said, confessed that he told many lies when singing the praises of the Emperor. This is not the place to discuss to what extent his remark was colored by his unbending and even hostile attitude toward lying. At any rate, Plato and the Stoics allow the wise man a beneficial lie. Are we not doing the right thing when by occasional false praise we fire up the hearts of boys to strive for excellence? Do not all the best doctors assure their patients that they are pleased with their condition and complexion, not because the patients actually are that way, but only to make them so? Besides, it is proper for a loyal subject to be blinded by his admiration for his ruler and to be boundless in his praise of one for whom his love should know no bounds. Also, it is in the best public interest that, even though a ruler may not be of the highest quality, his subjects should have the highest opinion of him. It is for them that a panegyric is intended, not for the ruler, if he should happen to be unworthy of praise. For a panegyric is delivered not merely to the person who is its theme, but also to the large number of people who form the audience. The orator should direct many of his remarks to them, as he does in a speech before a public assembly. For a panegyric is very closely related to that kind of speech, as is indicated by the Greek word itself, which refers to "a large gathering of the general public." Therefore even Fabius held that in no type of

2. Ovid, *Epistolae Ex Ponto*, 4.2.36.
3. Persius, 3.38.

oratory is there as much freedom granted as in those speeches wherein one can legitimately display all the devices and tricks of rhetoric in order to tickle the ears of an audience. Finally, such orations are also intended for future generations, for the whole world. And from that point of view it does not matter greatly under whose name the ideal of a good ruler is presented to the public, provided it be done judiciously, so that men of intelligence can perceive that its purpose was not to deceive, but to admonish.

TO JOHN COLET[1]

EE 181 (1–94)   Paris, [*ca.* December] 1504

If our friendship, my dear Colet, had resulted from commonplace motives, or if your character had ever suggested anything base, I would indeed have some fears that our long separation in both time and space might have caused our mutual affection to die out, or at least grow cold. But the fact is, I have no reason to fear what generally happens to people: namely, that I am no longer in your thoughts just because I am out of sight. For my attachment to you is the result of my admiration of learning and my love for piety, while your attachment to me is based on some hope perhaps, or rather expectation, of finding those same qualities in me. True, for several years I have received no letter from Colet. Perhaps you have been too busy, or have not known my whereabouts; in any case, I would prefer to attribute it to any other reason rather than that you have forgotten your humble friend. Although I have no right or wish to complain of your silence, still I do beg and entreat you all the more earnestly to steal a few moments from your intellectual pursuits and business affairs so that now and then you can send me your greetings. I am surprised that nothing as yet has appeared in print of your commentaries on Paul or on the Gospels. I am aware of your

---

1. See Letter 107, p. 29. The present letter comments in general on Erasmus' activities upon his return from England—his study of Greek, the different understanding of religion, his various publications, especially the *Adagia,* together with the practical problem of receiving moneys from the sale of that book in England.

modesty; but it is high time for you to overcome and eliminate it, in consideration of the public interest. As for your being honored with the doctorate and the deanship and several other distinctions which I am told have been conferred upon you for meritorious service,[2] I do not so much congratulate you personally, for I am sure that the only prerogative which you will demand from them will be hard work; rather, I congratulate the persons who will profit from your having those honors, and congratulate even those honors, which at long last are worthy of their name, for they have fallen upon a man who deserves but does not solicit them.

I cannot tell you, my excellent Colet, how intensely eager I am to devote myself to sacred learning and how distasteful I find everything that diverts my attention from reaching that goal or slows me down. But unkind Fortune, who constantly regards me with the same unfavorable expression, has been the reason why I have not been able to free myself from these entanglements. With this in mind I have returned to France, either to solve these problems or, at any rate, somehow to get rid of them. After that, I can freely and wholeheartedly turn to the study of theology, intending to spend the rest of my life on it.[3]

However, three years ago I did attempt something on Paul's Epistle to the Romans, and with a burst of enthusiasm did complete four volumes. I would have continued the work except for various interruptions, the main one being due to my ignorance of Greek, of which I was constantly made aware. And so for about three years now the study of Greek has completely occupied me, and I do not think it has been an utter waste of time. I also took up the study of Hebrew, but was discouraged by its strange mode of expression; and since the human mind in the course of one lifetime is incapable of doing several things equally well, I gave it up. I have read through a good part of Origen's works, and I believe his tutelage has proved quite valuable for me. He uncovers certain sources and points out fundamental principles of the science of theology.

2. Colet had been granted the deanship of St. Paul's in London.
3. This sentence seems to suggest that Erasmus had previously been unconcerned about theology and religion. My Introduction suggests as a preferable view of the significance of Erasmus' encounter with Colet and More that it exposed him to a *different* outlook on religion.

I am sending you as a little gift a volume containing a few works of mine. . . . I did not write the *Enchiridion*[4] to display my talent or rhetorical skill, but only to correct the error commonly made by those who base religion on ceremonies and on external observances to an almost greater degree than do the Jews, while they strangely neglect what pertains to the essence of piety. I have tried to propose a manual on the art of piety, following the practice of those who have composed handbooks containing a systematic explanation of the various branches of knowledge. . . . As for the *Panegyric*, I could not stomach it; in fact, I cannot recall having done anything more reluctantly. I realized that this literary form cannot be handled without flattering. However, I have adopted a novel approach—being very free in my flattering and very flattering in my freedom.

If you wish to have any of your writings published, just send me a copy. I will take care of everything else and will make sure that the printing is absolutely flawless.

I told you recently in a letter, as I think you recall, about the hundred copies of my *Adagia* which three years ago were sent to England at my own expense. Grocin had assured me in writing that he would very faithfully and carefully see to distributing them according to my wishes. I have no doubt that he has kept his word, for he is the most honest and the finest of all Englishmen. Will you lend me your personal services in this matter by reminding and spurring on those who, in your opinion, ought to be instrumental in finishing the business? Undoubtedly, during this long period of time, the books have all been sold, and the money must be in somebody's possession. And I need the money right now as never before. Somehow I have got to arrange to live for several months entirely for myself, so that I can finally disentangle myself from the projects which I have begun in the field of secular learning. I had hoped to do that this winter, except that I have been frustrated in so many of my hopes. It will not cost a great deal of money for me to purchase this freedom; it is only a matter of a few months.

Therefore I beg you to do whatever you can to help me in my passionate desire to work on theology and to liberate me from those studies which I no longer find attractive. I ought not to make any

4. This is the "Handbook of the Christian Soldier," mentioned in the Introduction.

request of my friend, Lord Mountjoy. Still, if he did give me some
assistance out of the goodness of his heart, his action would not be
pointless or inconsistent, for he has always promoted my intellectual
interests and also it was at his suggestion that I undertook a work
which I then dedicated to his name, that is, the *Adagia*. I am
dissatisfied with the first edition; because of the negligence of the type-
setters it is so full of errors, it seems to have been deliberately mis-
printed; moreover I was goaded on by some persons to rush the work
through the press, and only now, after reading Greek authors, have I
begun to realize how shabby and meager it is. I have therefore
decided to put out a second edition with a revision of my own errors
and those of the printers; at the same time I hope to provide scholars
with some very useful material. Even though I am presently handling
a subject that is perhaps somewhat lowly, still while strolling through
the gardens of the Greeks I have plucked many a blossom along the
way which will be of future service also in my theological studies.
From my experience I have learned one fact: in no area of learning
do we amount to anything without Greek. To venture a guess is not
quite the same as forming a solid judgment, and to believe your own
eyes is quite different from believing someone else's.

TO CHRISTOPHER FISHER[1]

EE 182 (1–8; 94–204)   Paris, [*ca.* March] 1505

Last summer, while I was hunting around in a very old library—
more fun than hunting in any woods—a most unusual quarry acci-
dentally fell into my snare: Lorenzo Valla's *Annotations* on the New
Testament. I immediately felt a strong desire to share it with every
scholar, thinking it would be a selfish thing to devour my game all by
myself and in silence. But I was deterred from that by the old

1. The recipient was from England, in the service of the Holy See, and in
1506 Bishop of Elphin, Ireland. He had met Erasmus in Paris. The letter
forms the preface to Erasmus' edition of Valla's *Adnotationes* on the New
Testament, published in Paris. Since Valla had begun to apply grammatical
and linguistic criticism to the text of the New Testament, Erasmus felt it
necessary to defend him against charges that he disturbed the biblical text. The
letter is not only in praise of Valla but a spirited defense of the need to apply
linguistic criticism to biblical text, and therefore of the kind of learning that
makes such critical scholarship possible.

prejudice against Lorenzo's name and also by the fact that this subject serves as a pretext for a considerable amount of odium. . . .

The only thing that some people have learned about Valla—and
this is altogether ridiculous—is that he is somewhat biting. In that
one respect they imitate or rather outdo him, since they bite at one
whom they don't know. In fact, men of wisdom prefer to be barbarians indefinitely, just because Lorenzo is mordant. Why don't we
follow that very fine rule of Epictetus and take hold of each person
by the handle that is most convenient, as Vergil did with Ennius,
Cyprian with Tertullian, Jerome with many, including Origen; and
Augustine with Tyconius?[2] Since there are so many handles by
which one can take hold of Lorenzo with profit, why do we grasp
only one, namely, his biting language? Why not balance a slight
defect by all his excellent qualities? Indeed, why in our ingratitude
do we pervert an inevitable freedom of speech by calling it vilifi-
cation?

But so much for that. To come now to a discussion of the points
pertaining to our subject. I imagine that some people, as soon as they
have read the title of the work, before knowing anything about the
contents, will promptly scream out like a tragic actor: "Heavens and
earth!" Although Aristophanes gives the very nice advice in his
Plutus: "Do not shout and yell before you know the facts."[3] And I
am inclined to think that those who will cause the wildest disturbance of all will be the very ones who can profit most from it,
namely, the theologians. They will say it is an intolerable act of
rashness for a grammarian, after plaguing all the other disciplines, to
apply his peevish pen to sacred learning. Nicholas of Lyra, whom I
would not call unlearned but certainly a man of recent times, engages
our attention as he even teaches St. Jerome and destroys many
opinions hallowed by the consensus of the ages, and this he does by
making use of the books of the Jews (although we grant that our
present text derives from that source, still I suspect those writings
were deliberately corrupted). But then what crime was it for Lorenzo
to collate some ancient, emended Greek manuscripts and to annotate
the New Testament, which unquestionably has its source in those
Greek texts? Those annotations concerned passages for which there

2. Tyconius, a late fourth-century Donatist about whom much is known. He
wrote a commentary on the Book of Revelation.
3. *Plutus* 477.

are variant readings or which were unsuitably rendered by the translator, or which are expressed more clearly in Greek, or, finally, where our text appears corrupt. Will they maintain that Valla the grammarian does not have the same privilege as Nicholas the theologian?[4] I could respond to this by saying that some important men list Lorenzo among the philosophers too, and among the theologians. When Lyra examines the meaning of an expression, surely he is acting not as a theologian but as a grammarian. In fact, this whole business of translating Scripture is clearly the role of a grammarian. It is not at all a silly thing to say that in some matters Jethro[5] is wiser than Moses.

I do not think that even Theology herself, the queen of all the sciences, will consider it beneath her dignity to be handled and be given due attention by her maid, Grammar. Although grammar is of lower rank than some studies, its services are just as necessary as any others. It is concerned with small details, but without them no one can turn out to be great. It deals with trifles, but the final product is something important.

If they protest that theology is too noble to be bound down by the laws of grammar and that the whole business of interpretation depends on inspiration from the Holy Spirit, it is indeed a novel honor for theologians if they alone are allowed to use barbarous language. Just let them explain what is meant by the remark which Jerome wrote to his friend Desiderius: "To be a prophet is one thing; to be an interpreter is quite another."[6] In the former, the Spirit foretells events; in the latter, erudition and command of language help to interpret the meaning. Then, too, what would be Jerome's purpose in laying down precepts for translating Scripture, if that ability is the result of divine inspiration? Finally, why was it said that Paul was more fluent in Hebrew than in Greek? And if it was possible for the interpreters of the Old Testament to err at times, especially in passages where faith is not affected, certainly the interpreters of the New Testament could have slipped, too. Jerome's work on the New Testament was not so much a translation as an emendation, and that to a limited extent, for he left some words

4. Nicholaus Lyra (*ca.* 1270–1333) was a celebrated biblical commentator.
5. The father-in-law of Moses.
6. Hieronymus, *Apologia adversus Libros Rufini* (J. P. Migne), *Patrologia cursus completus*, II, 520.

untouched as he himself testifies; and those words are the special object of Lorenzo's scrutiny. Surely we shall not attribute the errors that we have made to the Holy Spirit who is the author. Suppose the translations were accurate; still, an accurate translation can be corrupted. Emendations on the text were made by Jerome, but those emendations in turn were corrupted. One might object that in the present age half-learned men are not so brazen, or the knowledge of languages is superior, or corruption of a text is quite unlikely because of the art of printing, which can in a moment multiply one mistake among a thousand copies.

But, they object, it is blasphemous to make any change in the text of Scripture, because every little letter has some deeper meaning. Then it is all the more blasphemous to corrupt the text, and scholars must all the more carefully correct the errors caused by ignorance, but with that caution and restraint which all writings deserve, especially Sacred Scripture. But, they object further, Lorenzo was wrong in assuming a task which Jerome undertook at Damasus' command. However, each had a different purpose in mind. Jerome replaced the old text with a new edition. Lorenzo recorded his critical observations in personal notebooks, and he did not expect any change to be made in the text as a result, although the large number of variant readings in our present copies is clear proof that they are not free from error. Moreover, just as the accuracy of the Old Testament must be tested by comparison with the Hebrew, so too in the New Testament the Greek text must be employed as the norm of accuracy, as Augustine advises in words that are quoted in the *Decreta*.[7] As regards that passage, I doubt if anyone is so ruthless as not to pity, or so grim-faced as not to smile at, the silly gloss made by somebody who imagined that Jerome wrote in a letter to Desiderius that the Latin text was more accurate than the Greek and the Greek more so than the Hebrew. The fellow failed to notice that Jerome was proving his point by introducing an obviously absurd statement, and that the words preceding that statement, *aliud est si* ("it is quite otherwise if"), have exactly the same meaning as *nisi forte* ("unless perhaps"). Otherwise it would have been sheer madness to translate the one Testament from the Hebrew and to emend the other Testament from the Greek, if in both cases our Latin texts are superior. . . .

7. The reference is to the collection of ecclesiastical statutes, specifically those promulgated by Pope Clement V in 1311–1313. See Allen, I, 411.

But this, I think, is sufficient advice for scholars. I am told that the assertion is sometimes made that the ancient interpreters, competent in the three languages, have given an adequate explanation wherever it was necessary. Well, first of all, I would rather study the text with my own eyes than with someone else's. Secondly, though they did say very much, they also left much to future generations to say. Furthermore, some knowledge of the languages is required to understand their explanations. Finally, when a person meets texts of the ancient writings that are corrupt in every language—and so they are—where will he turn? Consequently, most learned Christopher, it is as true as can be, as you yourself have time and again said, that there is neither judgment nor shame in those who are bold enough to comment upon Scripture or upon any of the writings of the ancients without a moderate knowledge of both Latin and Greek. For it is just at the very moment when those fellows are toiling and struggling most of all to display their scholarship that they are most of all a laughingstock to skilled linguists, and all that turmoil is scotched by the mention of a Greek word. Now, whoever does not have the time to master Greek will still receive considerable aid from the work of Valla, who scrutinized the entire New Testament with extraordinary insight. He also introduces here and there not a few references even to the Psalms, whereas the text of the Psalms in common use is based on the Greek, not the Hebrew. And so scholars will be very much indebted to Lorenzo, and Lorenzo to you, through whom he has been introduced to the public.

TO FRANCIS THEODORIC[1]

EE 186   London, [end of 1505?]

You would be doing me a very great favor, dearest friend, if you would try your best to gather together my more carefully written letters addressed to various persons. I am planning to publish them in

1. The recipient had been a monk in a monastery near Steyn and then was prior of Hemsdonck. This connection prompted Erasmus' request to help him with the collection of his early letters.

This letter, coming from a relatively early period of Erasmus' scholarly life, conveys his first expression of intent to publish some of his letters. At the same time it offers some general advice about true learning.

a single volume, including especially the many letters I have addressed to Cornelius of Gouda, the large number addressed to my friend William, and the few to Servatius. Scrape together all you can from any and every source. But deliver them to me only in the hands of the person I tell you to.

On behalf of our friendship and your happiness, dear Francis, which means as much to me as does my own, I beg you to devote yourself wholeheartedly to the study of Scripture. Read the ancient interpreters. I assure you, that is the road that will take us to heaven, or we shall never arrive there. However, I am sure that you are already following this advice.

TO WILLIAM WARHAM[1]

EE 188 (20–63)   London, January 24, [1506]

The task of translating good Greek into good Latin demands an extraordinary craftsman, one richly endowed with a ready store of knowledge in both languages and also one who is unusually perceptive and alert. So true is this that no one has come upon the scene for centuries whose work of translation has met with universal approval in the world of scholarship. It is not difficult, then, to imagine what a job it has been to translate verse into verse, especially when the verse is so varied and unusual and written by a man in very ancient times—and a tragic poet at that—and also in a style so remarkably compressed and subtle and studied that it would be nothing short of a crime to eliminate or alter a single thing; furthermore, there is such a frequent and clever handling of the commonplaces of rhetoric that

1. This letter comes from the period of Erasmus' second stay in England (1505–1506). He came into contact with several scholars (Linacre, Latimer, Grocyn) who in turn helped him to meet high ecclesiastics. William Warham (ca. 1450–1532) was one of these—Bishop of London in 1501 and Archbishop of Canterbury from 1503. Other letters to Warham are 396 and 1828; see also p. 69 (in Letter 296) for light on his relation to Erasmus.

In the letter, which introduces Erasmus' translation of Euripides' *Hecuba et Iphigenia* from Greek into Latin, he deals generally with the problems of translating Greek.

the poet constantly seems to be declaiming. Then, too, there are the
choral odes, which are made so obscure by strange conceits that they
need an Oedipus or an Apollo for interpreting rather than a translator. Add to all this the corrupt state of the manuscripts and their
scarcity, and no translations to consult. It is no surprise, then, that
even in this enlightened age none of the Italians has dared to attempt
a translation of a tragedy or a comedy, although several have tried
their hand at Homer, such as Poliziano, and even he was dissatisfied
with his results. Somebody tried Hesiod, but with very little success.
Someone else tried Theocritus, with even much less success. And
finally, as I found out after beginning my translation, one of the
funeral orations of Francesco Filelfo contains a version of the first
scene of the *Hecuba*; talented as he is, he gave me no little encouragement after I had found my own work somewhat disgusting.[2]

But any deterrent arising from such formidable precedents and the
many difficulties of the work had less effect on me than did the
attractiveness of this poet's exceedingly sweet and honeyed eloquence, which even his enemies acknowledge. And so I was not
afraid to approach a task never before attempted. I had hopes that,
even if my results were poor, sympathetic readers would consider my
effort somewhat laudable, while the more critical ones would at least
excuse, in the case of such a difficult work, one who is a novice at
translating; especially since I purposely made the task considerably
more difficult by doing a conscientious translation, striving to reproduce as much as possible the figures of speech and the style of the
Greek, while making a line-for-line and almost word-for-word rendi-
tion and attempting constantly to adapt, with the utmost fidelity, the
weight and force of the original expression to the Latin ear. I did this
for two reasons: first, because I do not exactly approve the freedom in
translating which Cicero allows others, and which to almost an excessive degree he employed himself; second, because being a novice at
this craft I preferred to err by being too scrupulously literal rather
than too free, and to hug the shore at times rather than wreck my
ship and be forced to swim out in the deep. I would rather have
scholars criticize my work for lack of brilliance and beauty of style
than for lack of fidelity.

2. For details on these translation efforts see Allen I, 419.

TO RICHARD WHITFORD[1]

EE 191 (1-26)   The country, May 1, 1506

For some years now, my dear Richard, I have been completely occupied with the study of Greek. However, in order to become reconciled with Latin I recently took up declaiming in Latin; and this at the insistence of Thomas More,[2] whose eloquence, as you know, is capable of persuading even an enemy to do absolutely anything. My own love for the man is so deep that if he told me to do a rope dance I would not hesitate to obey. He has been treating the same theme, and in his treatment he carefully examines and elicits every possible argument. Unless my deep appreciation for him deceives me, it is my conviction that nature has never fashioned a mind that is more poised, more alert, more perceptive, more penetrating, in a word, more thoroughly endowed with every kind of gift, than that of Thomas More. Besides, his power of expression equals his mental abilities. Then, too, his is a remarkably happy disposition with a great abundance of wit but no sarcasm. In him you can find everything that the perfect advocate should have.

When I took up this task, therefore, I had no intention of trying to rival such a master, but only to engage in a match of wits with my very dearest friend, with whom I regularly enjoy a mixture of the serious and the light. I have also been motivated by my desire to have this incomparably fruitful practice restored some day to our schools. The lack of it, in my opinion, explains why in our day, when there

1. This letter, too, is a preface, this time to Erasmus' "Declamation" in reply to Lucian's *Tyrannicida*. The "task" Erasmus refers to was the competent handling of Latin in his translation from the Greek. Whitford was chaplain to Richard Foxe, a distinguished churchman and academician, founder of Corpus Christi College at Oxford.

2. This is the first extended reference to Thomas More, whom Erasmus had first met during his stay in England in 1499. As we noted in the Introduction, More exerted a lasting influence upon him, and the correspondence between the two men covered many years. From Erasmus' pen comes a lengthy portrait of his English friend in the setting of a letter to Ulrich von Hutten, see Letter 999, p. 142.

are large numbers reading the works of eloquent writers, there is still such a scarcity of men who are not altogether tongue-tied whenever there is a demand for an orator. But if we followed the authority of Cicero and Fabius and the example of the ancients and were diligently trained from boyhood in such exercises, then, in my opinion, there would not be such a dearth of eloquence, such a pitiful inability to speak, such a shameful mumbling of words, even in the case of those who are professors of rhetoric.

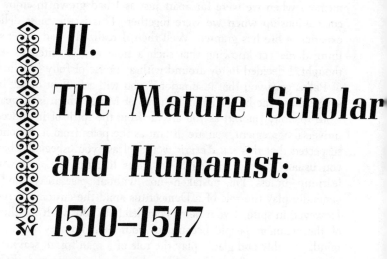

III.

The Mature Scholar and Humanist: 1510–1517

Now widely recognized, Erasmus continued his travels—England, Louvain, Basel, Antwerp—and his literary work, of which his Greek edition of the New Testament may well have been the most significant. He was at the zenith of his career.

TO THOMAS MORE[1]

EE 222 (1–77)   [Paris?], June 9, [1511]

In the course of my last trip from Italy to England, not wanting to waste all the time I had to spend in the saddle on simple and dull talk, I preferred from time to time to meditate on our joint studies or to enjoy myself by reflecting upon the friends—as sweet as they are learned—whom I had left behind in England. You were in my

1. Lived 1478–1535. More was the most eminent of the English humanists, famous for his *Utopia* (1516), who pursued a life of studies as well as of public service. See also Letter 191 (p. 55). For other letters and references to More see Letters 785, 999, 1162; also pp. 120, 142, and 155. The present letter forms Erasmus' own brief commentary on the reasoning that led him to write the "Praise of Folly."

thoughts most of all, my dear More, and I was wont to enjoy your memory when we were far apart just as I had grown to enjoy your companionship when we were together. This is the most delicious experience life has granted! Well then, I realized I had to get something done; yet knowing that such a time was ill-suited to serious thought, I decided to toy around with a "praise of folly." "What sort of Pallas gave you that inspiration?" you will ask. First of all, it was suggested to me by your family name of More, which is as near the word for folly [*moria*] as you are far from the spirit of it! Indeed, by universal agreement, you are distant as the poles from it. Secondly, I suspected that this *jeu d'esprit* would please you especially, because you usually take great delight in trifles like this, *i.e.*, not without learning—unless I'm mistaken—nor without pleasantry, and you generally play the role of a Democritus amid the customs of society. However, in spite of your being completely at odds with the thinking of the common people because of your extraordinary keenness of mind, you ably and gladly play the role of a man for all seasons with all men because of your incredibly charming manners and affability. Therefore you will be so good as to accept this little declamation as a remembrance of your friend and also to take it under your protection; after all, it has been dedicated to you and is now yours, not mine.

Probably there will be no lack of noisy critics to belittle it with the charge either that such lighthearted levity is unbecoming a theologian or that such biting satire is not in keeping with Christian self-control. Their persistent cry will be that I am reviving ancient comedy or Lucian and carping at everything with a biting tooth. But those who take offense at my frivolous, playful theme might well consider that I am not creating a new genre; this sort of thing has a long history among noted authors. Such trifles have been produced for centuries; think of Homer's *The Battle of Frogs and Mice*, Vergil's *Gnat* and *Salad*, and Ovid's *Nut-Tree*; Polycrates lauded Busiris, and Isocrates, the critic of Polycrates, did the same. . . .

Accordingly, if it please the fellows, let them think that I have just been playing a game of chess for recreation or, if they prefer, that I have been riding a hobbyhorse. But really, is it not a lack of balance to grant to every profession its own form of amusement but permit no fun at all to learning—especially if jests can lead the way to serious discussion, and if humor properly handled can be the source of considerably more profit for the reader who is not an utter blockhead than some people's crabbed and pompous compositions? I am thinking of some lengthy patchwork in praise of rhetoric or philosophy, or an encomium of some prince, or an exhortation to launch a war against the Turks, or predictions of the future, or a concoction of brand new quibbles over trifles. Just as there is nothing more nonsensical than a nonsensical treatment of a serious subject, so there is nothing more merry than a treatment of nonsense which discloses the fact that one has been doing anything but talk nonsense. As to my own case, the decision is in the hands of others; and yet, unless I am completely blinded by self-esteem, I have praised Folly and not altogether foolishly.

Now to answer the caviling charge of carping. Men of intelligence have always been granted the privilege of poking fun wittily and with impunity at the customs of society, provided this license did not lapse into raging passion. Therefore I am the more amazed at the sensitiveness of modern ears, which can endure almost nothing but solemn titles. What is more, one may observe men so wrongheadedly religious as to put up even with the most serious insults to Christ rather than have a pope or ruler touched by the slightest jest—especially if it concerns their pocketbook. If someone criticizes men's lives without censuring anyone at all by name—now, is such a person really carping, or is he not rather teaching and admonishing? If not, then on how many counts am I not censuring my own self? Besides, one whose criticism leaves no class of men untouched is obviously angry at no single man but at all forms of vice. Therefore anyone who stands up and cries that he has been insulted will betray either a guilty or a worried conscience. This type of satire was written by St. Jerome, who was much freer and more caustic and did not always refrain from mentioning names. I have not only completely avoided the use of names, but have also tempered my pen so that the intelligent reader will readily understand that my purpose is to amuse, not to hurt. Nor have I at any point followed Juvenal's example of churning up the dark dregs of sin; I have aimed to survey the funny rather than the filthy. If there is still someone not satisfied with this approach, at least he can bear this in mind: it is a fine thing to be scoffed at by Folly. Since I have represented her as the speaker, I had to make her words consistent with her character.

TO ANDREW AMMONIUS[1]

EE 226   Queen's College, Cambridge,
                                                   August 25, 1511

As to my situation, there is still nothing new to write about, except
that the trip was most uncomfortable and I still feel a little shaky
after that sweating sickness. I think I shall stay at least a few days at
this College. Out of concern for my health I have not as yet made
myself available for lecturing. I do not at all like the local beer, and
the wines are not very satisfactory either. If you could arrange to
have a cask of the best Greek wine sent to me, you will make your
friend Erasmus extremely happy; but it must be a very dry wine. As
for the money, do not worry; it will be sent you, ahead of time if you
wish. I am now experiencing the first of the blessings which result
from papal bulls; I am dying of thirst.[2] You can imagine what the
rest will be. This is only the beginning for me.

TO JOHN COLET[1]

EE 227 (1–22)   Cambridge, September 13,
                                                   [1511]

I am sending you, as you requested, the Mass of Chrysostom[2] and
also the letter,[3] in which if I am not mistaken there are some points
with which you will disagree, for you despise systems and rules. But I
consider them somewhat important, especially in the case of a
teacher. Regarding Linacre, be careful not to give rash credence to

1. The recipient was one of Erasmus' most intimate friends, a gifted Latinist
who came to England from his native Italy around 1505 and was in the service
of Lord Mountjoy. Erasmus comments here (he is back in England) on his
present whereabouts and activities and expresses some misgivings about his
situation at Cambridge.
2. Probably a reference to the efforts to obtain formal confirmation of the
dispensation granted to Erasmus by Pope Julius II in 1507. These efforts had
depleted his financial resources and thus made the purchase of wine difficult.
1. See Letter 107, p. 29. Along with sundry other matters, including words
about his own scholarly projects, Erasmus offers what might be called a
"character reference" for a mutual acquaintance.
2. *Missa Sancti Iannis Chrysostomi.*
3. Erasmus' *De ratione studii* ("On the Method of Studies").

what anybody says.[4] I have definite proof that he has the greatest
respect for you and that he is not greatly upset over the rejection of
his grammar; although it is natural for a person to be strongly biased
in favor of his own writings, as parents are toward their own children. But if this matter still bothers him, use your diplomacy and
hide your feelings and don't open up the wound; cheer him up with
a pleasant look and a lively manner, rather than try to offer an excuse
through a third party. In this way, his bad feelings will gradually
disappear in time. But, really, I am extraordinarily brash in telling
you this, like a moron addressing Socrates.

I have not as yet met anyone whom I would consider a suitable
assistant for your school. I shall continue my search, and as soon as I
find the right man I shall let you know. . . .

On occasion, I battle here on your behalf with these Thomists and
Scotists; but that we can discuss in person. I have begun a translation
of Basil's commentary on Isaiah; I do like the work very much. I am
going to show a sample to the Bishop of Rochester and see if he is
willing to soothe my toils with a little reward. "What a beggar!" You
are laughing now, I am sure. I do hate myself for this, and I am
absolutely determined either to hit upon a fortune that can relieve
me of all this begging or to follow the example of Diogenes.[5]

TO JOHN COLET[1]

EE 237 (71–89)   Cambridge, October 29,
                                                          [1511]

I mentioned the subject of an assistant teacher for your school to a
group of professors, and one of them, a man of no mean reputation,
asked with a smirk, "Who could stand spending his life in a school

4. The Englishman Thomas Linacre was a widely renowned Latinist and
physician.
5. The Greek philosopher Diogenes insisted that a man, in order to be
happy, must be aloof from all material goods and desires, and is said to have
resigned himself to live in a barrel. When he saw a boy use his hands to drink
from a well, he threw away his wooden goblet, and when Alexander the Great,
standing before him, told him he might ask for any favor, his response was
"Stand out of my sunshine."
1. See Letter 107, p. 29. Colet founded the famous St. Paul's School for
boys in London. In this letter Erasmus praises those who teach the young, as
against those who withdraw into monastic seclusion.

like that with little boys when he could live anywhere and in any fashion he liked?" I quietly answered that I thought it a very honorable position to train young men in character and learning, and that Christ did not show contempt for young people, and that that was the best age upon which to bestow kindness and from them one could expect the richest harvest, for there is the soil, the material, of our future citizens. I also said that all men of true piety believe they can serve God in no better way than by leading children to Christ. But the fellow only wrinkled his nose and sneered, "If a person really wants to serve Christ, he can enter a monastery or join a religious order." I replied that, for St. Paul, true religion depends upon acts of charity which consist in doing all we can to help our neighbor. This he tossed aside as a stupid statement. "Look," he said, "we have left all things; therein lies perfection." "No," I answered, "a person has not left all things if he can do much good for a large number but refuses because the position is considered too lowly." And so I left him, for fear of starting a quarrel.

TO JOHN COLET[1]

EE 260 (1–35)   London, April 29, 1512

I cannot help but speak in high terms, my dear Colet, of your extraordinary and truly Christian piety. For you have always devoted all your efforts, all your energy, not to the attainment of your own personal advantage, but to promoting the good of your country and your fellow citizens. And I have no less admiration for your choice of the two special means for accomplishing your goal in the fullest manner. First of all, you have realized that the richest fruit of love consists in this: to implant Christ in the hearts of one's fellow men by frequent sermons and teaching sacred doctrine. You have been engaged in this work for several years; how much praise you have received I shall not mention, for that is not what you are looking for, in fact, you do not even welcome it. Still, the results have been

1. See Letter 107, p. 29. This letter is the preface to Erasmus' *De duplici copia verborum,* an introductory Latin primer, and a panegyric on the scholarly accomplishments of Colet as Erasmus sees them.

outstanding. For that reason your own St. Paul, who is ordinarily very modest, can on occasion glory and boast with a holy pride. The second means you chose was to open up a very fine and most excellent grammar school, where the youth of Britain just at their tender age could, under the guidance of carefully selected teachers, drink in the spirit of Christ along with the best in literature. You deeply realized that these young boys are the tender shoots upon which the future of the state depends, and how important it is for their whole life that, right from the cradle, they be imbued with the very best.

Now no one can fail to admire the generosity and loftiness of your spirit and, I might say, the holy pride manifested in your willingness to perform this twofold duty to your country without recompense or self-seeking. As a result, all those years of laborious preaching have not made you one bit richer, and while sowing the seeds of your own spirit you have never reaped any material goods from other men. You have wished to bear yourself the burden of the school's expenses, which are so vast as to appall even a Persian potentate. And while the common run of men would be most ready to welcome a partner in such an enterprise, you preferred to expend your inheritance, your wealth, and even your household furnishings rather than admit anyone else to a share in this glory. Surely you are showing a more than fatherly attitude toward all those children of your friends, and toward your fellow citizens. You are robbing yourself to make them rich; you are stripping yourself to clothe them; you are killing yourself with hard work so that your sons may live in Christ. In a word, you are spending yourself completely so as to gain them for Christ.

TO KING HENRY VIII[1]

EE 272   [Cambridge, July 1513]

Although there is nothing that adds more pleasure to our daily life or is more essential for performing our tasks than a sincere and really true friend, still such a blessing is the rarest of happenings to men;

1. King of England. This was the preface to Erasmus' edition of Plutarch's De discrimine adulatoris et amici ("On the Distinction of Flatterers and Friends"), and describes, with various references to classical antiquity, the nature of true friendship. See Letter 104, p. 28, for an earlier dedication to Henry.

even as in other matters, the finest things are the rarest. Indeed, as Hiero in the writings of Xenophon wisely states, this valued prize of good fortune is desired most of all by rulers, who may otherwise be the most favored of men, since no one is in greater need of having numerous genuine friends. One who all by himself looks out for the good of thousands of other men must have extremely clear vision. Therefore it is proper for a ruler to be provided with many eyes, that is, with many prudent and loyal friends. This was clearly realized by Darius, king of the Persians. On one occasion, when an exceptionally large pomegranate was offered to him, he expressed the wish of having as many Zopyruses as there were seeds in that fruit. Zopyrus was an unusually upright man and a friend of the king, and so the king was quite right in esteeming him so highly as to say that he would rather have one honest Zopyrus than capture a hundred Babylons. He thereby openly declared that a friend is one's most precious treasure.

When Darius' son, Xerxes, was on the point of invading Greece, he could find only one frank and friendly adviser among all those thousands upon thousands of men, whose total number is still considered incredible; and that one man was Demaratus. Even his loyalty was not fully realized until it had been actually tested. . . . We read that Alexander the Great had only one friend amid his huge throng of hangers-on; that was Callisthenes, a pupil of Aristotle, and even he was more an outspoken associate than a friend. The only close associates of Dionysius of Syracuse were Dion and Plato, and of Nero, Seneca. And if Nero had been willing to accept Seneca as adviser, he would have enjoyed a longer reign and could have been counted among the good emperors.

But perhaps the behavior and temperament of those men did not attract candid friends. However, even if a ruler is very approachable, as you obviously are—and a more approachable person could not be imagined—the dazzling splendor of fortune, whose fascination draws a horde of friends, is what prevents one from distinguishing a true friend from a counterfeit. It is no idle saying that good times beget friends, bad times test them. Indeed, a genuine friend is a valuable possession; therefore he is all the more pernicious who steals upon us wearing the mask of friendship. We carefully test gold with a touchstone to see if it is pure or not, and there are ways of telling a real gem from an artificial one. Surely, then, it is highly absurd not to employ equal caution in a matter of much greater importance, so that we can clearly distinguish between a sycophant and a friend, that is, between the most pernicious evil and the most salutary good. But just as one does not detect poison by tasting it, so also it should not be necessary to determine a friend by putting him to a test involving grave consequences. With this in mind Plutarch, undoubtedly the most learned of Greek writers, devised a marvelous method for easily distinguishing between a candid, genuine friend and a mocking impersonator. However, in admonishing friends as in the practice of medicine, loyalty is not enough; one must also use discretion, or else, while ineptly trying to remedy a friend's mistakes, we may ruin the friendship. So for this reason, Plutarch added as a final touch to his work some advice on the need of tact in admonishing a friend when admonition is deserved. This very profitable work, then, I have presented in Latin garb to please Your Majesty, so that by it I might now reaffirm to you, the most glorious King of all, that same interest and feeling which I affirmed to you years ago when you were a boy of outstanding promise.

TO ANTONY OF BERGEN[1]

EE 288 (12–121)   London, March 14, 1513/4

Preparations for war have suddenly changed the spirit of this island. Daily the cost of living is going up, while generosity is dropping. And why shouldn't men be more sparing in their gifts when their numbers have been so often decimated? Good wine is scarce and as a result of drinking this vapid stuff I recently developed the stone and almost died. Living on any island is by its very nature a kind of exile, but we are being still more closely confined by these

1. The abbot of St. Bertin (northwestern France) and a former patron of Erasmus. This letter on the ravages and evils of war was occasioned by the conflict between England and France at the time. It was subsequently enlarged by Erasmus into a discussion of the adage entitled *Dulce bellum inexpertis* ("War is sweet for those who do not know about it"), which was included in the 1515 edition of the *Adagia*.

wars, so that we cannot even send out a letter. I can see great turmoil stirring, and what the outcome will be no one knows. May God in His mercy quiet this storm of Christendom.

I am frequently amazed as I wonder why it is that men—and I won't call them Christians—are driven to such a pitch of madness as to rush into mutual destruction with so much zest and at such a tremendous cost and risk. We spend our whole life fighting wars. Not even animals do that, except wild ones, and they do not battle with their own kind, but only with members of a different species; they fight with the weapons with which nature has provided them, not like us, with war machinery devised by the devil's art. Nor do they fight for any and every reason, but only to protect their young and get food, while our wars, for the most part, are the result of ambition or anger or lust or some such disease of the soul. Finally, animals do not mass together by the thousands, as we do, and then line up to destroy each other. We proudly bear the name of Christ, whose whole life in teaching and example was one of meekness. For us, who are members of one body, who are one flesh, are quickened by the same Spirit, nourished by the same sacraments, joined to the same Head, called to the same immortal life, and have hopes for that supreme union whereby Christ and the Father are one, so that we too may be one with Him—for us, then, can anything in this world be so important as to provoke war? War is so destructive and ugly that, even when it is most just, still it cannot be pleasing to a truly good man.

Only reflect on what kinds of men fight wars: murderers, debauchers, dicers, rapists, filthy mercenaries for whom a little money is more precious than life. Such men are the best fighters in a war, for what they have been used to doing at their own risk, they are now paid and even praised for doing. These dregs of humanity must be welcomed into your lands, into your cities, so that you can fight a war. In short, such men must we serve when we wish to gain vengeance on another. Furthermore, how many criminal acts are committed under the guise of war, since in time of war good laws are silenced! The plundering, the godless conduct, the raping, and all the other disgraceful things which one would blush to mention! This moral plague must last for several years, even when the war is over. And then count the cost; even the winner loses much more than he gains. What territorial conquest would you consider worth the bloodshed of countless thousands? Indeed, those who seem to have nothing to do with a war feel its worst shock, while the blessings of peace reach out to all men. As a rule, even the victor in a war sheds tears. War brings with it such a train of woes that poets rightly have imagined it as sent from hell by the Furies. I need not mention the plundering of the people, the secret agreements between generals, and the new conditions, which ordinarily are not rectified without extreme difficulty. But if it is the desire for glory that attracts us to war, it is not glory we are particularly aiming at by committing foul deeds. It is much more glorious to build cities than to destroy them, if one is looking for glory. Cities are built and developed by the common people, but destroyed by the stupidity of rulers. If money is our attraction in war, no war has ever been so successful as not to produce more evil than good. And no man can cause harm to his enemy by means of war without first bringing many woes upon his own people. Finally, when we view human affairs, which like the currents in Euripus channel change this way and that and are in great confusion, what is the point of all the struggling and straining to gain an empire which is destined on some occasion in the near future to fall into the hands of others? How much bloodshed did it cost to found the Roman Empire, and how soon did it begin to fall! . . .

Oftentimes a supreme right is a supreme injustice and there are some rulers who first decide what they want and then search for a pretext to justify their action. And amid all the changes in human affairs and the making and breaking of so many treaties, who can fail to find a justifiable reason? But if there is a violent dispute over the proper authority, why must there be so much bloodshed? No consideration is given to the good of the people, but only to whether this man or that man deserves to rule. There are pontiffs and bishops and men of prudence and integrity who could serve as mediators in handling such small matters and thus prevent the endless chain of wars and the embroilment of things both human and divine. It is the duty of the pope and of cardinals, of bishops and abbots, to settle the differences between rulers, and in such situations to express their authority and show how much respect they can command. . . .

Furthermore, we must keep in mind that men are free, especially Christians. When they have flourished for a long period of time under a ruler and now acknowledge him, what need is there to overturn the world with a revolution? A ruler is considered a ruler if he is long recognized as such; this is true even among pagans, and much more so among Christians, where being a ruler means service, not ownership; and so, if he is deprived of a part of his realm, he is relieved of a part of his burden, but not wronged. But, you say, suppose the other party refuses to accept the decision made by upright men; what do you want me to do in that situation? First of all, if you are a true Christian, I would want you to bear it and to acquiesce and to disregard whatever right is yours. Secondly, if you are only concerned with prudence, consider how much it is going to cost you to vindicate your rights. If the cost is excessive (and it is surely excessive if you vindicate your rights by force of arms), do not, at the expense of great disaster to the human race, defend your cause—which may be only a pretext—by endless butchery, by depriving families of their loved ones, and by the wailing of your own people. What do you imagine are the thoughts of the Turks when they hear of Christian princes raging furiously against one another merely for the sake of gaining the title to a throne? Italy has now gained revenge on the French. What has all that bloodshed accomplished except that where formerly a Frenchman was in charge, now there is someone else? And formerly there was more prosperity than at present?

I would not care to go more deeply into this subject. But if there are any rights that do justify a war, they are stupid and suggest that Christ has become degenerate and is weighed down by worldly wealth. I doubt if these rights justify the modern type of warfare. However, when Christian peace is defended against the onslaught of barbarians in order to protect the faith, then I realize that war is sometimes approved by men of piety. But why do these human thoughts come to mind rather than the many statements made by Christ and the apostles, and the orthodox and highly approved Fathers, about peace and the tolerance of evil? What position cannot be defended in some way, especially when those in charge of affairs are flattered by large numbers of persons even for their misdeeds and when no one would dare to correct their mistakes? But even so there is no doubt what noble hearts desire, and pray and sigh for. If one studies the matter more closely, one finds that the reasons why rulers begin a war are, for the most part, personal. Do you think it is human for the whole world to be stirred to arms whenever this or that ruler for any reason at all feels peevish at some other prince—or perhaps pretends to be?

TO SERVATIUS ROGER[1]

EE 296 (23–190; 205–232)   Hammes Castle, [near Calais] July 8, 1514

Although I realized that I was not at all suited for this type of life [i.e., in the monastery] and that I had entered it not freely but under compulsion, still, since public opinion today regards it as a crime for a person to abandon a way of life once he has entered upon it, I had made up my mind to endure courageously this portion of my unhappiness too. For you know that I have been unfortunate in many ways. But there is one aspect which I have always considered more distressing than all the rest: the fact that I had been shoved into a type of life for which I was completely unsuited, both mentally and physically—mentally, because I felt aversion for ceremonial observances and was a lover of freedom; physically, because even if I had found such a way of life most attractive, I did not have the constitution to endure such hardships. One might object that I had had my so-called year of probation and was mature in age. But that is absurd! For how could one expect a lad of sixteen, especially one reared in an academic life, to know himself—a great accomplishment even in an elderly man—or to be able to learn in a single year what many a grayheaded man has not yet grasped. However, I never approved of the life, much less so after having had a taste of it; but I was trapped in the manner which I have described, though I do admit that a really good man will live well in any calling. And I do not deny that I was prone to serious vices; but I was not so totally corrupt as to be incapable of being guided toward virtue, if only there had been

1. See Letter 7, p. 14. The present letter was a response to Roger's plea to Erasmus to return to the monastery. The latter justifies his withdrawal at length. The argument is developed along several lines: his own personal experience, the nature of monasticism, his scholarly interests.

available a suitable director, one who was a true Christian and not a follower of Jewish superstitiousness.

Meantime I have been on the lookout to see what kind of life I could live fairly well, and I really think it is the life I have been following. I have been living in the company of men of prudence, amid intellectual pursuits, which have kept me from many faults. It has been my privilege to enjoy the friendship of men who have a true delight in Christ and whose conversation has made me a better man. I am not at all boasting now of my writings, which you perhaps despise. But several persons have admitted that reading those works has made them not only more learned, but also better men. Desire for money has never influenced me. I am not the least bit touched by the glory of fame. As for pleasures, though at one time I was inclined toward them,[2] I have never been a slave to them. As for excess in eating and drinking, I have always felt an aversion for that and have avoided it. And whenever I thought of returning to your community, there would flash across my mind the spitefulness of many men, the contempt of all, the utterly dull and silly conversations without any delight in Christ, and the ungodly feasting—in fact, the whole manner of life, in which I can see nothing at all desirable left once you eliminate the ceremonial observances. Finally, there would occur to me the thought of my physical weakness, which has grown worse as a result of my age and illnesses and hard work; I would not prove satisfactory to you, and a return would mean suicide for me. For some years now I have been susceptible to the stone, an ailment that is quite serious and might prove fatal. For some years now I have drunk nothing but wine, and not any and every kind of wine; my ailment has made this necessary. I cannot take just any sort of food, nor even any sort of climate. For my ailment readily recurs and therefore demands great restraint in my living habits. I am well acquainted with the Dutch climate and with your manner of life, to say nothing of your moral practices. And so, had I returned, I would merely have succeeded in causing you trouble and bringing death on myself.

Now it may be that you consider it a great part of happiness to die amid one's brethren. But that is a snare and a delusion. You are not the only one to suffer from it; it is an almost universal sentiment. We

2. The term here is "inclinatus" (inclined toward, favorable to).

make Christian piety depend upon place of residence, upon the mode of garb and living, and upon certain external observances. We think a person is done for if he exchanges a white garb for a black one, or a cowl for a cap, or if he occasionally changes his residence. I would dare to say that serious damage to Christian piety has resulted from these religious formalities, even though it may have been out of a holy zeal that they were first introduced. But once introduced, they have gradually increased in number and developed into a million varieties. The situation had been aggravated by the authority of the popes, who were excessively lenient and indulgent in many cases. There is nothing so vile and impious as such lax religious practices. Even if one considers only those that are esteemed, or even most highly esteemed, I doubt if you can find any image of Christ in them, apart from some meaningless Judaical observances. Yet these are the reason why they put on airs and why they judge and condemn others. How much more in accordance with the mind of Christ it is to regard all of Christendom as one household, as one monastery, and to consider all men as fellow canons and fellow brethren, to think of the sacrament of baptism as the most important form of religious profession, and to give thought not to where one lives, but how well one lives! You want me to settle down in a fixed residence; my advancing years urge the same. . . .

I have never changed my place of residence unless forced by a plague or for reasons of scholarly work or health. And no matter where I have lived (it may be somewhat arrogant to say this, but it is true), I have been approved by the most highly approved men and have been praised by those most highly praised. Every single country—whether Spain, Italy, Germany, France, England, or Scotland—invites me to accept its hospitality. And if I am not approved by all men (which is not my ambition), at least I am pleasing to the most important persons. In Rome, every cardinal welcomed me as a brother, although I did not solicit anything of the sort. This was especially true of the Cardinal of St. George, the Cardinal of Bologna, Cardinal Grimani, the Cardinal of Nantes, and even the present pope,[3] not to mention bishops, archdeacons, and scholars.

3. Pope Leo X, concerning whom see G. Truc, *Léon X et son siècle* (Paris, 1941).

And that honor was not being paid to wealth, which I neither possess nor desire; nor to vaulting ambition, for which I have always felt a deep aversion, but to learning, which our countrymen mock and the Italians worship. There is not a single bishop in England who would not be delighted to receive a visit from me, who would not desire to have me as a guest at table, who would not want me to be a member of his household. The King [Henry VIII], shortly before his father's death while I was in Italy, even sent me a most affectionate letter in his own handwriting, and now he frequently mentions me with as much respect and affection as anyone does. And whenever I pay him a visit, he receives me most courteously and cordially; obviously his thoughts of me are just as kindly as his words. He has often instructed his almoner[4] to provide me with a benefice. The Queen has tried to pay claim to me as her tutor. As everyone knows, if I wished to spend just a few months at the King's court, I could pile up all the benefices I wanted. But my leisure and scholarly work take precedence over everything else. The Archbishop of Canterbury, who is Primate of all England and Chancellor of this realm, a learned and good man, could not treat me with more affection if he were my own father or brother.[5] To prove to you his sincerity: he gave me a benefice worth roughly one hundred nobles, which later, at my wish and upon my resignation, he exchanged for a pension amounting to one hundred crowns. Besides that, he has presented me with the gift of more than four hundred nobles within the past few years, and this without asking on my part. On a single day he once gave me a hundred and fifty nobles. From other bishops I have received more than a hundred nobles, which they freely and generously offered me. Lord Mountjoy, a baron of this realm and a former student of mine, gives me an annual pension of a hundred crowns. The King and the Bishop of Lincoln, whose present influence with the King is all-powerful, have been making me splendid promises. There are two universities here, Oxford and Cambridge, and both are trying to get me. You see, I have taught Greek and sacred letters at Cambridge for several months, but without accepting any pay, and that will always be my policy. They have colleges here where the religious mode of

4. Cardinal Wolsey. See A. F. Pollard, *Wolsey* (London, 1953).
5. William Warham (*ca.* 1450–1532). See Letter 188, p. 53.

living and the discipline are so extraordinary that if you could see it you would disdain any other form of religious life by comparison. In London lives John Colet, who is the Dean of St. Paul's. This man has joined a high degree of learning with admirable piety, and he is greatly respected by everybody. He loves me deeply, as everyone knows, and prefers my company to that of anyone else. There are countless other men whom I won't mention for fear of bothering you with my bragging and talkativeness.

To say a word now about my writings. I think you have read my *Enchiridion*, which many persons say has inspired them to a life of piety. I am not taking any credit for that, but am grateful to Christ if, through my efforts, some good has been accomplished as a result of his gift. I am not sure if you have seen the Aldine edition of my *Adagia*. The contents, of course, are secular, but it is a very useful work for any kind of learning. At any rate, it cost me an inestimable amount of toil and sleepless nights. I have published my *De Rerum Verborumque Copia* ["How to Express Things and Words"], which I dedicated to my friend Colet; it is a very helpful work for those preparing to preach. But such things are despised by men who despise good learning. During the past two years, in addition to many other things, I have emended the text of St. Jerome's Epistles. I have indicated the corrupt and spurious passages, and have explained the obscure ones in the notes. By collating the old Greek manuscripts I have emended the entire text of the New Testament, and have annotated more than a thousand passages, not without benefit to theologians. I have begun to do commentaries on Paul's Epistles, which I shall finish after publishing this other material. For I am determined to live and die in the study of Sacred Scripture. To these tasks I am devoting both my free and my working hours. Men of importance say that for these tasks I have an ability which others lack. Were I to live your way of life I could accomplish nothing. I have enjoyed the company of so many scholars and men who command respect, here, in Italy, and in France; yet I have never met anyone who advised me to return to you or who judged that to be the better course. In fact, your predecessor, Father Nicholas Werner of blessed memory, consistently discouraged me from doing so, urging me rather to attach myself to some bishop and remarking that he understood my own attitude and also the practices of his dear little brethren. Those were his own words, though he used the vernacular. And in this type of life which I am leading, I see what I should avoid, but do not see what might be a better course for me to follow.

There is one other point for me to make; and that is to give you a satisfactory explanation of my mode of dress. Up to the present I have always worn the garb of canons. While in Louvain I received permission from the Bishop of Utrecht to wear, without any scruple, a linen scapular instead of a full-length robe of linen, and a black hood instead of a black cape, as is done in Paris. But on my trip to Italy, I noticed all along the way that canons were wearing a black habit with a scapular; and so, to avoid giving offense by novelty in dress, I began to wear in Italy a black habit with a scapular. Later the plague broke out in Bologna, and those who nurse the victims of the plague in that city regularly wear a white linen shawl hanging down over their shoulders; and they avoid contact with other people. One day while I was on my way to visit a scholar friend of mine, some blackguards drew their swords and were getting ready to attack me and would have done so if a lady had not warned them that I was a cleric. On another occasion, when I was on my way to see the sons of the treasurer, men came rushing at me from all sides with clubs and assaulted me with murderous yells. And so at the advice of some respected men I hid my scapular, and I received permission from Pope Julius II to wear or not wear the religious habit according to my best judgment, provided I did wear clerical garb.

There you have an account of my life and of my aspirations. If I see something better, I am prepared to change my present mode of life. But I cannot see what I am to do in Holland. The climate and style of life will not agree with me; everyone will look at me. I will return as a white-haired old man, having left as a youth. I will encounter the contempt of the lowest, though I am used to the esteem of the highest. I will exchange the pursuit of learning for drinking brawls. You promise me help to find a place where I can live on an excellent income: I have no idea what you have in mind—except a place among some nuns in order to serve them. But I have never been willing to serve either kings or archbishops. I desire no remuneration. I desire no wealth and only funds sufficient for my bodily well-being and literary pursuits, so that I can live without being a burden to anyone.

[TO GREGORY REISCH][1]

EE 308 (1–39)   [Basel, September 1514]

I have been struggling and laboring so that the public may have a corrected edition of the letters of St. Jerome. The texts are in the worst condition imaginable. In my opinion Jerome is practically the only one deserving to be read by everybody, at least unique among Latin theologians. I have decided upon this order of arrangement. The first place will go to those letters which are genuinely his; the second place to those which are falsely ascribed to him, but still worth reading; the third place to those spurious letters forged by some senseless, shameless clown. I shall add the reasons why I do not consider them authentic. In this way the reader will not be deceived by false ascriptions and one who enjoys such silly drivel won't miss a thing in my edition. I have detected the style of writing of some loudmouth who also confused the works of Augustine with many additions, as for instance the desert sermons, and who added to the works of Ambrose a congratulatory sermon on the baptism of Augustine.

I see that we both feel the same way about this divinely inspired man; I do not reject your order of arrangement, and yet I could not follow it without a great deal of toil on my part, as I would have to unravel everything. Besides, my system of classification would then be destroyed. Finally, there are several letters that can be grouped together according to some other arrangement; Jerome himself wants his work addressed to Nepotianus to be joined with that addressed to Heliodorus. And so I shall accept the arrangement adopted in ancient times, with the exception of the spurious writings. To replace the arrangement you have devised I shall add an index, so there will be a twofold order of arrangement and a twofold benefit. I have added summaries of the individual works and also explanations, so that

1. A Carthusian monk and scholar (d. 1525), confessor of Emperor Maximilian I, author of *Margarita Philosophica*. This letter, with its somewhat complicated scholarly content, shows Erasmus' use of correspondence as a medium of scholarly exchange.

persons without much education can read them without trouble. I have explained scriptural allusions, at least those which would not be readily intelligible to anybody, not even a theologian.

I certainly do extend my best wishes to this holy man on the occasion of his appearance in print, in a text so thoroughly emended, thanks to the extraordinary pains taken by the learned young Amerbachs.[2] You will not be reluctant to share with us any emended manuscripts you may have, or any passages with a felicitous annotation.[3]

In the letter to Heliodorous which begins *Quanto amore* there is an alternate reading, *cui nos morituros relinquis?* etc. If it is not too much trouble, tell me what you think about that. In the letter to Rusticus which begins *Nihil Christiano,* etc., I am tormented by the passage concerning the sons of Ionadab, who, it says, are mentioned in the Psalms as being the first to endure captivity. I find mention of them in Jeremiah, but I do not recall anything about them in the psalmist.

TO THOMAS RUTHALL[1]

EE 325 (58–103)   Basel, March 7, 1515

The fact has not escaped me that there is no other type of toil [i.e., than editing] that causes more trouble for the author and brings him less glory. The reader reaps all the profit without even being aware of the service performed by the editor. Besides, although nothing is more completely wasted than what is done for an ungrateful person, it is a still greater waste to perform a service for one who is not even aware of it.

Although realizing this fact, nevertheless we did think this honor

2. On the two brothers Amerbach, see Letter 862, p. 130.
3. For the technical aspects of the problems raised by Erasmus, see Allen, II, 29.
1. This letter forms the preface to Erasmus' edition of Seneca's *Lucubrationes.* Thomas Ruthall (d. 1523) was Bishop of Durham and secretary to Henry VIII.
Erasmus uses this prefatory letter to sketch briefly the significance of Seneca, especially pointing to his moral emphases.

of editing ought to be paid to these two men [Seneca and Jerome]. First of all, Jerome is the only one we have in the field of theology whom we could compare with the Greek writers. And if we did not have him, I definitely do not know of anyone whom we could hold up as truly worthy of the title of theologian. This is a fact; let us admit it. Secondly, Seneca was so highly esteemed by Jerome that he is the only one of all the pagans listed by him in his catalogue of distinguished writers. His reason for doing so was not that famous correspondence between Paul and Seneca, which he, being a man of keen perception, knew very well was not genuine, although he did take advantage of it and use it as a pretext to win greater favor for Seneca. Rather, Jerome's reason was that he considered Seneca the only non-Christian worthy of being read by Christians. Seneca's advice is remarkably sound. With so much feeling does he encourage virtuous living that it is quite obvious that he practiced what he preached. He turns the mind toward heavenly things and arouses it to a contempt of the commonplace; he implants in the mind a loathing for moral baseness and fires it to a love of virtue. In brief, anyone who picks up the works of Seneca with the desire to become a better person, departs a better person. Nor am I deeply disturbed by the ancient malicious charges; not a single man who made such charges ever dared to attack Seneca's life. Only in the matter of his style do they express disappointment. Caligula described Seneca's style as "sand without lime." But the fact is, he also had such a contempt for Vergil and Livy that he came very close to removing their statues from all the libraries. . . .

However, there are some things which I too would prefer to see changed. Offense is caused by his use of homely language, and his senile loquacity in some passages is rather annoying. Also his jests are on occasion somewhat wanton, his exclamations are artificial, and there are sudden interruptions in the vigorous flow of speech. On the other hand, he is not an honest critic of other people's talent, though he attributes an abundance of such talent to himself. In disputes it is remarkable how seldom he commends another and how often he mocks other men as if he were superior to them. Consequently, as I see it, he set a precedent which, as happens, bounded back against himself. But has there ever lived an author so perfect as not to have some failings? There is such a high degree of moral goodness in him that, even if he were absolutely lacking in eloquence, he would still deserve to be read by all men who desire to live a good life. However, such was his eloquence, in that most eloquent age, that he was regarded as a prince of eloquence and Quintilian ran the risk of being considered jealous of Seneca. I am very well aware that a large number of errors still remain in the text; but without the assistance of ancient manuscripts they could hardly be removed even by Seneca himself.

TO DOMENICO GRIMANI[1]

EE 334 (99–156)   London, [May 15], 1515

For a long time now I have been toiling at the cost of many sleepless nights to bring about a complete rebirth of St. Jerome. In the West we regard him as our supreme theologian; in fact, we say he is virtually the only one deserving that name. But at the same time the text of his writings is so disfigured, chaotic, and corrupt that, although no other author is so worth reading, he is the one least possible to read, much less understand. My first concern has been to arrange all his writings in proper order, especially the letters, which presented the most difficult problem. Next, with the aid of old manuscripts and my own ingenuity I removed the errors which not only bespattered but completely engulfed him. Along with summaries I have added helpful explanations of various passages to make them readable even for persons of average education: formerly—this is a bold but true statement—they were not intelligible even to the most learned. For, as it was said of Romulus of old that his boasting of distinguished deeds was as magnificent as his performance,[2] so one can see in Jerome a unique combination of broad erudition and saintly showmanship. I have taken great pains to restore Greek and Hebrew passages which earlier were either altogether omitted or so badly handled that they should have been. I have banished to a

1. An eminent patron of literature (1461–1523), who occupied high ecclesiastical positions as cardinal and patriarch. This letter describes Erasmus' work on his edition of St. Jerome, the difficulties he encountered in obtaining the authentic text, the best place of publication. It is also a request for help, with books—and with patronage.
2. Livy, *Ab urbe condita*, 1.10.5.

special volume the spurious works and forgeries which form a considerable part of the material, so that the reader with more appetite than discrimination will not miss a thing. At the same time, such silly trivia will never again be circulated under the name of so peerless a writer.

I have been considering Italy, with the resources of its libraries and its great prestige, as the place to publish this edition, but fortunately I stumbled upon some men in Basel who were equipped for the task and had, in fact, already undertaken it: Johann Froben, in particular, whose competence and resources are in great part responsible for the work, but also three learned young Amerbach brothers who have command of Hebrew, which Jerome uses extensively. In this respect I needed a Theseus, for I had barely a taste of Hebrew. After admitting them to partnership in my labor, I undertook the project with Herculean verve. The workshop hums as St. Jerome appears in most elegant print. Truly he is reborn, but at such a high cost in labor and money that it was less of an expense to Jerome to compose his works than for us to revise them. At any rate, I have gone through such labor here that I all but died in the effort to bring him back to life. The complete set will probably run to ten volumes.

You may wonder how all this pertains to you.

First of all, I knew that with your unfailing interest in good learning you would extend your best wishes to Jerome and at the same time support our efforts, that is to say for Christian piety, which I hope will be greatly furthered by the writings of Jerome. However, a project of this kind cannot be properly completed without the resources of many well-supplied libraries. So, if there is any item in your library—which contains a variety of books in all languages—or in that of the Pope, or of anyone else, I would consider it an expression of your graciousness to share it for the common good of the world. Moreover, I thought it most appropriate that the works of this supreme theologian should be published under the happy auspices of the Supreme Pontiff and in such complete and restored form as they apparently have not been hither to. Thus, the most learned of all writers would be commended to the world by one whose family (de Medici) has produced so many literary notables. Jerome would receive much luster and merit from the lofty authority of the Pope, and in turn Leo would acquire no little glory from the celebrity of a most eminent teacher. In fact, I do not know of any other monument

more suitable for immortalizing Leo's illustrious deeds. Therefore, I
shall dedicate the rebirth of Jerome to him, and do so especially if
your vote supports my decision.

TO POPE LEO X[1]

EE 335 (70–234)   London May 21, 1515

When Pope Leo was placed at the helm, the world was conscious
that by a sudden revolution a worse than iron age had become a
golden one. A great and providential change revealed to all the hand
of God. The waves of war were calmed and the mutual threats of
rulers were repressed. The minds of great kings, sundered by bitter
hatred, were led to Christian concord. The baneful schism was removed, in such a way as to leave no scars. You have restored several
Italian rulers to their subjects and many exiled citizens to their
homes. You have reinstated your own family, long afflicted by the
injuries of Fortune: Florence, which flourished many years through
the prudence of your forefathers, is flourishing more than ever
through you. It was an answer to the ancestral name of Medici—to
cure at once so many ills of the whole world, not by severe measures,
not by amputations or brandings or disagreeable medicines, but by
good counsel and prudence, by gentleness and moderation. . . .

Let other men extol the wars which Julius II either effectively
stirred up or successfully fought;[2] let them review the victories won
by force of his arms; let them sing the praises of his regal triumphal
celebrations. It matters not how much glory they attribute to those
events; they must still admit that they entailed the grief of many
people. I need not mention the fact that a large share of military
glory is claimed by the princes under whose command and guidance
the action occurs, and that perhaps a larger share is claimed by the
soldier who risks his life in personal combat on the field of battle, and
that the largest is claimed by Fortune, whose reign is nowhere

1. This letter constitutes a praise of Pope Leo X. Part of Erasmus' argument
has to do with the current political situation, especially in Italy, and here he
shows little perception of the real nature of the circumstances. Pope Leo was
much involved in the political struggle in Italy, as was evident in his Holy
League, with which he sought to counter King Louis XII of France.
2. Erasmus comments here on the conflict between France and Spain over
northern Italy.

mightier than in battle. However, no one mutters or complains of the honor given to Leo, nor is there any danger that he, like so many other men, will be condemned by posterity after receiving the plaudits of his own age. Furthermore, your glory is not only beneficial to everyone and an occasion of joy to everyone, but it is also a feature completely appropriate to yourself and the power of heaven, inasmuch as it has involved the common welfare and is the result of God's blessing and your own extraordinary wisdom. And this glory is all the more appropriate to you for the very reason that it comes as the gift of Him who never favors the undeserving.

A war that was almost world-wide may have been proof that Julius was a very great man; but at all events the restoration of world peace is evidence that Leo is a greater one. Your greatness is more clearly proved by the complete surrender made to you by Louis, the renowned King of France, than is Julius' by the fact that he defeated Louis or at least annoyed him with warfare.[3]

Therefore, with perfect right does Christendom rejoice at having this Leo, on whose lips the world finds more than honeyed sweetness. For what is sweeter than peace? Especially after the wearisome long turmoil of wars in which we have clashed with one another with endless shedding of Christian blood, to the deep sorrow of noble minds and to the great joy of the Turks. The mind shudders at the mere recollection of those times. But no matter to whose account this disaster is laid by posterity, we are indebted to one of the Medici for remedying it. . . . We trust that in the near future, with Christ's blessing on all your works, that phrase of the Apocalypse will find its fulfillment in you, namely: *Vicit Leo de tribu Iuda.*[4] All of us have already felt the sweet effects of your wisdom and temperate rule, and clearly within a short time we shall be viewing Leo as that conqueror.

This hope of ours is based on your unparalleled virtues; its omen is also found in both your names, the one you brought with you to the papacy and that which you chose upon being elected pope. Indeed, when we hear the names John and Leo, we think of extraordinary goodness coupled with invincible strength of spirit. In fact, there

3. The contrast between Leo's peacefulness and Julius' belligerence is important for understanding the dialogue of *Julius Exclusus.* This dialogue, a satirical account of how Pope Julius is refused entrance to heaven, was published anonymously, but promptly attributed to Erasmus. See Letter 622.

4. Revelation 5:5: "The Lion of the tribe of Judah has conquered"—this is a pun on the Latin meaning of "Leo."

seems to be a happy omen also in the fact that not only do we have a
Leo (and every Roman pontiff bearing that name has been worthy of
eminent praise), but we have Leo the Tenth. The ancients used to
apply the word for "tenth" to anything that was unusually outstanding. Therefore the various virtues that are found to an eminent
degree in each of the other Leo's, we expect to find one and all in Leo
the Tenth: Leo I's successful influence; Leo II's learned piety and
interest in sacred music; Leo III's beneficial eloquence and also a
spirit unshaken by fortune, whether good or bad; Leo IV's simple
prudence, a virtue praised by Christ; Leo V's holy tolerance; Leo VI's
efforts to restore universal peace; Leo VII's sanctity, worthy of
heaven; Leo VIII's moral integrity; Leo IX's kindness poured out on
everyone. All these hopes of ours are based not only on interpretation of the omens found in the names themselves—and such auguries
should not be slighted—but also on what we have observed in your
past performance and in your present plans. A good beginning
portends a good end. Furthermore, our hope of victory is made more
certain by the fact that you in your wisdom clearly perceive that the
war, like the victory, is twofold: on the one hand, against vices, truly
the single deadliest enemy of the Christian faith; on the other,
against the impious and barbarous adversaries of Christianity and the
Roman See. The former warfare is more necessary and the more
difficult of the two; it depends most of all upon ourselves and therefore demands our deeper concern. Once it is successfully completed
by us, the other one, with Christ's assistance, will easily be fulfilled.

I do not mean to say, however, that these two types of warfare are
different in character. The one is disapproved by some good men, the
other is universally praised. Without a doubt Christ encourages us
and Paul spurs us on to battle against vice. But as for war with the
Turks, Christ is not instigating it, nor do the apostles encourage it.
Granted that both wars are necessary; certainly the one which the
Holy Spirit has declared demands much greater exertion than that
begun by men. I tend to think that, just as Christ along with His
apostles and martyrs subdued the whole world by kindness, patience,
and holy teaching, so too we can more effectively subdue the Turks
by piety of life than by armed force. Thus Christendom would be
defended by the same methods by which it was once established. But
if both wars must be approved (and undoubtedly we must approve
whatever the Roman Curia approves), still in neither instance, most

blessed Father, is there any negligence on your part. With unprece-
dented devotion you are repairing and restoring, I am told, by means
of beneficial synodal constitutions[5] the religion of the Christian
people, which in many ways broke down long ago and continues to
do so more and more. These constitutions are not such as reek of
financial profit or a passion for power or despotism, but truly reflect
the spirit of the apostles, and anyone can recognize them as coming
from men who are fathers and not masters; pious minds can revere
them as Christ's own words.

In this way does Your Holiness endeavor to make the Church of
Christ rich with a true wealth that is proper to her, shine with a
glory that is her own, enjoy the authority that belongs to her, and, in
a word, wear those heavenly gifts which are sometimes most abundant when we are deprived of others. And yet, you are obviously not
neglecting that other function of virtue; you seek the reconciliation
of all rulers and the settlement of existing problems among Christians. Thereby you are building a fine and safe path that will lead to
subduing or crushing the impious Turks. Eventually those savage
beasts will not endure the roaring of our Lion [Leo]; they will
experience, I insist, that unconquerable strength of a most gentle
Lion, wild and fierce though they be. They will be no match for a
Pope whose weapon is piety, not armed force, and who is accompanied into battle by a power that is eternal.

I have long observed, most blessed Father, what a vast opportunity
lies open before us for singing your praises, but my little talent is no
match for such a lofty theme. My eloquence, or rather lack of
eloquence, does not aspire to such divine deeds. May scholars
everywhere be granted the desire and ability to express in fitting
language the merits of Leo X, which deserve a lasting memory. Your
loftiness, however, drives me far away with fear, and who would not
be frightened away by it? And yet, for some mysterious reason, I feel
a passionate desire to make every effort to direct all the forces
of genius toward this one goal, namely, that the valuable services
performed by Leo for the Christian people may be regarded and
celebrated by posterity as they deserve, so that they will never be forgotten in future ages. . . .

A work of no small importance is actively pursued at Basel, where
Jerome is "restored to life" in Froben's printing shop. There is no

5. A type of ecclesiastical legislation.

more accurate printer or one producing a greater number of good
books, especially relating to theology. This is not done by one man's
labor or at one man's expense. The other remains of Jerome which I
have not included in my own effort (though I contribute some
occasional assistance) have for some time been given attention by
several learned men. Among them is that distinguished scholar,
Johann Reuchlin, skilled in Greek, Latin, and Hebrew and so versed
in every branch of learning as to be a match for its greatest professors.
He is honored and revered by all Germany as a phoenix, and their
special pride. No little assistance has been received from Kühn of
Nürnberg, a Dominican, whose intimate knowledge of Greek is
equaled by his indefatigable pursuit of literary work. Then there is
Beatus Rhenanus of Schlettstadt, a young man who combines thorough learning with critical judgment. Our most important assistants
are the brothers Amerbach, at whose expense and efforts the work is
mainly undertaken. One may well believe that this family has been
raised up by Fortune to be the means of bringing Jerome back to life.
Their father, the best of men, had his three sons instructed in Greek,
Hebrew, and Latin for this purpose. When he died, he bequeathed
to his children a legacy, dedicating his fortune to its fulfillment.
These excellent young men are diligently discharging the commission
imposed on them by their father.

TO MARTIN DORP[1]

EE 337 (86–120; 395–429;   Antwerp, [end of May] 1515
  569–572; 587–627; 660–
  750; 768–789)

The purpose in my *Folly* is exactly the same as in my other
writings, though the approach is different. In my *Enchiridion* I presented in a straightforward manner a plan for Christian living. In my

1. This letter might be called an apologetic response to the critical reaction
to the *Moriae Encomium*, or "Praise of Folly." Dorp (1485–1525), theologian
at the University of Louvain, criticized Erasmus' "Praise of Folly" and later his
project of a Greek New Testament. Erasmus succeeded in overcoming his
objections and the two men remained on cordial terms. This letter (with
certain additions) was subsequently printed together with the "Praise of
Folly."

Education of a Prince I openly offer advice as to the type of training a prince should receive. In my *Panegyric* the praise is only a cloak for treating indirectly the same theme that I treated in the previous work in a straightforward manner. In my *Folly* I am ostensibly joking, but my real purpose is the same as in the *Enchiridion*. My aim has been to advise, not to pain; to help, not to hurt; to promote human conduct, not to thwart it. The staid philosopher Plato approves of having several rounds at a drinking bout for the reason that some defects can be routed under the cheerful influence of wine which could not be corrected by a stern rebuke. And Horace is of the opinion that humorous advice is no less profitable than serious.

What is wrong with telling the truth with a smile?[2] This point was perfectly clear to wise men of old, who preferred to embody their salutary rules for living in funny fairy tales, because a truth which in itself is severe does penetrate more easily into the hearts of men, when embellished by the charm of pleasure. Undoubtedly this is what Lucretius meant by the honey which doctors, in treating children, smear on the edge of a cup of wormwood. And princes of old employed court jesters for the simple reason that their outspoken remarks could reveal and correct slight faults without offending anyone. Perhaps it is improper to add the name of Christ to this list. But if one may make a comparison of divine with human things, do not His parables have something in common with the fables of the ancients? The truth of the Gospels, when dressed up so attractively, does slide into the heart more gently and remain rooted there more firmly than if presented in all its nakedness. This is the very point pursued at great length by St. Augustine in his work on Christian education." I had often noticed how the common people were corrupted by stupid opinions, in all the various areas of human life; the promise of a cure given to them was more real than the prospect. And so I thought I had found in this device a means for stealing into sensitive hearts and correcting even while pleasing them. And I have often observed that this lighthearted and humorous method of giving advice does have very happy results with many people. . . .

Not even under the mask of *Folly* did I dare to mention the sort of thing I often hear men deploring, who are theologians themselves,

2. Horace, *Sermones,* 1.1.24.

true theologians, men of character, seriousness, and learning, men who have deeply imbibed the teaching of Christ from the sources. Whenever these men are with a group where they can freely air their views, they deplore this modern brand of theology that has assailed the world and yearn for the good old-fashioned kind. For no other sort is more sacred or more august; no other reflects or savors to an equal degree those heavenly teachings of Christ.

As for this modern brand—to say nothing of the barbarous, unnatural, vulgar style and monstrous expressions, or the complete lack of good learning, or the ignorance of languages—it is so polluted with the teachings of Aristotle, with paltry human inventions and even with pagan precepts, that I doubt whether it savors of the true, genuine teachings of Christ. Too close attention to the explanations handed down by men results in a failure to follow the original pattern. Therefore, the more intelligent theologians are frequently compelled to tell the people something different from their personal convictions or from what they would discuss with their friends. And sometimes they cannot answer those seeking their advice, for they observe the inconsistencies between the teaching of Christ and precepts dictated by the mere explanations of men.

What does Christ have in common with Aristotle? Or the mysteries of eternal wisdom with quibbling sophistries? Where does that maze of questions lead? So many are idle and baneful, if for no other reason than that they lead to wrangling and factions. True, some things do demand further investigation, and decisions must be made on some. I do not deny that. But, on the other hand, there are many matters which it were better to leave untouched than to investigate (it is a part of knowledge not to know certain things). And there are many things where uncertainty is healthier than a decision. Finally, if any decision is to be made, I would like to see it done with reverence, not arrogance, and based on Sacred Scripture rather than the petty fabricated arguments of men. Today there is no end to quibbling questions; and yet what violent dissension they cause among friends and among factions! Every day a new decree is born from an old one. In short, the situation has come to this: the whole discussion depends, not on what Christ taught, but on the definitions given by the scholastics and on the power of the bishops, no matter what sort of men they are. As a result the whole situation has become so involved that there is not even a hope of recalling the world to true Christianity. . . .

I would not want even a joke to come from my pen if it would cause any harm to the piety of Christians. I only ask that a person understand what has been written, that he be fair and unbiased and try to grasp the meaning, and not make it his aim to misrepresent it. . . .

As for my *Folly*, it is not worth a straw, in case anyone thinks this matter has upset me. However, it is not surprising if detractors such as I have just been describing excerpt passages from a long work and then interpret some of them as scandalous, others as irreverent, some as badly expressed, others as blasphemous and smacking of heresy; not that they really find these foul defects in the work, but they read into the work their own defects! It would be a much more gentle approach and more in keeping with Christian openness, to support and encourage the efforts of scholars, and in the case of any thoughtless, accidental slip, to disregard it or give it a kindly interpretation, rather than evil-mindedly to look for something to criticize and behave like a backbiter rather than a theologian. How much happier it would be to instruct or to learn by a mutual sharing of ideas and, to use Jerome's phrase, to frolic in the field of Scripture without causing us grief! But these fellows show an amazing lack of moderation. In reading some authors they will use the silliest excuse to defend the most obvious error; but they are so unfair toward other writers as to find some way to misinterpret even the most carefully phrased expression. How much more profitable it would have been for them to learn Greek or Hebrew or at least Latin instead of doing this sort of thing, tearing apart and being torn apart, while wasting their own precious time and that of others! A knowledge of those languages is so important for an understanding of Scripture that I definitely think it highly impudent for one who is ignorant of them to claim the title of theologian.

Therefore, my excellent Martin, out of the good will I bear you I shall not cease urging you, as I have often done in the past, to add at least a knowledge of Greek to your scholarly pursuits. A happy talent such as yours is a rare thing. A style of writing that is strong and vigorous, yet supple and rich, indicates a mind that is not only well balanced but also fertile. You are now in the prime of life and your powers are in full bloom. You have successfully completed the regular course of studies. If you would crown such a brilliant beginning with a knowledge of Greek, I would dare to promise myself and everyone else that you will produce something extraordinary, something which no recent theologian has as yet produced. If you are of the opinion that for love of true piety all human learning is to be spurned, and if you believe that this type of wisdom can be reached by a shorter route through a sort of transformation into Christ, and that everything else worth knowing can be more fully viewed in the light of faith than in the books of men, then I shall readily subscribe to your opinion. But if, considering the present state of human affairs, you expect to attain a true knowledge of theology without skill in languages, especially in that language in which a large portion of Sacred Scripture has been handed down, then you are completely wrong. . . .

Let me take up the second point discussed in your letter. You highly approve my efforts to restore the text of Jerome, and you urge me on to similar projects. The fact is, you are urging one who does not need any pricking. I do not need encouragement for this work so much as I need assistance; it is a very difficult job. But I do not want you to accept my word for anything hereafter except where you catch me telling the truth. Those who are so deeply offended by my *Folly* will not approve of my edition of Jerome either. And their attitude toward Basil, Chrysostom, and Nazianzen is not much fairer than it is toward us,[3] except that they are less restrained in raging against us. And yet on occasion when they are aroused they are not afraid to utter idiotic remarks which those luminaries do not deserve. They do dread good learning and they have fears for their own despotic power. So that you won't think this a rash judgment on my part: after I had started on my project and my fame had already spread abroad, some people who have the reputation of being serious-minded men and consider themselves distinguished theologians rushed to the printer and pleaded with him by all that is sacred not to allow any Greek or Hebrew words to be included; for there was great peril attached to those languages, and no profit was to be gained from them; they were intended merely for the sake of curiosity. Also on a

3. The reference is to other eminent theologians of the early Church.

previous occasion, when I was in England, I happened to be having some drinks with a Franciscan who was a first-class Scotist. In popular judgment he was a man of great wisdom and in his own judgment he knew absolutely everything. After explaining to him my plans for the works of Jerome, he expressed great surprise that there was anything in Jerome's works that was unknown to theologians. This fellow was so ignorant that I would be amazed if he could grasp the meaning of any three lines in Jerome's works. . . .

Now I ask you, Dorp, what would you do with such a theologian? What would you pray for, except perhaps for a reliable doctor who could cure his mind? And yet this is often the stuff of which those men are made who scream the loudest at theological conventions; these are the men who issue pronouncements on Christianity. They fear and dread as dangerous and pestilential the works which St. Jerome or Origen produced (the latter with great toil in his old age, in order to become a true theologian). Augustine, when he was a bishop and advanced in years, expressed his regret in his *Confessions* that he had, as a boy, shirked the study of that language which could have been very helpful to him in his commentaries on Scripture.[4] If there is any danger involved, I would not be afraid to venture on something to which such wise men aspired. If it is curiosity, I would not want to be holier than Jerome; and as for the kind of treatment those fellows have given him by calling his work a curiosity, well, that is their problem. There does exist an ancient decree of a papal commission concerning the appointment of professors for the public teaching of some languages; although there was never any provision made for the study of sophistry or Aristotle's philosophy, except that in the decretals doubt is expressed as to whether the learning of such subjects is the right thing to do.[5] Besides, their study is condemned by a large number of important authorities. Why do we neglect what papal authority has commanded, and favor only that upon which doubt has been cast—in fact, which has been condemned? Although the same thing did happen to those fellows with regard to Aristotle as in the case of Sacred Scripture. The goddess Nemesis, who avenges the neglect of language, is everywhere present. In other areas also

4. *Confessions* 1.12.
5. See Letter 182, p. 48, n. 6.

those fellows are lunatics; they are in a dream world. In their blindness they stumble around and have nothing to offer but weird ideas. We owe it to these brilliant theologians that so few authors have survived of all those listed by Jerome in his catalogue. The reason is that our professors could not understand what the writers had to say. We owe it to these same men that our text of Jerome is so corrupt and mutilated that it is almost more of a problem for other men to restore it than it was for Jerome to produce the original.

To come now to the third subject discussed in your letter, namely, the New Testament. Your remarks amaze me. What has happened to you? You are usually very clear-sighted; now you have turned your gaze somewhere else, but where? You would prefer that I change nothing except perhaps what might be more meaningful for the Greeks; and you deny that there is any defect in our Vulgate edition. You consider it a crime to rip apart something that has had the approval of many centuries and many synods. But, my very learned Dorp, if what you say is true, then why are the quotations cited by Jerome and Augustine and Ambrose so frequently different from our present text? And why does Jerome censure and correct in detail much that is found in our edition? What will you do when so many sources are in agreement—that is, when the Greek manuscripts give a different reading and Jerome cites the reading of those manuscripts and the oldest Latin manuscripts agree with it and that reading is more appropriate to the sense of the passage? Surely, you are not going to condemn all this evidence and follow a text which was probably distorted by some scribe. However, no one maintains that Sacred Scripture contains any falsehood. . . . But the facts themselves make it perfectly clear (as is obvious even to a blind man) that the Greek text has often been badly rendered because of the ignorance or carelessness of the translator, and that often the genuine, true reading has been corrupted by unskilled copyists—this we know is a daily occurrence. Moreover, sometimes the text has been changed by half-learned copyists who were not very alert. Now which person gives more support to falsehood: the one who corrects these errors and restores the text, or the one who prefers to include the error rather than remove it? It is the very nature of error for one mistake to beget another. And as a rule the things we change pertain to emphasis rather than the sense, although the emphasis is very often an important consideration in determining the sense. Still, it is not a rare occurrence for the meaning to be completely missed. Whenever that was the case, Augustine and Ambrose and Hilary and Jerome had only one recourse: the Greek sources. Although such recourse has the approval of ecclesiastical decrees, you try to evade that fact and to refute it, or rather to escape it by some neat little distinction. . . .

Besides, when you say that it is unnecessary to go back beyond our Vulgate text because it has been so authoritatively approved, you are talking like the common brand of theologians. They regularly claim the Church's authority for anything that has crept into general usage. Name just one council that has approved this text. Who approves of something when its origin is unknown? Jerome's own prefaces testify that it is not his work. But suppose that some council did approve it. Surely such an approval would not completely forbid later emendation based on the Greek sources. And surely such an approval would not apply also to all the errors which could in various ways creep into the text. Assuredly the Fathers of the council in promulgating their decree would not have used such language as the following: "We do not know the authorship of this edition, but still we do approve it. Nor shall we permit any interference from variant readings found in the Greek copies, no matter how faultless they may be; nor from variant readings found in Chrysostom, Basil, Athanasius, or Jerome, even if those readings are more appropriate to the sense of the Gospel. Nevertheless we do give out hearty approval to those authors in other matters. Furthermore, we also approve with the same authority any future defect or mistake or addition or omission that may be introduced in any way whatsoever by copyists who may be half-learned or a little foolhardy or ignorant or drunk or careless. And it is our will that no one is to make any change in the text of Scripture now that it has been established once and for all." A silly decree, you would say. But that is what it would have to be if you are going to employ the authority of a council to deter us from our work. . . .

Now I was aware of what you reminded me, namely, that Lorenzo Valla had anticipated me in this work on Scripture; in fact, I was the first to arrange the publication of his annotations, and I have also seen the commentaries of James Faber on the Pauline Epistles. I only wish that those men had done a very thorough scholarly job so that my work would not be necessary. As for Valla, whose interest is philology rather than theology. I regard him as worthy of the highest praise for having diligently compared the Greek and Latin texts of Scripture, and this at a time when many theologians have never read through the entire Testament. However, I do disagree with him on several points, especially where a theological matter is concerned.

TO JOHN SAPIDUS[1]

EE 364 (8–40)   Basel, [*ca.* October 1515]

[Here in Basel] I definitely feel that I am dwelling in some very lovely home of the Muses. I would not speak of them as a group of learned men, but of men learned in no ordinary fashion. Everyone knows Latin; everyone knows Greek; several of them also know Hebrew. One has an outstanding knowledge of history; another is well versed in theology. One is an expert mathematician, one a scholar of ancient culture, and one is competent in law. Now you see what a rare experience this is. I, at any rate, have never before had the good luck to share in such a fortunate association. And apart from their learning, they are all so genuine, and delightful, and harmonious. One would swear they are all controlled by one mind.

And yet you have no reason to grieve over your separation from our board. To use an expression of Plato—you are present with us as much as anyone. At every luncheon, at every dinner, on every stroll, in every conversation, Sapidus is with us. And as for your lot—while I admit it is a toilsome one, I deny that it is tragic, as you call it, or deplorable. To be a schoolteacher ranks second, in service, only to being a king. Or do you consider it a lowly occupation to imbue the tender years of your fellow citizens with the best literature and with the spirit of Christ and then to hand them over to your country as men of solid virtue and sound character? In the opinion of fools it is a

1. Johann Witz, or Sapidus (d. 1561), Latin teacher, friend of Beatus Rhenanus, Wimpfeling, and other humanists. In this letter Erasmus not only describes his learned associations at Basel, where he had recently moved, but also comments on the role of the schoolteacher, whose work and true remuneration he praises.

lowly task, but actually it is a very splendid one. Even pagans have always considered it a glorious distinction to be of service to the commonwealth, and, to put it boldly, no one does a greater service than he who fashions the raw material of youth, provided he has learning and sound character. And both of those qualities you possess in such equally high degree that I cannot say in which one you excel.

As for the cut in your salary—Christ Himself will repay you from His own store in full measure, since virtue is its own quite ample reward. And do not let yourself be upset at seeing the large annual salary allotted by the government to abominably lazy individuals who live only for themselves or are toadies to men in power, but are of no value to the commonwealth; at the same time as such a poor salary is paid to one who is the common father of all children and, in what is most essential of all, struggles and strains to advance the public interest. Such an office demands a man of genuine integrity, a man who values devotion to duty, even without recompense. Otherwise, the offer of a high salary and the prospect of honor would attract the most unprincipled characters to this kind of work.

TO THE READER[1]

EE 373 (12–49; 202–224)   Basel, [*ca.* December] 1515

I have made a recension of the text of the New Testament with all the diligence that was possible and with all the fidelity that was appropriate. First of all, I consulted the authentic Greek text; that is the source to which we are urged to have recourse, for any situation, in the precedent set by eminent theologians; we are also frequently advised to do so by Jerome and Augustine and are ordered to do so by the decrees of the Roman pontiffs. Second, I consulted the text of very ancient Latin codices, two of which were lent me by that distinguished member of the guild of theologians, John Colet, Dean of

1. This epistolary greeting is addressed to the reader of Erasmus' edition of the New Testament. In it he explains his approach to the task and also seeks to dismiss possible criticism raised against it.

St. Paul's in London; their script was of such an early date that I had
to learn how to read again and start all over, like a little boy, with the
alphabet. A third codex was provided by that most illustrious sturdy
woman, Margaret, aunt of Prince Charles. In my edition I have
frequently adopted the reading of this manuscript, called the *Aureus
Codex* because it is completely bound in gold and beautifully written
in golden letters. Later I was offered the use of some remarkable
ancient manuscripts by the old and very famous College of St.
Donatian at Bruges. Earlier the priory at Corsendonk had supplied
me with a neatly emended manuscript, in addition to those made
available to me by Basilius and Boniface Amberbach.

The emendations which I have made, therefore, were not the
result of any idle whim but were based on the text of these manuscripts which I examined, and also of other manuscripts which are
not important enough to mention. Finally, I have used as a basis for
my recension certain citations, emendations, or interpretations made
by those authors who are universally approved, namely, Origen,
Chrysostom, Cyril, Jerome, Ambrose, Hilary, Augustine, Theophylactus, Basil, and Bede. I have included their testimony in several
places so that the observant reader, after noticing that my emendation
of certain passages agrees with the opinion of these authors, will then
trust my judgment in other passages where, perhaps, they have made
no comment at all or have favored another reading.

I was aware that people are customarily offended by an innovation
in any matter, especially in the field of scholarship, and that for the
most part they prefer the old familiar flavor and taste they know so
well. I realized too that it would be much easier, in the present age
particularly, to corrupt emended texts rather than to emend corrupt
texts, and so I have added certain guideposts, so to speak, to my recension of the scriptural text. My reason for doing so is, first of all, to be
of service to the reader by offering a sufficient explanation of what
changes were made and why, or at any rate to appease him in case he
is offended, for men vary in talent as well as in taste. My second
reason is to take security measures for the preservation of the work, so
that it will not be easy for anyone in the future to vitiate a text whose
restoration—such as it is—cost so much toil. . . .

Therefore, kindly reader, I ask you to bring pious ears and a
Christian heart to the reading of this work. No one should approach

it in the frame of mind with which he perhaps approaches the *Attic Nights* of Gellius or the *Miscellanea* of Angelo Poliziano, namely, in order to gauge the depth of thought or rhetorical power or hidden erudition. We are concerned here with something that is sacred, something that is commended to the world primarily by its simplicity and purity. In such a work it would be ridiculous to try to display human erudition and irreverent to vaunt human rhetoric. Even if that were present, it would be more proper to ignore it, for fear that one might rightly be charged with "pouring sweet oil over lentils." In offering this work to the attention of Christians my purpose is pure and simple, namely, that in the future more persons will apply themselves to the study of this sacred wisdom, and do so with greater willingness, and not only with less trouble but also with more profit. I call upon Christ Himself, who has been both witness and assistant to this task of mine, to withdraw His favor from me if in any way I have sought personal gain in this toil; the fact is, I have knowingly and willingly suffered even great and very definite financial loss. Besides, so little pleasure do I find in the tickling sensation of fame that I would not even have attached my name to the work, had it not been for the fear that its omission might detract from its value, since an anonymous work is generally suspect. I am equally prepared for either contingency: to explain any good instruction I have offered or to admit my error honestly wherever I am caught in a mistake. I am a human being and nothing that is human do I regard as foreign to me.

TO PRINCE CHARLES[1]

EE 393 (1–40)   [Basel, *ca.* March 1516]

Although wisdom itself is something extraordinary, still, in the opinion of Aristotle the most outstanding form of wisdom is that which gives instruction on how to be a good ruler. Consequently

1. Of Spain, grandson of Emperor Maximilian. This is the dedication of Erasmus' *Institutio Principis Christiani* ("Institution of a Christian Prince"). In this brief excerpt Erasmus sketches the importance of the proper education of rulers, noting that nothing is more important than teaching them how to rule.

Xenophon is perfectly right when maintaining in his work entitled *Oeconomicus* that the ability to govern subjects who are free and willing is something superhuman and a gift of heaven.[2] Assuredly this is the wisdom that should be the goal of rulers, the wisdom which the youthful Solomon with all his prudence chose in preference to all other things and which he wished to have as constant adviser to his royal throne. Wisdom is that beautiful and yet chaste Sunamite girl whose embraces gave unique delight to David, wise father of a wise son. It is Wisdom who speaks in the Book of Proverbs: "By me princes govern and nobles establish justice,"[3] As often as kings employ wisdom for their counselor and reject such wicked advisers as ambition, wrath, greed, and flattery, the state flourishes in every way and, while crediting itself with the happiness of its prince's wisdom, can deservedly congratulate itself with the words: "All blessings have come to me along with wisdom."[4]

For this reason, Plato is more careful about the education of the guardians of the state than about any other matter. He wants them to surpass other men, not in wealth or jewelry, dress, or possession of statuary, or retinue, but in wisdom alone. And he maintains that states will never be happy unless they are governed by a philosopher or philosophy is embraced by those who happen to be their rulers. By philosophy Plato does not mean the kind that argues about principles, prime matter, motion, and infinity, but that which liberates the mind from the crude opinions of the populace and from ignoble passions, and following the eternal pattern laid up in heaven points the way to good government. A similar thought, I believe, is also found in Homer, in the passage where Mercury gives Ulysses the moly herb to counteract the magic potions of Circe.[5] With good reason does Plutarch hold that no one serves the state better than he who instructs its ruler, whose charge is to be the common good, in the noblest and most worthy principles.[6] On the other hand, no one causes such terrible disaster to human affairs as one who corrupts the

2. *Oeconomicus*, 21.12.
3. Proverbs 8:16.
4. Ecclesiastes 7:11.
5. *Odyssey*, 10.305.
6. *Moralia*, 778 D.

heart of a ruler with false opinions or desires; such a man is like him who poisons the water of a public drinking fountain. Very much to the point also is Plutarch's note of the famous statement made by Alexander the Great, who after a discussion with Diogenes, the Cynic, felt great admiration for his philosophical, lofty, and invincible mind, which never seemed depressed and rose above all human affairs; and he said, "If I were not Alexander, I would want to be Diogenes."[7] The more his vast realm was exposed to violent storms, the more he should have desired the mind of Diogenes so as to be equal to all those mighty problems.

TO WILLIAM WARHAM[1]

EE 396 (332–376)   Basel, April 1, 1516

The one fear I have is that my mediocre talent has not done justice either to Jerome's deserts or to your excellence. I am never made more aware of the leanness of my poor little talent than when I strive to make a return to you, as best I can, for your distinguished qualities and your abundant kindnesses to me. What other course was there for me—since I was so deeply in debt to you that not even by putting myself up at auction could I have paid any part of it? I have done what people usually do when they are completely insolvent: they offer an amount of money, be it ever so small, and then obligate themselves all the more, thereby testifying that they are lacking in cash, not in heart; they are in debt to bad fortune rather than to bad faith; and they ordinarily receive a favorable court sentence for the reason that they are unlucky rather than irresponsible. In this kind of matter one method of making compensation is for a person to admit

7. *Alexander,* 14.
1. See Letter 188, p. 53. The present letter is the preface to Erasmus' edition of Jerome, *Hieronymi Opera.* Warham was Archbishop of Canterbury. Quite in keeping with the nature of his communication, Erasmus comments here on the importance of Jerome, the Church Father, and the benefits to be derived from reading his works.

frankly and willingly that he is in debt—by acknowledging his creditor he makes a partial payment. Or to use a better analogy, I adopted the plan used by people who prefer to take out a loan to pay a debt rather than go to jail; I borrowed from Jerome so that I might repay you. And yet, would one call that borrowing, when it really belongs to me? Often a piece of real estate becomes someone else's property either by occupancy or by prescription. Besides, in this matter Jerome himself has laid down the rule for us to follow in the preface to his edition of the Book of Kings, where again and again he calls that work his own, for the reason that we can lawfully claim for ourselves anything we have made our own by correcting and reading and frequent study. On the basis of this rule, why can I not lay claim to the works of Jerome, which for centuries had been considered derelict? They were without occupant when I came upon them, and apart from appraising the toil involved I declared them the property of scholars of true theology.

Whoever has a single volume of Jerome has a golden river, a well-stocked library. On the other hand, whoever has Jerome in the jumbled and corrupted condition in which he has been up to now does not really have Jerome; not that I would dare assert that there are none at all of the old errors, or that there remain no traces of the former dilapidated condition. I doubt whether Jerome himself could guarantee that, unless he had access to more accurate manuscripts than have been available to us up to now. As a result of our strenuous efforts there is not much left to be done. At the very least, our attempt will prompt others to be more critical in what they stumble upon in their studies, and will prevent them from taking up and reading and approving and quoting—as if from an oracle—anything at all, no matter how badly corrupted by some imposter, no matter how spurious. And it is my wish that all scholars should devote their full energy to this task of restoring the original text, as far as is possible, of all the good writings left to us, no matter how shattered their condition. However, I would want only those men to enter this field who are distinguished for their trustworthiness, exactness, good judgment, and painstaking ability as well as for their learning; for no plague does more damage to good books than a corrector who is half-learned, listless, thoughtless, or lacking in judgment.

TO WILLIAM BUDÉ[1]

EE 421 (43–119)   [Antwerp, *ca.* June 19, 1516]

In this work [the edition of the New Testament] I have done what I ordinarily did in my other works. It was my intention to do the whole job superficially, dwelling on some small details but in general touching only lightly upon the various passages. But just when the work was ready for publication, some people urged me to revise the Vulgate edition with emendations or interpretations of my own. I thought the additional work involved would be very slight, but as a matter of fact it turned out extremely burdensome. Then they kept pressing me to expand the annotations. Finally, as you know, the whole undertaking had to be reworked. And then there was a further problem. I expected to have access at Basel to some emended manuscript copies. Being disappointed in that hope, I was forced to make my own correction of the manuscripts which the printers were going to use. And something else; two learned men had been hired to handle the correction of the proof—one a lawyer, and other a theologian with a competent knowledge of Hebrew. But being inexperienced in this sort of work, they could not fulfill the obligation they had assumed. Consequently, it was up to me to do the final proofreading. The editing and printing of the work went on simultaneously, and each day one ternion came off the press.[2] Even so, I was not free to devote my entire time to this task. My work on Jerome was being run off the press at the same time, and that claimed a good part of my attention. But I was determined either to extricate myself from all that drudgery by Easter or die on the job. In the end, we were wrong about the size of the volume. The printer had insisted

1. An eminent French humanist (1468–1570), in the service of the French court. See J. Bohatec, *Budé und Calvin* (Graz, 1950). The work discussed here by Erasmus is the *Novum Instrumentum,* his edition of the New Testament. He comments on the problems encountered, noting his own contribution in resolving them. He also speaks briefly of several of his other works, mentions the criticism directed against them, and then affirms the significance of his labors.
2. Three folio sheets.

that it would total about thirty ternions. It amounted to eighty-three, if I'm not mistaken. And so, after spending most of the time in matters which either did not pertain to me directly or had not been carefully planned beforehand, I was exhausted and had almost broken down when it came to doing the annotations. Considering the limitation of time and the state of my health, I accomplished what I could. I deliberately passed over some things, and wittingly winked at many others concerning which I held a different view shortly after the work was published. Consequently, I am preparing a second edition and I earnestly beg you to help me with it. I shall consider it my charge to be severely criticized by men like yourself. Do be careful about one point, my excellent Budé; don't let the public ever get a sniff of this. . . .

Some people accuse me of being foolhardy for attempting such lofty projects although I am a mere nonentity. In the *Enchiridion* I dared to disagree with our age, undeterred by anyone's authority! In the *Chiliads*,[3] a very slight work, I frequently wander off into the fields of philosophy and theology and, apparently forgetting all about the subject at hand, soar far beyond the proper limits! This will be all the more obvious if one reads the proverb: "One should be born either a king or a fool." Or, "Sparta is your share, now rule it!" Or, "War is sweet to one who has never known it." . . . In my pamphlet on the Christian prince I set down precepts for matters which no theologian would even dare to mention. Perhaps by "trifles," you mean the *Dialogues* of Lucian and the tragedies of Euripides, with no theologian would even dare to mention. Perhaps by "trifles," you one brief day on it. But trifles that they are, I do prefer them to those insignificant production of darkness. Now, as for my *New Testament,* I am very much aware and admit that many small details are introduced. But that was demanded by the subject matter. And yet if one would reflect, or better, himself experience what it means to translate and annotate such a text, he will realize that it would not have cost much more effort to produce a complete commentary than it cost me to write those pretty trifles.

These "trifles," such as they are, are being warmly received by

3. The *Adagiorum Chiliades* (Venice, 1508), best translated as "Thousands of Adages."

eminent theologians, who admit that they are deriving many insights from them. Of course, perhaps I am only flattered by all those men of high character. I would list their names and produce their letters except for my violent dislike of vainglory.

On the other hand, if I should want to measure myself by my own talent, I would undertake nothing but trifling tasks and would shun every burden that would overtax my tiny spirit and body. In fact, I find more pleasure in mingling the serious with the trifling than in trifling with matters of importance. I think it is utterly trivial to babble away over those quibbling questions in which many students of divinity consider themselves divine.

In this field, I think I have outstripped all my predecessors, if not in learning, then at least in industry. In Jerome's emendation of the Psalter, how many of his annotations are paltry little things! I shall do my duty as long as I have life and strength. I have done a preface on the Psalm: *Beatus vir*.[4] I shall tackle St. Paul. Jerome will see the light of day completely reborn. These projects are so enormous that I can hardly stand up under the malicious attacks of some men. How vast they seem to you, I do not know; at any rate, I admit and realize that they are too much for my strength.

TO POPE LEO X[1]

EE 446 (1–30; 53–76)   London, August 9, 1516

I would have considered myself extremely happy, most blessed Father, if Your Holiness had merely interpreted favorably my rashness or importunity in not hesitating to address, though unrequested, a letter to Your Papal Highness, and especially to Leo's most vener-

4. The reference is to the Latin opening of Psalm 1, "Blessed is the man."
1. See Letter 335, p. 80. In this letter Erasmus expresses his appreciation for the various honors he has received on account of his scholarly contribution, including approbation from the Pope, which he says he values most highly. He also comments on his edition of the New Testament and defends himself against certain charges. Though written in London, the reference "now that I have returned to my homeland" [!] indicates that Erasmus drafted the letter while still in Antwerp.

able and peerless majesty. But this boldness of mine, I see, has turned out most happily for me. Your extraordinarily paternal affection has surpassed all my expectations and prayers in the two briefs which you have sent without solicitation. One of them honors me and my scholarly activity by a rich store of weighty testimony; the other, a recommendation to the King's Majesty, shows your affection as well as your considerateness. It is of paramount importance to merit the approbation of Eternal Deity; next to that comes certainly, in my opinion, a commendation from the lips of the Supreme Pontiff—even the more when he is a man like Leo, who while holding the highest office among men graces it with every kind of virtue and learning.

If those briefs had reached me while I was still in Basel, not even the perils of travel would have deterred me from flying to the feet of Your Holiness. But now that I have returned to my homeland, I am not only hindered by my advancing years, which are becoming more burdensome, but am also detained by the generosity of the rulers and feel obligated by the rare affection shown me by my native land. For the most illustrious Prince Charles, Catholic King,[2] the peerless light and glory of our age, under whose dominion I was born and to whose father Philip I was not only an acquaintance but a dear friend, issued to me in my absence a most gracious invitation with the offer of an annual salary, and this without any soliciting or expectation on my part. When I returned—and I had just barely come back—he conferred upon me a rich and distinguished benefice. On the other hand, I know from good evidence how much the recommendation of Your Holiness has added to the earlier favor shown me by the King of England, and to the good will of the Cardinal of York[3] and the long-standing interest of the Archbishop of Canterbury.[4] Your recommendation has been not only very pleasing to me but also influential with these men, especially as it was not wrung from you by entreaty but freely given. . . .

My revision of the Greek and Latin texts of the New Testament along with my *Annotations* came out in print some time ago under

2. Charles was now king of Spain. As such he enjoyed the appellation "Catholic King."
3. Thomas Wolsey.
4. William Warham.

the patronage of your auspicious name. Whether this work is universally approved, I do not know; at any rate, up to now I am sure it does have the approbation of the recognized and outstanding theologians; most of all, of that peerless prelate Bishop Christopher of Basel, under whose eyes the book was printed. I am not trying in this work of mine to do away with the ancient Vulgate edition; I have only emended some corrupt passages and clarified several others where the text is obscure. This work is not the fanciful product of my own imagination, nor did I approach it without proper training. . . . It is based in part on the evidence of very ancient manuscripts and in part on the opinion of those men whose learning and holiness have been approved by the authority of the Church, namely, Jerome, Hilary, Ambrose, Augustine, Chrysostom, and Cyril. At the same time, however, I am always ready to give a modest explanation of any point which I have made correctly, or to correct without hesitation any point in which, being human, I have inadvertently slipped into error.

TO PETER GILLES[1]

EE 476 (36–79)   Brussels, October 6, 1516

Most of our ailments are mental in origin; the hard work demanded by the intellectual life will cause you fewer troubles if you control your studies by reason. Have a definite storage place for your collection of books and your letters and all your papers. And do not rush, without good reason, from one author to another. Rather, select a work of one of the very best authors and stay with it until the very last page, and as you read along note any observations you consider worth remembering. Set down a definite schedule for yourself,

1. Gilles (1486–1533), secretary of the city of Antwerp, was editor of various humanist texts. Thomas More dedicated his *Utopia* to him. This is another of the letters of advice written by Erasmus, here dealing with the proper distribution of time, the best ways of reading and of keeping a diary, the value of friendship and a good family life. Other letters to Gilles are 715 and 2260.

arranging the things you plan to do according to the various hours of the day. Do not pile one job upon another unless you have accomplished the previous work. In this way you can make the day longer for yourself, whereas now practically the whole day is lost. And since you find fault with your memory, I think it would be profitable for you to keep a diary for each year (it involves very little trouble) and note down every day any happenings which you do not want to forget. I know people who have profited very much from such a practice. . . .

But before all else, I plead with you to let yourself be guided in the conduct of life by good judgment rather than by impulse. If anything upsets you, stop and reflect to see if there is any means to remedy the pain or at least to lessen its effect. Such reflection will be more fruitful for you if undertaken with a tranquil mind rather than in a state of excitement. If there is some remedy, use it; if not, then what good is it to feel angry or bitter and thereby increase the pain through your own fault? In the name of our friendship I beg you not to consider anything more important than your life and health. If you can maintain your position without harm to your health, then do so; but if not, you will lose much more than you gain by guaranteeing the maintenance of your position at the cost of your health or peace of mind. . . . Do not spend too much effort on insignificant matters. The years are fleeting and health is a fragile thing. Some things must be disregarded, and we must elevate our thoughts to what is important. Make Seneca and Plato your close friends; frequent conversation with these men will prevent your soul from feeling depressed. It is truly the sign of a great mind to ignore some injuries and not to listen to or answer the insults of some people. Experiment occasionally to find out how much more effective are deference and a judicious use of gentle language than a wild display of emotion.

As for your wonderful father, continue to lighten the burden of his aging years by kindly attentions, not merely because he is your father but even more because he is such an excellent father. Enjoy the company of sincere friends and avoid associating with false ones. As for your dear wife, live with her in such a way that she will love you not merely for the sake of sexual desire. Live with her so that she may not only love you, but also respect you. Take her into your confidence and share with her all matters that pertain to your home and to the enjoyment of life. Maintain your authority over your home, and let your personal relations with the members of your family be seasoned by gentlemanly manners. As for the rearing of your children, it would be idle for me to offer you advice, since you have a perfect model in your own father.

TO STEPHEN PONCHER[1]

EE 529 (53–100)   Antwerp, February 14, 1516/7

While I have been reflecting upon the strenuous efforts made by His Royal Highness and You, Reverend Father, to honor your land of France by attracting men who are eminent for virtue and learning, there suddenly occurs to me the name of Heinrich Glareanus.[2] This man was a very intimate friend of mine some time ago at Basel, and in my opinion he is the man to suit your wishes, if anyone can. I shall give you a brief but accurate description of him. He is by birth a Swiss (that nation has begun to add distinction for intellectual pursuits to its military renown); he is in the prime of life, just short of being thirty years old. He is in excellent health and capable of hard work. He has taught liberal arts for several years, first at Cologne, then at Basel, with considerable distinction. He is a doctor of liberal arts, but in his case it is not just a title as with the common run of men in that profession. He was once very skilled in sophistry, but since regaining his senses has abandoned it and is now its enemy. He has more than a passing acquaintance with theology; in fact, at one time he entered right into its inner sanctuary. But later he withdrew, disgusted partly with those chilly subtleties which are almost the only thing that wins approval in the schools today, and

1. A distinguished humanist, churchman, and politician, Bishop of Paris (d. 1525). This is a letter of recommendation for a friend and at the same time a splendid portrait of the latter: Heinrich Glareanus.
2. Heinrich Loriti (1488–1563), or Glareanus, after his home canton of Glarus—humanist, musician, historian, author of *Helvetiae descriptio* (1517–22). From 1524 he was professor at Basel. His opposition to the Reformation led to his move to Freiburg in 1529.

partly with the endless fighting and disagreement going on among the theologians. He preferred to drink in Christ from the sources rather than from the ditches of those fellows. For this purpose he began with great enthusiasm to devote himself to the study of Greek. His poetry is not without elegance; in his early youth he received the poet's laurel from Emperor Maximilian at Cologne. His prose style reveals both talent and learning, although on occasion one may observe a lack of experience and practice. He has a broad knowledge of history; in music, cosmography, and in the mathematical sciences he is thoroughly proficient, for that is the area in which he is supreme.

As for his morals, he is extremely chaste and pure, a virtue seldom found in men of this profession; in fact, not only his thoughts but even his ears shrink from filthy suggestion, for he is really ardently devout. Not even Momus could find any fault in him, except for the wild and unrestrained language he uses against the sophists and their thorny problems, if indeed that is to be considered a fault rather than a matter of discretion. For you realize how brash and insolent such men can be unless they have added a higher type of learning to that kind of study. In doing battle with such men Glareanus shows no less courage than did Hercules in ancient times when battling with monsters. He has the lungs and the voice and the invincible spirit of a Hercules to handle those fellows, no matter how loud they scream. And for this reason there is very little agreement between him and the theologians; I am not referring to learned theologians, with whom he is very much in agreement, but to those who have never learned anything beyond a barbaric form of literature and some chilly, trivial questions. Such men he can rout and tear to pieces with greater facility for the fact that he once belonged to their camp. However, even this passionate violence and what I might call "divine frenzy" of his are gradually becoming more controlled, as time goes by. Besides, he is far removed from anything like arrogance or pride. He is very good-natured and sociable under all circumstances. Ask him to sing, and without hesitation he will sing. If you prefer to have him read, he will read. If you want light talk, he can be very witty and funny. If you wish a serious discussion, he will quickly change for you. And yet, with all his congeniality he is incapable of flattery.

TO WILLIAM LATIMER[1]

EE 540 (22–44; 80–91)   Antwerp, [February 1517]

Furthermore, in regard to the Bishop of Rochester,[2] I disagree with you even more. You consider it preferable not to begin any project at all unless one can finish it. You advise getting an outstanding Greek scholar from Italy who could remain with the Bishop until he reached the point where he would be proficient in the study of Greek. The point of your suggestion, my dear Latimer, is desirable but not very practical, and therefore we have decided to do, as the Greek comic poet puts it, "as much as we can." Italy is some distance from here and has far fewer eminent scholars today than it had when you were there. And there is also the risk that, instead of a distinguished scholar, we may get some busybody. You know, too, how those Italians are; they demand an exorbitant salary to move from their country to a land of savages, and this is true even of the mediocre ones. I might also mention the fact that those who are competent in good learning sometimes bring along morals that are not so good. And you know the high moral standards of the Bishop. And so while we are looking around to see who would be the best person to get, and while we argue over the salary and discuss the traveling arrangements, much time is being wasted.

I realize it is a wise and true saying that a person should stop and reflect before acting, and once he has reflected should quickly carry out his decision. But I see many people who do nothing but reflect until it is too late to put their final decision into effect. They are like some men who deliberate whether they should marry or not, and then which girl they should select for marriage; and meanwhile the

1. At the time a widely known English humanist (*ca.* 1460–1545). See Allen, I, 438. This brief excerpt displays a variety of concerns: the difficulty of getting a good Greek scholar to come to England, the need to make decisions in life at the proper time, and how one should not be bashful when it comes to scholarly writing.

2. John Fisher (*ca.* 1469–1535), humanist, Bishop of Rochester, later cardinal, executed by Henry VIII.

years are surreptitiously fleeing by, and before they can come to a definite choice they are too old to marry. . . .

I should conclude with this one piece of advice. Do not let your excessive bashfulness—I might almost call it immoderate modesty—prevent you from helping to publicize scholarly work. Some people like myself are lacking in sufficient restraint. But I am not quite sure which are more at fault, those who attempt nothing for fear of making a mistake or those who in their imprudent efforts to be helpful sometimes stumble into error. Members of the latter group disclose many excellent things, even though not everything turns out according to their desires. Besides, their scholarship encourages and inspires other men to intellectual activity. But those who keep their knowledge all to themselves are, in my opinion, more deserving of blame than disreputable misers, who are guardians rather than owners of their money. For the money which such men have piled up can at least after their death be transferred to others to be used, whereas scholars can leave nothing after death to any heir unless they have committed their thoughts to writing.

TO WOLFGANG CAPITO[1]

EE 541 (1–9; 29–93; 118–   Antwerp, February 26,
125; 133–151)   1516/17

It is not part of my natural disposition, dear Wolfgang, to be excessively fond of life. Perhaps I have lived long enough, having entered my fifty-first year, or possibly I see nothing so splendid or delightful in this life as to merit desire by one who is convinced that a happier life awaits those who in this world earnestly seek after piety. But I almost wish to be young again, and this for the reason that I expect the coming of a golden age: we clearly see how rulers, as if changed by inspiration, devote all their energies to the pursuit of peace. . . .

1. Ca. 1478–1541. A cleric and Hebrew scholar at Basel, later reformer at Strasbourg. This letter contains a general assessment of the temper of the time, including the imminence of a "golden age." Erasmus notes the recent termination of war, the qualities of the ruling sovereigns, the renascence of learning, including theology, and the dangers of a resurgence of paganism under the disguise of a revival of learning.

I see that the leaders of the world—King Francis of France, Charles the Catholic King, King Henry of England, and Emperor Maximilian—have made a drastic cutback on their armaments and have established a secure and, I hope, lasting peace. Therefore I am encouraged to entertain the expectation that there will be a renascence or even an efflorescence, not only of good morals and Christian piety, but also of the purer and genuine kind of learning and the finest branches of knowledge. The basis for my hope lies in the fact that this goal is being pursued with equal enthusiasm in various parts of the globe: in Rome by Pope Leo, in Spain by the Cardinal of Toledo,[2] in England b King Henry VIII, a scholar himself of no mean ability; in our country by King Charles, a young man of superhuman gifts; in France by King Francis, who was born so to speak for this very purpose, and who is also offering rich rewards to invite and attract from other lands men who are eminent for virtue and learning. In Germany this is the goal of many outstanding rulers and bishops, and especially of the Emperor Maximilian, who, aged and weary of many wars, has decided to seek rest in the arts of peace, a decision more suitable for a man of his years and also more fortunate for all of Christendom. It is due to the piety of such rulers that we see gifted men all over the world awakening to the sound of the signal and rising up and joining forces to revive the best learning. How else can one explain the fact that all these learned scholars from various lands are sharing their efforts, and pursue this wonderful work not only with vigor but also with a fair degree of success, with the result that there is almost a sure hope that all branches of learning will blossom forth in a much purer and more genuine condition? First of all polite letters, which were long ago all but extinct, have for some time now been cultivated and cherished by the Scots, the Danes, and the Irish. And medicine—think of all the champions it has! In Rome, Nicolaus Leonicenus, in Venice Ambrose Leo of Nola, in France William Cop and John Ruell, and in England Thomas Linacre. Roman law is being revived in Paris by William Budé and in Germany by Ulrich Zasius, and mathematics in Basel by Heinrich Glareanus.[3]

2. Francisco Ximenes, outstanding Spanish churchman and reformer, from January 1516 regent of Castille and Aragon. See H. de Montherlant, *Le Cardinal d'Espagne* (Paris, 1960).
3. See also Letter 529, p. 105.

On the other hand, theology has presented a little more of a problem, because until now professors of theology have generally had a
deep abhorrence of good learning and have covered up their ignorance all the more successfully by doing so under the guise of piety.
As a result these fellows have convinced the illiterate masses that it is
a violation of religion for anyone to assail their barbarism. They
complain bitterly to the unlettered populace in particular and appeal
for stoning whenever they see any danger of their ignorance being
exposed. But I am confident that this situation too will turn out well,
once the study of the three languages gains public acceptance in the
schools, as it has begun to. The most learned and least spiteful
members of this profession are either actively supporting this project
or are favorably inclined toward it. Jacques Lefèvre of Étaples, as
well as others, has devoted considerable energy to this matter; you are
like him not only in name but also in your rich endowments.[4] As for
me, the humblest portion of this task has fallen to my lot, and rightly
so; I am not sure if I have made any real contribution. At any rate I
have so roiled these fellows who are opposed to having the world
regain its senses that apparently my poor little efforts have had some
effect. However, I did not undertake this labor in the belief that I
had some extraordinary teaching to propose; rather, it was my desire
to pave the way for those destined to strive toward higher things, so
that they could more easily convey their brilliant, lofty discoveries
without stumbling over rough spots or through swampy places.
Nevertheless, not even these poor efforts of mine are spurned by men
who are learned and open-minded. The only ones who carp at them
are a few fellows so stupid that they are hooted at even by those of
the common rabble who have a little intelligence. Not long ago a
man complained bitterly to the people here, in a tearful voice, and of
course in a sermon, that the Scriptures were done with, as also the
theologians who up to now had borne the Christian faith upon their
shoulders—now that men had appeared who were emending the text
of the Holy Gospel and even of the Lord's Prayer—as if I were
finding fault with Matthew or Luke instead of discovering the
original correct text. In England, one or two persons are screaming
that it is a shameful thing for me to try to teach an outstanding man
like St. Jerome—as if I were altering and not restoring his original

4. Erasmus refers to the fact that Capito's middle name was Fabricius,
which paralleled Lefèvre's Latinized name Faber Stapulensis.

text. And yet these growlers with their dirges, which a common fuller with an ounce of intelligence would laugh to scorn, consider themselves mighty theologians. . . .

It is not that I want the kind of theology which is commonly accepted in the schools today to be completely abolished, but I want to have it enriched and purified by the addition of the ancient and true learning. Neither the authority of Scripture nor of the theologians will be shaken if some readings are emended which up to now have been considered defective, or if some texts are more correctly understood which up to now have been the occasion of sheer drivel on the part of the common run of professors. In fact, their authority will be all the greater if their understanding of Sacred Scripture is more genuine. . . .

There is one thought that causes me anxiety; it is the fear that under the appearance of a renascence of ancient learning paganism may attempt to rear its head, for even among Christians there are some who acknowledge Christ practically in name only, while within their hearts they breathe the spirit of paganism;[5] I am also afraid that Judaism may plan to use the renascence of Hebrew learning as an occasion for revival. There is no plague so opposed and so hostile to the teaching of Christ. Such has always been the condition of human affairs. Whenever anything good has succeeded, something bad has immediately used it as a pretext for trying to intrude itself. I would like to see those chilly subtleties completely lopped off—or at least they should not be the only interest of theologians—and Christ in all His simplicity and purity deeply planted in the hearts of men. I think the best way to accomplish this is to use the knowledge of the languages in order to penetrate deeply into the meaning of the sources themselves. I only hope we can avoid this evil without perhaps falling into something else that is worse. Recently some works have been published that smack of pure Judaism. I realize how hard St. Paul worked to liberate Christ from Judaism, and I am aware that some people are quietly slipping back into that position. Then, too, I hear that some have other plans in mind which would add nothing whatsoever to an understanding of Christ and would only throw up a cloud of smoke before the eyes of men.

5. Erasmus' dialogue of 1527, *Ciceronianus*, while addressing itself to the problem of the conflict of two cultures, ancient and modern (Christian), was a warning against the unquestioning worship of classical antiquity.

TO JOHN CAESARIUS[1]

EE 622 (1–7; 12–30)   Antwerp, August 16, 1517

But the most annoying thing of all is the report, if true, which was brought to me by my servant James upon his return from Cologne.[2] He said that several persons in that city have in their possession some sort of pamphlet which satirizes Pope Julius, describing how after his death he was excluded from heaven by St. Peter.[3] I had heard some time ago that a play on this theme had been staged in France, where there has always been an unrestrained indulgence in this sort of nonsense. I suppose somebody translated that play into Latin. I wonder what gets into the mind of such fellows when they waste so much time and effort on that sort of thing. But I am also surprised that some people suspect that this notorious bit of tomfoolery came from me; I imagine the reason might be that the Latin style is a little better than average. I admit I did some ridiculing in my *Folly*, but without drawing blood; and I censured no person by name. I mocked the conduct of men; I did not attack their reputation. If my servant has told me the truth, though I cannot as yet quite believe it, then please, my dear sir, do all you can to suppress such ungodly nonsense

1. *Ca.* 1468–1550. A humanist scholar, a student of Lefèvre, who taught at the University of Cologne. This letter, which Erasmus intended to be widely circulated, appeared subsequently in a volume entitled *Epistolae Obscurorum Virorum* ("Letters of Obscure Men"), a satire on the foibles and esoteric subtleties of scholasticism which grew out of the Reuchlin-Pfefferkorn controversy. The letter concerns the authorship of the satirical dialogue *Julius exclusus a coelo* and conveys the general assertion that he should not be suspected as its author—without denying the charge outright! Other letters to John Caesarius are 701 and 1528.

2. The "famulus" was James Teyng (d. 1530), a humanist scholar.

3. The reference is to the satirical dialogue *Julius exclusus a coelo*. As the letter shows, Erasmus was unwilling to acknowledge the authorship, which remains disputed to this day. See R. H. Bainton, "Erasmus and the Dialogue Julius Exclusus," *Vierhundertfünfzig Jahre lutherische Reformation* (Leipzig, 1967), 17–26. A modern edition of the dialogue was published by W. K. Ferguson, *Erasmi Opuscula* (The Hague, 1933), while an incomplete English translation is found in J. A. Froude, *Life and Letters of Erasmus* (London, 1894).

before it can be put in print; not that such rascals deserve this kind of service, but because it is our duty to safeguard the public esteem of scholarship which these fellows are trying to mar shamefully by such displays of wit. As far as I am concerned with this matter, I am sure that anybody who really knows me is well aware that such dreary lullabies have always displeased me to an extraordinary degree, inasmuch as they are unworthy of men of learning and virtue.

TO JOHN CAESARIUS[1]

EE 701 (13–38)   Louvain, November 3, [1517]

That scholars are giving their support to Reuchlin is clearly a sign of their good culture. But for them to be engaging in written controversy with that mangy pest Pfefferkorn, that trumpeter of the Furies and tool of certain men masking as theologians and actual representative of Satan—that I cannot approve. The fellow is a concoction made up completely of abusive language; he cannot be vanquished by insults. He is incapable of blushing; he has never learned how to say a kind word. And that brazen-faced clown thinks it will be to his glory if in any way he can gain publicity from the writings of scholars. He prefers to win the approval of the populace rather than of the very best men. But if the world perceived his hypocrisy, and realized that while pretending to defend the Christian faith he was going to destroy the Christian religion, he would win great favor among his circumcised brethren by doing for them the same service that Zopyrus did for Darius. If his body were dissected, by damn, I bet you'd find inside of him not just one Jew but a thousand! Beware of an angel of Satan when he is transfigured into an angel of light.

1. On Caesarius, see Letter 622, p. 112. Erasmus is commenting here on the Reuchlin affair, i.e., the feud of Reuchlin, an eminent Hebrew scholar, with Pfefferkorn, a renegade Jew who called for the destruction of all Jewish books. The controversy turned into a virtual clash between the humanists on the one hand and the scholastic theologians on the other. The "Letters of Obscure Men," already mentioned on p. 112, came out of this conflict. Its two authors were Crotus Rubianus and Ulrich von Hutten. A recent edition of the "Letters" is *On the Eve of the Reformation* (New York, 1964).

Would to heaven that old saying were not so true, that a bad Jew always makes a worse Christian. Consequently, I would desire scholars to be above engaging such a dirty monster in a contest out of which they can emerge, whether they win or lose, with only mud and venom. It amazes me that civil authorities, bishops, and the Emperor do not put a stop to such a plague. It is a very easy thing to cause mischief, and the common people do not have any judgment. A tiny spark can cause a conflagration that will do endless damage. And what would be more desirable to the Jews, whose case he is pleading while pretending to oppose it, then to have Christian concord so completely disrupted? Provided the New Testament remained intact, I personally would prefer to have the entire Old Testament done away with rather than have peace among Christians destroyed for the sake of the books of the Jews. Would to heaven that fellow were still completely a Jew, and that we would be more cautious in admitting others!

TO DOMENICO GRIMANI[1]

EE 710 (95–110)   Louvain, November 13, 1517

But what would St. Jerome say if he saw Rome today with all its churches and cardinals and bishops? If he were to see all the princes of the world seeking responses from this one thoroughly reliable oracle of Christ? And men streaming in here for religious reasons from the farthest corners of the globe? And each individual hardly regarding himself as a Christian unless he has seen Rome, unless he has seen the Roman Pontiff, who is like some earthly divinity, since all the affairs of mortal men seem to depend upon his approval or disapproval? Finally, what would Jerome say if he were to perceive that under Leo X the tempests of wars have been calmed and the city of Rome is flourishing in learning no less than in religion, since this one city possesses so many eminent ecclesiastical dignitaries, so many men distinguished in every branch of learning, and so many shining

---

1. See Letter 334, p. 78. This is from the Preface of Erasmus' *Paraphrasis ad Romanos,* a paraphrase on St. Paul's Epistle to the Romans. Erasmus comments here on the contemporary atmosphere in Rome.

lights of the human race, so that one would more accurately call it not a city but a world? The one prayer that we should say for our Pope is that his life may always be in accord with the praises he receives, that his piety may always transcend his felicity, and his goodness excel his majesty. That will come about if he does his utmost to express the spirit and life of Saints Peter and Paul under whose auspices and protection he reigns.

TO PETER GILLES[1]

EE 715 (8–50)   Louvain, [ca. November 16, 1517]

If it is a blessing to live a long life, your father reached his eightieth year so sound of limb and with vision so good that he needed neither a cane nor reading glasses, and his black hair was just beginning to be sprinkled with touches of gray.[2] And what is the greatest and also the rarest blessing of all, he remained in complete possession of his faculties. And if it is a blessing to have a happy marriage, that happened to him twice. His second marriage was more fortunate in that it presented a wonderful man with several wonderful children. Many of them survived their father, and after reaching an honorable position in life he saw them all grown to adulthood.

And just as he himself lived his entire life among his fellow townsmen without ever sullying his fair name with any foul rumor, so too he raised all his children in such a way that none of them ever caused him any regret or shame. Your father was the embodiment of goodness, your mother the ideal of innocence. What love he had for his wife, and what respect she had for him even after she married him! But even so the best parents do not always have the best children. How little he was disturbed by the thought of death, when he realized that he would live on in his children! In fact, whenever he hugged and kissed his darling little grandson, your own son, named

1. See Letter 476, p. 103. This letter, like the former, presents a sensitive eulogy of the father of the recipient, in this case apparently on the occasion of his death. At the same time, Erasmus exhorts his friend to translate the lessons of this life into practice—by rearing his children the way his father reared his.

2. Little is known about Nicolaus Gilles, whom Erasmus commemorates in the letter, except that he was treasurer of the city of Antwerp.

Nicolaus after his grandfather, he thought of himself as not really dying. His wealth was not vast, but it was sufficient and was—an extremely rare occurrence in these times—honestly acquired. He had chosen a profession which without any fraudulent practices provided him with enough income to support his family, and also to help the poor, toward whom he was most generous. He left enough money to provide a decent livelihood for each of his children, even if there were no further source of income. He held several civic offices, and would have held others, and more important ones, if he had in any way sought them. His conduct in the offices that he did hold was such that no one had any reason to complain.

Domestic discord was as abominable to him as the plague. Nor did he ever quarrel with any of his fellow townsmen, being very able to adjust himself to others. He preferred to give up his own right if he saw that was the only way to preserve harmony. No one ever heard from his lips any word that was idle or indecent or disparaging. Though living in a large city he did not have a single enemy. When he passed away, many, many people, especially the poor, mourned him as a father. And how patiently he bore very painful sufferings through several days! For no form of death is more excruciating than that which results from an obstruction of the urinary passages. The only advice he had for his children as he lay dying was to preserve harmony and to pursue piety. He left his inheritance distributed in such a way that it did not matter who had chosen what portion. And no one appeared who could say that he was owed a single penny. Would not people rightly consider you ungrateful if you mourned such a father? Enjoy his happy memory, and congratulate him on having been transported from the stormy waves of this life into the haven of immortality!

Remember to commemorate your father by the integrity of your character, as you have done hither to. Bring up your son from his tender years to recall his grandfather not only by the name he bears but also by the piety of his life, commemorating at the same time his father and uncle by his erudition. Let him drink biblical wisdom as the milk of his soul; let him drink in literature, both sacred and profane, and greet his parents with charming talk in Greek and Latin. May you, Peter, live with Cornelia to a happy old age and in the best of children find that satisfaction which brings with it the highest honor.

IV.
The Challenge of Luther and the Reformation: 1517–1529

At the height of Erasmus' fame came the outbreak of the "Lutheran controversy," and even though he continued to travel, notably to Basel, Louvain, Antwerp, and also to write—paraphrases of various New Testament books and the Diatribe on Free Will, for example— Luther and the Reformation increasingly overshadowed his thought and life. In 1521 he settled at Basel, where he remained until 1529, enjoying the association with fellow humanists and the publisher Froben.

TO JOHN OF LOUVAIN[1]

EE 749 (3–32)   Louvain, January 2, 1518

As for my *Folly* I offer sufficient explanation to the reader, partly in the preface to the work itself and partly in my letter to Dorp,

1. Nothing is known about the recipient of the letter.

which is now included in the edition of the *Folly*. But what can one do with people who cannot be appeased by any amount of reasoning, and who in fact loudly condemn what they have never read? Their screaming and shouting reveals their utter insanity. If I had known beforehand that these fellows would be so deeply offended, perhaps I might have arranged to suppress the work. For it is my resolve if possible to try to please everybody, so far as that can be done without flattery. But now any regrets on my part are bootless, since the work has already gone through more than a dozen editions. One thing does puzzle me. Why are monks and theologians the only ones who take offense at it? Is it that they all recognize that they fit the descriptions I give in that work? The Pope read the *Folly* and it made him laugh. He merely added this one remark: "I am glad that our friend Erasmus is also included in the *Folly*." And yet there is no group that I handle more harshly than popes. The last thing I would do would be to indulge in abusive language. But if I wanted to portray theologians and monks as very many of them really are, then *Folly's* remarks about them would obviously be very polite.

However, I had never heard before that the book is being read in the schools. Even so, I cautiously avoided putting anything in it that could corrupt persons of that age. As for your fears that students by reading it may develop a total aversion for religion, I do not quite understand what that means. Can it be that some remark directed against those who are superstitiously religious could thereby jeopardize the whole of religion? Indeed, I wish that all those who are now called religious might be worthy of that name! Let me speak out more openly. I wish that even secular priests and the common people would follow the true religion of Christ in such a way that those who now alone are termed religious would not seem to be religious. The world is full of monasteries everywhere. However, I am not condemning any specific type of religious institution. But just figure out for yourself how few there are in this way of life who, apart from the liturgy and ceremonials, practice true religion. The behavior of most of them is extremely worldly. I have never blackened the reputation of any man. I have made fun of common defects of mankind which are well known to everybody. Even so, in the future I shall be more moderate in this matter.

TO WILLIAM BUDÉ[1]

EE 778 (222–250)   Louvain, February 22, [1518]

When I am attacked by name and called in writing an adversary of Christ's glory (whereas I would not hesitate, unworthy sinner that I am, to risk my life or even to die in defense of His glory), will you still bid me hold my tongue? But for goodness sake, do tell me, do you consider reprehensible the fact that I am defending myself? Or the way in which I am doing it? If, out of your sense of fairness, you do not reproach me for defending myself, then you cannot complain of my way of doing so either, since my mode of self-defense is such as to show all possible favor even to my adversary. Why then do you think I should be rebuked, unless you consider it my destiny to be the only person in the world who must submit to being mauled and trampled on by everybody without retaliating? And so, from now on, no dog will be so cowardly as not to dare to bark at Erasmus, no ass so stupid as to be afraid to bray at him, and no pig so hesitatant as not to grunt at him. Mice do all they can to protect themselves with their tiny teeth. Little bees when annoyed vent their anger with their sting. Am I the only one who has no right even to shield himself, especially in a matter of the faith? Believe me, Budé, any man who can bear the charge of impiety with composure has very little piety in him. Notice all the thunder and lightning with which St. Jerome rose up against Rufinus, once a very close friend of his, merely because he was drawn into some odious association by Rufinus through an artful figurative expression of praise. And the anger with which he answered and threatened Augustine for having dared to tear up his interpretation of one passage! What if he had been

1. On William Budé see Letter 421, p. 99. The setting of this letter is Erasmus' dispute with Lefèvre, which arose over Lefèvre's public disagreement with one of Erasmus' notes on the Epistle to the Hebrews. The feud was brief but exceedingly vehement.

doused with vinegar as I was by Lefèvre? Whether he did it as a
friend or as an enemy, intentionally or unintentionally, whether
under urging or of his own accord, jokingly or seriously, sober or
otherwise—that is his worry. At any rate, he did it. The fact is all too
obvious. If only both of us could deny it! In no way am I to be
compared with Jerome, neither in holiness nor learning, nor prudence nor self-control. Yet note how much more cruelly I have been
assailed than he, but how much more polite I am in defending
myself.

TO THOMAS MORE[1]

EE 785 (21–36)   Louvain, March 5, 1518

The Pope and several rulers are staging some new farces mas-
querading under the horrors of war against the Turks. Poor devils,
those Turks! May there not be too much thirst for blood in us
Christians! Even wives are feeling the effects of the war. All married
men under fifty and over twenty-six will be recruited into the armed
forces. For the time being the Pope forbids the wives of men away at
war to indulge in any pleasure at home; they are to avoid finery, not
to wear silks or gold or jewelry, nor use cosmetics, nor drink wine,
and are to fast every other day—so that God may look favorably upon
their husbands engaged in this bloody war. If any married men are
kept at home on necessary work their wives are to follow the same
regulations they would have had to follow if their husbands had gone
off to war. They may sleep in the same bedroom, but in separate
beds. No kissing is allowed until the day when this awful war is
brought to a successful conclusion under Christ's protection. I am
aware that these regulations will prove irksome to many wives who
have not sufficiently reflected upon the seriousness of the situation;
although your wife, I know, with her good sense and devotion to a

1. See Letter 222, p. 57. The letter above reflects conditions attending the
crusade then proposed against the Turks.

matter of concern to the Christian religion, will even be glad to comply.

TO MARCUS LAURINUS[1]

EE 809 (9–38; 78–126)   Louvain, April 5, 1518

No group is more in need of the results of my toil than those fellows who carp at my scholarly work, which is really for their own benefit. And no group is more wild and savage in its carping than those who have never seen even the outside of the book. Just put it to the test, my dear Marcus, and you will find I am telling the truth. When you meet such a man, let him go on raging against my New Testament. Then when he has ranted himself hoarse, ask him if he ever read the book. If he puts up a bold front and says he has, insist that he produce the passage he is criticizing. You won't find anyone who can do that.

Consider whether it is the mark of a Christian, or worthy of the profession of monks, to tear a man's reputation to pieces before an illiterate mob. They could not repair this reputation even if they wanted to, since they are utterly unaware of what they are criticizing. They do not reflect upon the truth of St. Paul's statement: 'Slanderers will never inherit the kingdom of God."[2] The most criminal charge to make against a man's good name is that of heresy and that is the charge these fellows fasten upon anyone who offends them, be it merely by the way he nods his head.

Whenever in Switzerland a person in a crowd points his finger at some individual, so it is said, the whole crowd points their finger in the same direction and they all swoop down upon their prey. Similarly, as soon as any person in that gang begins to grunt, they all start grunting, and then with their wild screaming they egg the people on

1. Dean of St. Donatian at Burges. Erasmus is reflecting on the opposition of the scholastic theologians, in particular the faculty at Louvain, to his textual work on the New Testament. Their argument was that tampering with the text of Scripture would inevitably lead to rejection of the faith.
2. I. Cor. 6:10.

to throwing stones. They seem to forget their religious profession and act as if their only trade were to defile the names of good men with their foul tongues. They completely fulfill the words of the psalmist:

> They make their tongues as sharp as serpents'
> with viper's venom on their lips.[3]

Thus, men who should have been preaching Christian piety deliberately disparage the piety of others; men who profess to be ministers of the gospel confess that they are slanderers. And quite paradoxically, men who are absolutely speechless when it comes to saying a kind word have a tongue for backbiting and calumny; and while otherwise complete strangers to the Muses and the Graces, when defiling the reputation of good men they consider themselves witty and charming. . . .

Let them think lightly of my work provided they do admit that it contains explanation of countless passages which hitherto have not been understood even by men of more than ordinary learning.

Finally, why do my detractors condemn a work which is not condemned by the Pope, to whom it was dedicated? I sent him a copy; he accepted it, read it, thanked me in writing, and also expressed his gratitude by his very action. But some loudmouthed critics, being naturally stupid and then blinded by the disease of foul language, are of the opinion I suppose that I intended to reject as obsolete the entire Vulgate translation, whereas I do prefer it in many places to the reading of the Greek text. As a matter of fact, I translated only the text I found in Greek manuscripts, and I pointed out in my notes the readings I approve and disapprove. Now, suppose that I had done nothing but merely translate the text of the Greek manuscripts so that those who are ignorant of Greek could compare this translation with the Vulgate, then what reason would they have to criticize? But what I did was to show by evident proofs that in very many places our Vulgate text is corrupt, though with no danger to the faith. I show that Cyprian, Jerome, and Ambrose agree with the text of the Greek manuscripts. Still, my detractors scream as if some wicked crime had been committed. But what good is it, my dear

---

3. Ps. 139:4.

Marcus, to use proofs with men who deliberately shut their eyes so that they cannot see and close their ears so that they cannot hear. There is an abundance of explanation available to them in my *Apologies,*[4] in case they are willing to look for it. If not, then it would be bootless for me to try to offer a satisfactory explanation to people who prefer to slander rather than learn.

Now my stern judges notice a lack of stability in me because they have heard that I am going to make a trip to Basel. . . . How remarkably unstable I am for wanting to go to Basel rather than guzzle with these fellows! But they themselves rush off to Rome and rush back again; they go gadding over every land and every sea—not of course at their own expense, since they profess to be mendicants, but with money they have raked together by fleecing widows, whom they crush with feelings of guilt and then drive out of their minds; by robbing holy virgins and by cheating simple-minded brethren out of their pleasures. And this they do just to cause damage and to bring disgrace upon men who have done good service to the Christian commonwealth. Of course, my opponents are considered stable and serious-minded. But I, since I serve the public welfare at my own expense and my own inconvenience—I am unstable. Let him choose, they say, some city in which to reside. What? Do they think I live here in a Scythian solitude? Or do they think the only people who exist in this world are those whom they constantly see at their drinking parties? Home for me is where my library is and whatever furniture I have. If public service demands a change of residence, then I would say I should be praised for being dedicated and not damned for being unstable. If I could have been released from the obligation of making that trip even at the cost of three hundred gold pieces, I would not have been reluctant to pay that sum. But circumstances forced me to go. Nor have I ever changed my place of residence except when driven out by a plague or at the demands of health or for some worthy purpose. Italy is the only place I ever visited on my own initiative, partly because I wanted to go to the holy places at least once and partly because I wished to enjoy the libraries and to meet the scholars of that country. For this lack of stability I do not as yet have any regrets.

4. *Apologiae ad J. Fabrum Stapulensem* (Louvain, [1517]) and the *Ratio verae theologiae* ("The Way of True Theology") of the same year.

TO JOHN LASCARIS[1]

EE 836   Louvain, April 26, 1518

Jerome Busleiden, a man of learning and influence and an incomparable ornament of this realm, who died on a trip to Spain, bequeathed several thousand ducats to establish a college at Louvain, which is today a very flourishing university. In this college instruction is to be given without charge in the three languages, Hebrew, Greek, and Latin. A salary of about seventy ducats, quite a handsome sum, is to be paid to each professor. That amount may be increased according to the qualifications of the person. The chairs of Hebrew and Latin are already filled. There are several applicants for the chair of Greek. However, it has always been my suggestion to accept for this position a native Greek, from whom the students could immediately absorb the correct pronunciation of the language. All the officials involved have concurred with my view and have granted me the authority to send, in their name, for anyone I considered qualified for the position. Therefore, because of your usual courtesy toward me and because of your interest in good learning, I request this favor of you: if you know anyone who in your estimation would be a source of honor to you and me, please arrange for him to hurry here at once. He will be given traveling expenses, a salary, and a place of residence. He will associate with men of high moral standards and deep culture. He should put no less confidence in this letter of mine than if the matter were being transacted by a hundred official contracts. Business between honest men can be efficiently handled without signing any documents. If you make sure that you select a qualified man, I shall make sure that he never regrets coming here.

1. On John Lascaris (ca. 1445–1535) see Allen, I, 523. He was a humanist and an official in the service of the French court. From 1513 onward he was academician at Rome. This letter is related to Erasmus' involvement in the establishment of the Collegium Trilingue at Louvain. The Collegium had been endowed by Busleiden for the express purpose of further study of Hebrew, Greek, and Latin. As matters turned out, the usefulness of the study of Hebrew was promptly attacked by James Latomus, a member of the Louvain faculty.

TO PAUL VOLZ[1]

EE 858 (21–77; 134–171;   Basel, August 14, 1518
230–239; 292–297)

A great part of holiness consists in desiring with all one's heart to
become holy; I do not feel that we should look down on a person
striving for such a goal even if the attempt sometimes falls short of
success. This challenge should be faced in every man's life; frequently renewed efforts at length beget a happy issue. For whoever
has carefully conned the map has completed much of a journey along
a confusing route. Therefore I am not at all upset by the taunts of
certain people who spurn this little book as being not very learned
and maintain that it could have been written by any novice, since it
fails to treat of Scotistic questions, as though without these nothing
at all would be scholarly. It may not be very profound, if only it
inspires. It may not train men for combat at the Sorbonne if only it
does train them for Christian tranquility. It may not be useful for a
theological disputation, if only it is of use for theological living.
What would I achieve by discussing what everybody discusses? Who
in these times does not engage in theological questions? What other
purpose is there for examinations in the schools? There are almost as
many commentaries on the books of the *Sentences*[2] as there are
names of theologians. How estimate the number of *summulae* by
writers do hash and rehash the material of various authors? In the
fashion of druggists, they are forever compounding and remixing old
potions from new, new brews from old, one substance from many
elements, or one divided into many. How then can a pile of volumes
of this kind train us to live properly when there is not enough time
in the whole course of life even to open them? It is as though a
doctor should prescribe for someone presently suffering from a disease

1. This letter is the preface to the edition of the *Enchiridion* published at
Basel in 1518, which gave the book its European renown. Paul Volz (1480–
1544), a Benedictine monk and member of the humanist circle of Wimpfeling,
was later a Protestant reformer in Strassburg.
2. The reference is to the *Sentences* of Peter Lombard.

that he study the books of James Despars and all similar works, so as to find in them how to restore his health.[3] Meanwhile death takes him victim, and there is no way to help him.

Since the years of life fly by so quickly, we need a ready and prompt remedy. In how many volumes do theologians treat of restitution, confession, vows, scandals, countless other things? They minutely weigh each detail; they define each item as if they distrusted the goodness of Christ, in prescribing explicitly what reward or punishment He owes to every action. And yet they do not agree among themselves and never explain their notions clearly if you press them for clarification. What a wide variety there is of talent or of circumstances! But let us grant that all those definitions are true and correct, overlooking the fact that the discussions are dull and dry; even then, how many people have time to read through all those volumes? Or who could carry around the *Secunda Secundae* of Aquinas?[4] And yet, to live well is a matter of concern to every individual, and Christ wanted everyone to have easy access to it, not through the complicated labyrinths of disputations, but through genuine faith, unfeigned love, and a hope which does not disappoint. Finally, let those mighty volumes be the occupation of mighty professors, though they should be few in number. At the same time, we must remember the unlettered masses, for whom Christ died. The most important part of Christian piety is taught by him who inflames men with a love for it. A wise king, in educating his son for true wisdom, spends much more time on motivation than on information, as if the love of wisdom were almost the attainment of it. Doctors and lawyers have the shameful practice of deliberately making their profession very difficult so that their profits may be more lucrative and their renown also more extensive among the uninitiated; but far more shameful would such a practice be in the case of the philosophy of Christ. Rather, our efforts should be in the opposite direction: to make this philosophy as uncomplicated as possible and intelligible to all. We should not strive to appear learned, but to win over as many as possible to the Christian way of life. . . .

3. "Iacobi a Partibus" Despars (1380–1458) edited the writings of the Islamic philosopher and physician Avicenna.
4. The second section of the second part of Aquinas' *Summa Theologica*.

I am well aware that every font and vein of Christian wisdom is stored up in the Gospels and the apostolic writings. However, a work written in a foreign tongue, in a style that is often confusing, with involved metaphors and figures of speech, is so difficult that even we professionals often have to struggle and strain before we can understand it. So, in my opinion, it would be most helpful to assign such a task to men as holy as they are learned, men who could draw the complete philosophy of Christ from the pure sources of the evangelists and the apostles and from the most approved interpreters, and then reduce it to a summary statement in a manner that is simple but learned, brief but clear. Dogmas of faith would be handled in as few paragraphs as possible. Directives for daily life would be spelled out in equally few words, but in such a way that the Turks, for example, would understand that Christ's yoke is mild and agreeable, not burdensome, and that they have found a father, not a tyrant; a shepherd, not a robber; and that they are called to salvation, not dragged into slavery. They too are human beings; they do not have iron or adamant in their breasts. They can be softened, they can be won over by kindnesses, which tame even wild beasts. And the most efficacious means is the Christian truth. But to whomever the Pope decides to entrust this responsibility, by the same token he will order them not to swerve from Christ their model, and to disregard the passions or lusts of men.

Some such work, poor though it was, I had in mind when I published the first edition of my *Enchiridion.* I could see that the rank and file of Christians had been led astray not only by inordinate desires but also by false views. I considered that a large number of those who professed to be shepherds and teachers were using to their own advantage the privileges they have in the name of Christ—not to mention the number of those who by a nod or a refusal turn human affairs upside down. And as for their vices, obvious though they be, it is barely permissible even to utter a sigh over them. In the deep darkness of our age, amidst its great confusion, with all the conflicting views of men, what better refuge have we than that truly sacred anchor, the gospel teachings? What truly pious person does not sigh as he views this modern era, by far the most corrupt ever? When did tyranny, when did greed ever enjoy a wider sway, and with greater impunity? When was more attention ever given to ceremonial observances? When did wickedness ever flourish with greater license? When has charity grown so cold? Is anything presented, read, heard, decided except what smacks of ambition and profit? O unhappy generation, has Christ not left us some traces of His teaching and of His spirit?

Do not infect that heavenly philosophy of Christ with human decrees. Let Christ remain what He is, namely the center, while various circles surround Him. Do not remove the target from its position. Those who are nearest to Christ—priests, bishops, cardinals, popes, and those whose duty it is to follow the Lamb wherever he goes—let them have a thorough grasp of what is the absolutely pure center, and then, as much as possible, transmit that spirit to those next to them. Let the second circle contain the secular princes whose arms and laws in their own way do service to Christ—whether in just wars they overcome the enemy and safeguard public order, or by legitimate punishments they restrain criminals. . . .

In the third circle let us gather together the common people; true, they form the grossest part of our series of circles, but even so they do belong to Christ's body. For the eyes are not the only members of this body. So are the legs, the feet, the genitals. A kindly consideration must be shown to them so that they may always be encouraged, as far as possible, to the things that Christ prefers. For in this body, he who was once a foot, can become an eye.

TO ANTONIO PUCCI[1]

EE 860 (31–72)   Basel, August 26, 1518

To prevent you from having any doubts about this matter, I shall briefly explain the method followed in my work [edition and translation of the Greek New Testament]. After collating several Greek

1. An eminent churchman (1484–1544), subsequently bishop and cardinal. In this letter Erasmus explains the principles that guided his work on the text of the Greek New Testament. At the same time he shows his awareness of possible objections against his labors and expresses his desire for papal approval.

manuscripts, I adopted what I considered the most genuine text; then I made a Latin translation of it and arranged my version so that it ran parallel with the Greek text, thus enabling the reader to compare the two. In doing the translation I aimed first of all, as far as I could, at a pure Latin style, while preserving the simplicity of the original language. My next aim was to make sure that all those things would be made clear and lucid which the reader formerly found perplexing either because of ambiguity or obscurity of language or because of faulty or unsuitable expressions; at the same time I departed very sparingly from the original words and never from the sense. However, the sense is not something we have dreamed up by ourselves,[2] but was derived from Origen, Basil, Chrysostom, Cyril, Jerome, Cyprian, Ambrose, and Augustine. Annotations were added, which have now been further enriched, to inform the reader whose authority is followed in each instance, and I have always depended upon the opinion of ancient authors. I am not tearing up the Vulgate and destroying it. However, we do not know its origin, although it is certainly not the work of Cyprian, Ambrose, Hilary, Augustine, or Jerome. But I do indicate where it is corrupt. I also drop a gentle hint whenever the interpreter showed his bias, and explain all complicated or perplexing expression.

If it is desirable for us to have the text of Sacred Scripture in the most accurate state possible, my work not only removes the errors from the sacred texts, but will also prevent further corruptions in the future. If it is desirable that the text be properly understood, I have disclosed the meaning of more than six hundred passages which were not understood previously even by eminent theologians. They admit it themselves; they cannot deny it. If it is desirable that a knowledge of the sources be added to the disputatious type of theology which has almost too much authority in the schools, my work is especially valuable for that purpose. Therefore no intellectual activity is harmed by this work of mine; rather every kind is helped by it. Although I have made a complete translation of the Greek text, still I do not approve of the Greek text in every instance. In fact, in some passages I prefer our Vulgate version, though I regularly indicate where the orthodox Latin writers agree or disagree with the Greek.

2. Erasmus is thinking here of scholars in general.

Moreover, the variety of textual readings is not only no impediment to scriptural studies, but, on the authority of St. Augustine, even promotes them. These variant readings are never so crucial as to endanger the orthodox faith.

In conclusion, either my love for the work completely deceives me, or it is destined to be of no little value for sacred studies and to win no small degree of fame for Pope Leo among future generations, when envy will at last be at rest and the value of the undertaking will be realized. This fruition will be richer and will come more quickly if the work receives the approbation of the Supreme Shepherd. My only reason in wanting his approval is that he may make it plain that he is pleased with this labor because of its value for sacred studies.

TO BONIFACE AMERBACH[1]

EE 862 (5-42)   Basel, August 31, 1518

Approximately eighty years ago, men were mute and tongueless who professed a knowledge of those arts which Vergil in his own day (when learned eloquence especially flourished) termed the silent arts. Moreover, grammar, the teacher of correct speech, and rhetoric, guide to a rich and sparkling eloquence, could only stammer shamefully and woefully. And these arts which in former times had been well supplied with so many languages, could express themselves only in Latin, and indeed in very bad Latin. Shortly after, as a better form of learning gradually developed, Italy was the only region possessed of a tongue, but even there the only branch of learning was oratory. Today in all the nations of Christendom, learning of every sort, with

1. This letter commends the *Lucubrationes* of Ulrich Zasius (1461–1535), the distinguished South American jurist and humanist. Boniface Amerbach (1495–1562), one of Erasmus' closest friends, was a distinguished jurist and humanist at Basel and a student of Zasius. Another letter to him is No. 2684; see also references to the Amerbach brothers on pp. 76, 79, 84, 94. Erasmus here summarizes the advance of learning in the various disciplines during the recent past and notes that theology has not kept pace with this advance.

the kindly favor of the Muses, adds the grandeur of eloquence to the usefulness of learning.

Medicine has begun to find expression in Italy through the efforts of Nicolaus Leonicenus, an old man worthy of immortality, and in France through the efforts of William Cop of Basel. In England, thanks to the zeal of Thomas Linacre, Galen has recently begun to have such fluency that by comparison he seems to have very little in his native tongue. Also through the efforts of Linacre, Aristotle is so eloquent in Latin that, though an Athenian, he barely speaks with the same grace in his own language. Prior to him, Argyropoulos, Trapezontius, Theodora Gaza, Marsilio, and Pico in Italy and Jacques Lefèvre in France had guaranteed that philosophy would not appear mute. Further, in France William Budé has happily restored to Roman law its original splendor and elegance and glory; and in Germany the same has been accomplished by the truly incomparable Ulrich Zasius, whose flow of eloquence in the Roman tongue is so rich that one would think Ulpian was speaking[2]—not a jurist of our own age.

For some strange reason theologians have not had the same success, though there is no lack of those who passionately speak out. However, I hope that in the near future this profession too will be rid of its rust and lay claim to its original splendor. Until now men whose language was somewhat more polished have been barred from the ranks of the university faculties; the professors have not considered anyone worthy of being lifted with them unless he stammered in the same shameful way as themselves and had never once laid his finger upon anything written in a chaste style. There was always at hand a prompt rebuff, such as, "He is a grammarian, not a philosopher." "He is a rhetorician, not a jurist." "He is a public speaker, not a theologian." However, in a short time, unless I am mistaken, just the opposite will be true and only those will be admitted into their ranks whose works are written in a more elegant style and thereby reflect these ancient writers in the various disciplines. And it will be impossible for anyone to claim Wisdom unless Eloquence is also present to act as her maid—for St. Augustine insists that she never wants to be separated from her mistress.

2. A distinguished Roman jurist in the third century.

TO CHRISTOPHER ESCHENFELDER[1]

EE 870   Louvain, October 19, 1518

What more can one hope for than to find our learned Eschenfelder at Boppard—a customs officer who cares for the Muses and good learning! Christ reproached the Pharisees and said that tax collectors and harlots would enter before them into the kingdom of heaven. Is this not a disgrace to priests and monks who live in ease and luxury, while the civil servants spend their time in study? They only think of what they shall eat and drink, while Eschenfelder divides his hours between His Imperial Majesty and his books. I myself could easily see what an idea you had formed of me beforehand; I hope that the sight of me has not spoiled your dream. Your red wine found favor with the captain's wife, a great bouncing woman with a formidable thirst. She gulped it down and would give no one else a chance. This made her quarrelsome, and she nearly slew her servant girl with a big spoon. Then going up on deck, she attacked her husband and almost toppled him into the river. That is what comes of your wine!

TO ERARD DE LA MARCK[1]

EE 916 (55–75; 285–323)   Louvain, February 5, 1519

As for the points concerning the liturgy of the Church which St. Paul touched upon here (and mentioned only in passing), I wish he had given a fuller and more detailed account. How brief he is when mentioning the Eucharist, or synaxis, as if afraid to say any more than he should about so deep a mystery, although on that same

1. A customs officer whom Erasmus had encountered at Boppard when he was traveling down the Rhine on his way to Louvain. An admirer of Erasmus, this local official invited him to his house and sent some wine to the sailors of the boat on which Erasmus was traveling. The letter reports on what happened.

1. De La Marck (1472–1538), scion of an important noble family from the region between France and Burgundy, was later bishop and cardinal. This letter was the preface to Erasmus' *Paraphrasis ad Corinthios*. In it, Erasmus reflects on various issues raised by the Apostle Paul in his Letter to the Corinthians, laments the fact that in some respects Paul did not throw sufficient light on certain issues, and finally makes a comparison between the state of the Church in the apostle's and his own time.

subject some more recent writers without proper training will teach and decide anything! I wish that Paul had at least disclosed by whom, at what time, with what sort of liturgy and rite, and with what words the mystical bread and the sacred cup of the Lord's blood are consecrated. Paul does tell us that numerous diseases and deaths come from an unworthy handling of it. These words should make us more cautious, too, lest the plague which has been rampant for the past several years may have had its cause for us right here. An unworthy handling is committed not only by him who approaches the body and blood polluted with lust, but even more by him who is defiled with envy, hatred, and venom, with detraction and a passion for vengeance, and other similar vices which by their very nature are diametrically opposed to Christian charity, which we portray by this mystery. Paul discusses somewhat more fully the gifts of tongues, interpretation, prophecy, and others which were later replaced by Church hymns, scriptural reading, and a homily. For the gifts of healing and of revelation have left us bereft long ago, ever since charity grew cold and faith languished and we came to depend more on human supports than on heavenly aid. . . .

And I also wish that St. Paul had shed considerably more light for us on these questions: whether souls exist separated from the body, and where they exist; whether they enjoy the glory of immortality; whether the souls of the wicked are already suffering torments; whether our prayers or other good works can help them or they can suddenly be liberated from their punishment by an indulgence granted by the Pope; for I see that many people have doubts about these questions, or at any rate discuss them, which would have been unnecessary if Paul had definitely decided them.

A further point. Although it is proper for those who are reborn in Christ to put off their old self along with its behavior, we notice that even in the days when the gospel was still fresh and under the guidance of Paul, lust, avarice, quarrelsomeness, self-seeking, disagreements, and other plagues that infest piety and good morals had crept in among the people. Certain vices which remained from their earlier life could not be completely uprooted. So no one should be surprised that in our own day charity has grown cold in some people and therefore sinfulness abounds. In fact, even during Paul's lifetime false apostles had elbowed their way in, men who turned the gospel to their own gain, who made use of the glory of Christ for their own despotic ends, who preached themselves rather than God, who taught not Christ but the world, not the spirit but the flesh; who introduced the teachings of men into the heavenly teaching and built an unworthy structure upon that foundation which is Christ. These enemies of the Church did all the more damage because they were acting under the disguise of Christ and were commended by the title and dignity of apostles.

Would to heaven that the Church of Christ today had no false apostles! Would to heaven that all men who assumed the duty of preaching the gospel followed the example of Paul in preaching Jesus Christ, not for personal gain, not out of self-seeking, not to win the favor of men of influence, not out of ill will or to gain the approval of men, but with single-minded sincerity. Paul himself, when in prison and in chains, boasted that the word of the Lord cannot be chained down. But today, unfortunately, one may see men who are paid salaries by influential persons and act as if they were obligated by contract to perform this kind of service; and so they do not preach the things that serve Christ's glory and true piety, but rather those that are helpful for securing benefices, for snaring ecclesiastical dignities, and for trapping bishoprics. They are strong and vocal when flattery is safe and profitable as well. But when the truth hurts, they are even more mute than fish. But if the salt loses its savor, how can the unseasoned common people be salted? If light turns into darkness, what will dispel the gloom for the unlettered mob? If the shepherds turn into wolves, what hope is there for the herd? If the guides along the way are blind, who will keep men from wandering off the path? If those who should have been fathers are peddlers, will there be any place for genuine sincerity?

TO ELECTOR FREDERICK OF SAXONY[1]

EE 939 (87–128)   Antwerp, April 14, 1519

Finally, since there are so many ancient and modern writers in all of whose works admittedly dangerous errors are to be found, why do we quietly and calmly read the rest of their works, but savagely rage

1. Frederick, Elector of Saxony (d. 1525), was Luther's territorial ruler and as such played an important role in the early Reformation. Here is one of Erasmus' first responses to the controversy precipitated by Luther. He reflects on the true place of conflict within the Christian community and on the true spirit of the Christian religion.

against just one or two? If we are defending the truth, why are we not equally offended by everything that is contrary to the truth, no matter where it appears? It is very sacred to protect the integrity of faith and religion, but it is very sacrilegious to serve our own passions under the pretense of defending the faith. If they want everything that is accepted in the schools to be treated as an oracle, why then do the schools disagree with one another? Why do the scholastic doctors engage in violent controversies with each other? In fact, why does one theologian dispute with another in the very Sorbonne? Indeed, one would find but few who do agree except in collusion. Besides, it is not unusual for them to be caught red-handed condemning in books of recent authors what they do not condemn in Augustine or Gerson—as if the truth varied with its author. When reading the authors they favor, they so distort the meaning as to excuse everything. When reading those who offend them, they so read as to leave nothing uncondemned.

The most excellent part of Christianity is a life worthy of Christ. When that is present, the suspicion of heresy should not be easy. But in these times men are inventing new fundamentals, as they call them—that is to say, new criteria by which they proclaim as heretical anything they do not like. One who accuses another person of heresy should exhibit in his own life a demeanor worthy of a Christian, charity in admonishing, mildness in correcting, open-mindedness in judging, and deliberation in pronouncing sentence. Since no one of us is free from error, why are we so merciless in railing at the slips made by others? Why would we rather gain a victory than work a cure, rather crush than instruct? And yet He who alone was free from all error did not break a bruised reed nor quench a smoking wick.[2] When dealing with the Donatists, who were more than heretics, Augustine refused to employ coercion without instruction.[3] He removed the swords of the officials from the necks of those whose daggers were daily aimed at himself. But we, although our proper function is to instruct, would rather employ coercion, because it is easier.

2. Isa. 42:3.
3. Erasmus' point is that the Donatist Circumcellians were not only guilty of heresy but of violence as well; still, Augustine disapproved of the use of force against them. It is to be noted, however, that he subsequently modified his position.

I write this all the more freely, most illustrious ruler, since I am not involved in Luther's cause. Besides, as it is your responsibility to protect the Christian religion through your own piety, you must be concerned not to deliver an innocent man who is under your protection to impious men on the pretext of piety.[4] Pope Leo wants the same, for he has nothing more at heart than the safety of the innocent. He loves to be called Father, and he does not love those who under the protection of his name act in tyrannical fashion. No one acts more in his spirit than he who is concerned for justice. I do not know what they think about Luther in Rome. I see, however, that his books are read eagerly by the most eminent men, though I myself have not had an opportunity to read them.

TO WILLIAM CROY[1]

EE 959 (95–118)   Louvain, [ca. May 1519]

However, I think it best not to involve Christ in this discussion. Just because He wanted His apostles to be poor men, that does not mean that, according to His teaching, wealth is evil. He simply did not want the glory of the gospel to be attributed to the influences of this world. And yet I do not deny that on many occasions these things must be set aside if piety so demands.

Now you tell me this. If these things are not good, then how can we offer up prayers, even public prayers, for them and seriously request them from Him who is neither willing nor able to grant anything but what is good? Far be it from us to call those men unhappy who are endowed with virtue; in fact, we call them most happy. Still, happiness is more complete for those who have such things, whether they were freely given or honorably acquired, unless circumstances suggest doing without them.

I shall stop my philosophizing if you will answer one little question. Suppose there are two men. One of them looks like Thersites, is

4. Erasmus' appeal is of immense significance for subsequent developments, since it confirmed the policy which Frederick was already pursuing.
1. Ca. 1498–1521. English cardinal and archbishop, he died prematurely from a fall from his horse. See Allen, III, 68. This brief excerpt contains Erasmus' reflection on wealth: if properly used, it is not evil.

as poor as Irus, has wretched health, a stammering tongue, a worthless memory, a dull wit, a shameful origin, is hated by everybody, is an outcast, and is indeed a worn-out old man. The other is in his youthful years, is dignified and respected, in good health, has a sonorous voice and a fluent tongue, a faithful memory, a clever wit, great wealth, distinguished birth; indeed, he is the object of highest esteem in the eyes of all. Then suppose you have a mind worthy of a good man, a mind that loves the best things and desires to be of the best possible service to all men. And then suppose some god is here, bidding you choose whichever one you prefer, for you will promptly turn into the one you choose. Now tell me in all honesty, will you choose the first man or the second?

TO HENRY GUILDFORD[1]

EE 966 (10–33)   Antwerp, May 15, 1519

The world is regaining its senses as if awakening from a very deep sleep; and yet some persons are still putting up a stubborn resistance, while clinging tooth and nail to their old ignorance. But these men will be ashamed of their folly when they observe how mighty kings and the nobility cherish and promote and protect good learning.

The strange vicissitudes of human affairs! Once upon a time enthusiasm for learning belonged to men whose profession was religion. But today these men are for the most part occupied with their belly, with debauchery, and with money, while love of learning has passed to secular rulers and nobles at court. What school or monastery anywhere has as many men distinguished for character and scholarship as does your court? It is not perfectly proper for us to be ashamed of ourselves? The dinner parties of priests and monks are soaked in drink; they are filled with boorish jests; they echo with drunken frenzy; they reek of venomous slander. But the tables of princes are marked by restrained discussion of matters which can be

1. A friend and trusted counselor (1489–1532) of Henry VIII. Erasmus speaks in this letter of the despicable quality of clerics and monks, and at the same time voices a slight hint concerning his own future well-being.

of service to learning and piety. Little wonder then that everybody is eager to follow the example of an excellent King. Those qualities which he has in common with other kings I shall not mention; in many of them he is superior, in none is he inferior. But his penetrating mind in discussion, his happy ability for making discoveries, his soundness of judgment, and his charming eloquence—these qualities show him preeminent.

At one time, when I was fascinated by the luxury of having leisure for scholarly work, I shunned the courts of kings. But I would love to move with all my belongings (which consist mainly of notes and books) into such a court as this, were I not dissuaded by my poor health and the ever increasing burden of my years.

TO THOMAS WOLSEY[1]

EE 967 (105–132; 180–192)   Antwerp, May 18, [1519]

Germany has some young men who offer great promise of learning and eloquence, and I predict that as a result of their efforts Germany will one day be able to boast the same accomplishments as those Britain has every right to boast of at present. None of them is known to me personally except Eoban, Hutten, and Beatus.[2] These men are using every method of attack in their battle with the enemies of language study and good learning, which all good men promote. Their tactics I too would call intolerable, if I did not know what atrocious methods are used to provoke them, both publicly and privately. Their opponents feel free to scream out anything they please before the unlettered crowd, in sermons and in the schools and at dinner parties, and they stir up thereby violent hatred and, in fact,

1. Wolsey (1474–1530) was cardinal and papal legate, also chancellor to Henry VIII. To him Erasmus had dedicated his translation of Plutarch's *De utilitate capienda ex inimicis*. This letter offers a few brief reflections on the younger scholars and humanists in Germany and closes with Erasmus' insistence on the seriousness of his writings.
2. Eoban Hess, Ulrich Hutten, and Beatus Rhenanus were humanistically oriented scholars.

trouble. And they consider it an unbearable crime if one of these young men dares to say anything, although even bees have stings with which to strike when they are hurt and little mice have tiny teeth with which to protect themselves when attacked. Whence this new race of gods? They make heretics of whom they will, but they go on a rampage if anybody calls them slanderers. And although they do not hesitate to say what would make even Orestes blush, still they demand that we address them only with the titles befitting their dignity. To such an extent do they trust the stupidity of the crowd, not to mention that of rulers.

As for myself, though I have never reached the goal of good learning, I have always loved it. Its champions have my support, as they have the backing of good men everywhere except for some asinine fellows who, like Midas, will someday be the subject of a tale. But this younger generation has my endorsement to the extent that I appreciate their virtues, but not their defects. Yet if one considers how steeped in vice were those who some time ago assisted in the rebirth of ancient studies in Italy and France, one cannot help but support this modern group, whose morals deserve to be imitated rather than denounced by those theologians who are their critics. These critics suspect that everything published by this younger group is mine. The same is also the case with you in England, if the businessmen traveling from your country to this place are telling the truth. . . .

I have never yet written any work without attaching my name to it, nor do I intend to. Some time ago I did indulge in some ridicule in my *Folly*, but without drawing blood, though I may have been too outspoken. But I have always been cautious not to publish anything that could by its obscenity corrupt young people or in any way be detrimental to piety or engender revolt or party spirit or harm anyone's reputation. All my toil till now has been spent on furthering solid studies and promoting the Christian religion. Men all over the world are expressing their thanks to me, except a few theologians and monks who refuse to learn any more or become any better. I call down Christ's eternal wrath upon my head if it is not my desire that all my talent and all my eloquence be dedicated entirely to His glory and to the sacred studies of the Catholic Church. Whoever wants to inspect my heart more closely will find that this is true.

TO MARTIN LUTHER[1]

EE 980 (1–29; 35–54)   Louvain, May 30, 1519

I was very much pleased by your letter, which revealed a penetrating mind and breathed a Christian spirit.[2] No words of mine
could express what tragedies have been stirred up here by your
pamphlets. Not even now can the false suspicion be uprooted from
their minds that your works were written with my aid and that I am
the standard-bearer of this faction, as they call it. They thought they
had been offered an opportunity to crush not only good learning—for
which they have a mortal hatred, since it would thwart the majesty
of theology, which they esteem much more highly than Christ—but
also to crush me, too, whom they regard as having some influence on
the renewed interest in intellectual things. The whole affair has been
handled with wild shouting, rash statements, trickery, detraction, and
slander, so that if I had not witnessed and, in fact, experienced it
personally I would never have accepted anyone's word that theologians are such idiots. One might have called it a deadly plague.
And yet the infection of this disease which began with a few has
wormed its way into many persons, to such an extent that a great part
of this university has been driven crazy by the contagion.

I have asserted that you are a complete stranger to me and that I
have not yet read your books, and that therefore I neither disapprove
nor approve of anything in them. I only warned them, inasmuch as
they had not yet read your books, not to scream indiscriminately
before the people in such a hateful way, but to refer them to those
whose decision should have the greatest authority; in fact, they
should ponder the expediency of exposing before the general public
things that should more properly be refuted in print or discussed

1. The German reformer and theologian (1483–1546). Erasmus comments
in this letter on the various consequences of the publication of Luther's
writings and speaks of how, in his opinion, reform of religion might be
accomplished.
2. The letter is found in D. Martin Luther's Werke. Briefe, I, 361.

among scholars, especially since the author's manner of life met with universal praise. I accomplished nothing. Up to now they continue to rave on in their disputations, with indirect remarks and even downright slander. How often have we concluded peace, and how often have these fellows formed some little rash suspicion and then set off a new uproar! And they consider themselves to be theologians. Theologians here are loathed by the men at court; and they blame that on me, too. All the bishops are very favorable toward me. . . .

Some men in England think very highly of your writings, and they are men of great importance. Some persons here too, including the Bishop of Liege,[3] are favorable to your views. As for myself, I remain impartial so far as I can, in order to be of more value to the renascence of good learning. In my opinion, more can be accomplished by polite restraint than by vehemence. That is the way Christ brought the world under His sway. That is the way St. Paul abrogated the Judaic law, by basing everything on an allegorical interpretation. It is more advisable to scream out against those who abuse papal authority than against the popes themselves. The same approach I think should be used with regard to kings. We should not so much disdain the schools as call them back to a more sensible form of scholarship. As for matters that are too commonly accepted to be suddenly uprooted from men's minds, we should discuss them and employ sound and convincing proofs and not make rash assertions. It is better to disregard the venemous contentions of some individuals than to refute them. On all occasions one must be cautious not to say or to do anything with arrogance or a party spirit. Such conduct I think is pleasing to the spirit of Christ. At the same time one must keep his mind from being corrupted by anger or hatred or thirst for glory. For these vices usually try to trap us when we are engaged in the pursuit of piety.

I am not trying to advise you to act in this way, but only to continue to act as you do. I have dipped into your commentaries on the Psalms.[4] I find them delightful and hope they will prove very useful.

3. On Erard de la Marck, see Allen, III, 167, and Letter 916, p. 132. While concerned about ecclesiastical reform, he was not a partisan of Luther's.

4. The reference is to Luther's second academic lectures on the Psalms, the *Operationes in Psalmos,* printed at Wittenberg in 1519.

TO ULRICH VON HUTTEN[1]

EE 999 (97–110; 121–173;
271–276)   Antwerp, July 23, 1519

Thomas More seems to have been born and made for friendship, which he cultivates in a genuine and persistent manner. Nor is he afraid of that "abundance of friends" which Hesiod viewed with disfavor. The way is open for every person to form a friendly relationship with him. He is not at all fastidious in choosing friends; he is most obliging in cultivating them and most constant in holding on to them. If he happens upon someone whose defects he cannot remedy, he parts with him when opportunity presents itself by gradually untying the bond of friendship, not by snapping it. The company and conversation of those he discovers to be genuine and congenial he enjoys so much that he seems to find here the principal pleasure of life. He shuns ball games, gambling, cards, and other forms of amusement which the majority of gentlemen employ to while away the time. Moreover, while he is rather careless about his own interests, no one is more careful in attending to the affairs of his friends. To sum it up neatly: if someone were looking for the ideal of true friendship, he would find it nowhere more perfectly than in Thomas More. . . .

No matter what human situation he encounters, he always tries to find some pleasure in it, even in the most serious matters. If he is dealing with men of learning and intelligence, he relishes their native wit; if with illiterate and simple-minded men, he enjoys their simplicity. Nor is he offended by natural-born fools, for he has a marvelous facility for adapting himself to any kind of disposition. With women in general and even with his wife he is always jolly and joking. One might say he was another Democritus—or better, that Pythagorean philosopher who strolls around the market place, com-

---

1. Lived 1488–1523. A German nationalist and humanist. See H. Holborn, *Ulrich von Hutten and the German Reformation* (New York, 1966). This letter constitutes a splendid verbal portrait of Sir Thomas More.

pletely detached, and observes all the hubbub among the buyers and sellers. Nobody is less influenced by the judgment of the masses, but on the other hand nobody is closer to the feelings of the common man.

He finds special pleasure in studying the external features, characteristics, and instincts of various kinds of living things. And so he keeps practically every species of bird at his home and also different kinds of animals that are ordinarily rare, such as monkeys, foxes, ferrets, weasels, and the like. Besides, whenever he comes upon any article that is made abroad or otherwise attractive, he is very eager to buy it. So his home is completely filled with such objects, and when visitors come there is everywhere something that meets their eye and catches their attention. And he finds new pleasure each time he notices other people enjoying these things. In his youthful years he was not averse to loving girls, but never in a dishonorable way; he found joy in a love that was offered rather than in one obtained by flirting. He was attracted more by an exchange of friendly feeling than by physical love.

He imbibed good learning from his earliest years. As a young man he devoted himself to the study of Greek literature and philosophy; in this he got no help from his father, who was otherwise a sensible and honest man. In fact, for these efforts of his he was left without any form of assistance from his father and was almost disinherited, since he seemed to be deserting the studies which were his father's interest; English law, you see, was his father's profession. Though this profession is alien to true learning, in England authorities in the field are among the most highly regarded. It is not without reason that the English consider this the most suitable path to fame and fortune, for this branch of study has produced a very large part of the gentry on that island. And they say that no one can become perfect in it unless he works hard at it for several years. Therefore the talented young More, who was born for better things, with good reason felt an aversion for that profession. Nevertheless, after acquainting himself with the disciplines taught in the schools, he engaged in the study of law with such success that no one else's advice was more readily sought by litigants and no one of those who concentrated solely on the practice of law had a more profitable business; such was his vigorous and quick intellect.

Furthermore, he devoted considerable energy to studying the works of the orthodox Fathers. When barely more than a young man he gave a course of public lectures on Augustine's *City of God* before a packed audience. Priests and mature men felt neither embarrassment nor regret at learning about sacred subjects from a young layman. Meantime he also devoted himself wholeheartedly to the pursuit of piety, and while contemplating the priesthood he prepared himself with vigils, fasting, prayers, and other similar practices. Indeed, in this matter he was considerably more sensible than the great number of those who thoughtlessly rush into such a difficult profession without first putting themselves to the test. The only obstacle that prevented him from consecrating himself to this way of life was the fact that he could not shake off his desire for a wife. He preferred to be a chaste husband rather than an unchaste priest.

However, when he did marry he chose a young girl of honorable background, though without education, since she had always lived in the country with her parents and sisters. His reason for this choice was that it would be more possible for him to mold her according to his own tastes. He saw to it that she received a training in letters, and he had her well versed in every form of music. He had all but fashioned her to be the sort of person with whom he would have been happy to spend his entire life, when an untimely death carried her off while she was still young, though she had borne him several children. . . .

He practices true piety with great diligence, though he shuns any form of superstition. He has definite hours in which to offer his prayers to God; these are not said perfunctorily, but spring from his heart. When he talks with his friends about the next life, you can see that his words are sincere and inspired by the most solid hope. And such is More even when he is at court. And some people think that Christians are found only in monasteries!

TO ALBERT, OF BRANDENBURG[1]

EE 1033 (46–66; 69–88; 96–   Louvain, October 19, 1519
179)

I was sorry that Luther's works were published. When certain of his books first began to appear I exerted all my influence to stop them from being printed, mainly because I feared they would cause turmoil. Luther had written me a letter in what I at least would call a truly Christian tone. I answered it and warned him to write nothing seditious, nothing against the Pope, nothing in an arrogant or angry tone, but to preach the gospel with sincerity of heart and in all meekness. I did this in a courteous way so as to be more effective. I added that some men here were supporting him, so that he would all the more adapt himself to their judgment. Certain simpletons interpreted this to mean that I was supporting Luther, though none of these fellows has made any attempt to remonstrate with him. I am the only one who has warned him. I am not accusing Luther nor am I defending him nor am I responsible for him. I would not dare to judge his motives; that is very difficult, especially if it means an unfavorable view. And yet suppose I were to befriend him because he is a good man, as even his enemies admit— Or because he is a defendant, an action which is legally permissible even for sworn judges. Or because he is being crushed, which humanity would demand. Or because he is being crushed by men who are employing false pretenses in their determined opposition to good learning? Then, in sum, why should I incur ill will so long as I do not involve myself in his cause? Finally, it is Christian, in my opinion, to befriend Luther for the reason that, if he is innocent, I would not want him to be crushed by the factions of the wicked; on the other hand, if he is in error, I would want him to be cured, not destroyed. . . .

1. Albert of Hohenzollern was Archbishop of Magdeburg and administrator of the diocese of Halberstadt as well as Archbishop of Mainz (in 1514). The sale of indulgences which prompted Luther's Ninety-five Theses (and thereby precipitated the Reformation) had to do with his appointment as archbishop.
   This letter contains one of Erasmus' first detailed reactions to Luther and his teaching as well as observations on the proper response to dissenting opinion.

I would desire that a heart which seems to possess some brilliant sparks of the evangelical teaching be not crushed, but that it be properly guided and then invited to preach the glory of Christ. But at present, certain theologians whom I know are neither advising nor instructing Luther. They are only exposing him to public ridicule by their mad howling and are tearing the man to pieces with their savage, venomous slanders; the only words they can say are "heresies" and "heretics." It cannot be denied that the most hateful sort of outcry has occurred right here on the part of men who have never seen Luther's books. It is a known fact that some persons explicitly condemned things which they had not understood. Here is one example. Luther had written that we are not bound to confess mortal sins unless they are manifest, and by "manifest" he meant those which are known to us at the time of confession. A certain Carmelite theologian interpreted "manifest" to mean those sins which are openly committed,[2] and so he screamed in an astonishing fashion about a matter which he did not comprehend. It is a known fact that some things in Luther's writings are condemned by these fellows as heretical although the same teachings may be found in the writings of Bernard and Augustine, where they are considered orthodox, in fact pious.

I advised them from the beginning to refrain from such outcries and to handle the matter by means of writing and discussions. And I told them, first of all, that they should not publicly condemn what they had not read, in fact, what they had not studied; I did not like to add, what they had not understood.

Although every thinking man agreed with this very view, still, as a result of my kindly advice the suspicion arose that Luther's books were to a great extent of my own composition and that they had been brought forth here at Louvain. But not a single iota of those writings is mine, nor were they published with my knowledge or consent. And yet, relying on this false suspicion, some men have ignored every expostulation and have stirred up several tragic incidents here; I have never seen anything more frenzied in all my life. Besides, though it is the function of theologians to teach, I can see several whose sole activity is to constrain or destroy or crush. Augustine did not approve

2. Egmondanus (Nicholas Baechem). See Allen, III, 416. He was one of Erasmus' most vehement opponents.

of those who do not explain but merely employ constraint, even if they were opposing the Donatists, who were not only heretics but also savage robbers. Men who have a special obligation to be kindly seem to be thirsting only for human blood and have only one desire: to have Luther apprehended and destroyed. This is to play the hangman, not the theologian. If they want to prove themselves mighty theologians, let them convert the Jews, let them win over to Christ those who are separated from Christ, yes, let them improve the public morals of Christians. These men are the acme of corruption, worse even than the Turks. How is it just to indict a man who proposed points for discussion which have always been the subject of dispute and of doubt in all the schools of the theologians? Why must he be hurt who is eager to be taught and who submits to the decision of the universities? It should not be surprising if he refuses to entrust himself to the hands of certain people who would rather have him destroyed than be a good man.

We must first of all study the sources of this evil. The world is bowed under the burden of human regulations, of the opinions and dogmas of the scholastics, of the tyranny of mendicant friars. Although these friars are satellites of the Roman See, they have become so powerful and so numerous that they can strike terror into the pope himself and even into kings. When the pope acts in their behalf, they rank him above God; but in matters which work against their convenience, he has no more influence than a phantom. I am not condemning them all, but many can be classed as beings who, for the sake of gain and tyrannical power, would deliberately ensnare the consciences of men. And they have boldly begun to disregard Christ and to preach only their own novel and even shameless doctrines. As for their interpretation of indulgences, not even the unlettered could stand that. For these and many other similar reasons the gospel teachings have gradually lost all their force. And it was bound to happen, as matters continued to slide from bad to worse, that eventually the spark of Christian piety would be completely extinguished which could have rekindled the flame of charity. Under this deterioration the perfection of religion came to mean a set of ceremonials more complicated than those of the Jews. Good men mourn and deplore this situation. It is acknowledged in private conversations by theologians who are not monks, and even by some of the monks.

These conditions, I believe, first roused Luther to dare to oppose the unbearable effrontery of certain men. What other motive could I suspect in one who has no ambition for honors, no greed for money? As for those points with which they are taunting Luther, for the present I am not discussing them; I am only discussing the manner and occasion of their presentation. Luther dared to cast doubt on indulgences, but others had previously made excessively bold assertions about them. Luther dared to speak in rather restrained language about the power of the pope, but these fellows had previously written in a far too unrestrained manner on that topic, especially three Dominicans: Alvarus Pelagius, Silvester Mazolini, and Cajetan.[3] Luther dared to show little esteem for the doctrine of St. Thomas, whom the Dominicans place almost above the Gospels. Luther dared to dispel some scruples with regard to matter for confession, but therein monks would want endlessly to ensnare the consciences of men. He dared to neglect in part the teachings of the scholastics to which they themselves attribute too much, although they themselves disagree on these teachings; in fact, from time to time they change their doctrine, introducing new views to replace the old discarded ones.

Pious minds were tormented when they heard almost nothing in the schools about the Gospel teachings. They were told that those sacred authors so long approved by the Church were considered outmoded; very little was heard about Christ in sermons, almost everything was about the power of the pope and the opinions of recent men. The whole discourse was openly employed for profit, flattery, advancement, and deception. Here is where the blame must be put, in my opinion, even if Luther did on occasion express himself in rather unrestrained language. Whoever supports the teaching of the gospel supports the Roman pontiff, because he is the primary herald of the gospel, though other bishops are also its heralds. All bishops are representatives of Christ, but the position of eminence among them is held by the Roman pontiff. About him one ought to feel this way: that his chief concern is the glory of Christ, whose servant he boasts of being. They do him a great disservice who obsequiously attribute to him powers which he himself does not recognize and which are not beneficial for Christ's flock.

And the men who are causing these tragedies are not acting out of

3. Three of Luther's conservative opponents.

interest in the pope; rather they are perverting his power for their own gain and despotic rule. We do have, in my opinion, a devoted pope. But amid all the disturbances of the times there are very many things which he does not know. There are certain things which he cannot control, even if he wanted to. But as Vergil says: "The driver is swept along by his steeds nor does the chariot respond to the reins."[4]

The piety of the Pope can be helped by one who encourages him to act in the way most worthy of Christ. It is no secret that some men are arousing His Holiness against Luther, in fact, against anyone who dares to mutter a word against their dogmatic teachings.

TO GEORGE SPALATIN[1]

EE 1119 (27–40)   Louvain, July 6, 1520

I pray that the supreme and wonderful Christ will so temper Luther's pen and spirit that he can be of very great profit to evangelical piety, and that Christ will give a better mind to certain men who are seeking their own glory at the cost of ignominy to Him and who are seeking their own gain with loss to Him. In the camp of Luther's opponents I see many men who breathe the spirit of the world rather than of Christ. And yet sins are committed on both sides. . . . I would like to see Luther take a brief respite from all those wranglings and handle the evangelical matter with single-mindedness and not with such a mixture of motives. Perhaps then the matter would turn out somewhat more successfully. As things now stand, he is encumbering good learning with an ill will that is disastrous to us and of no profit to himself. And there is danger that the public corruption of morals, which everyone admits needed a public remedy, may, like a plague that has taken hold, be gaining strength.

4. Maro, *Georgica*, I.514.
1. George Burkhard (1482–1545), or Spalatin, after his birthplace Spalt, near Nürnberg, was chaplain and secretary to Elector Frederick of Saxony. In this position he exercised an important pro-Lutheran influence on the Saxon ruler. See I. Höss, *Georg Spalatin* (Jena, 1951). The letter is another brief comment on Luther and at the same time an expression of apprehension of an ominous future.

TO WILLIBALD PIRCKHEIMER[1]

EE 1139 (63–85)   Louvain, September 5, 1520

You congratulate me on having very many friends who are no less learned than influential; you congratulate me on having an immortal name begotten by good deeds; you consider me to be above envy. All this you do out of love, I am sure, my dear Willibald, while attempting with what you think are soothing words of consolation to support a friend who is in danger of being assailed on all sides by the tricks of slanderers. As regards that immortal name, I am not at all interested. As for good deeds, I do not recognize them; I have only striven to be of some value to the world of scholarship by my hard work, and to arouse the hearts of men to embrace Christ's teaching. But I am afraid that things may turn out just the opposite. Up to now God-fearing men have been left cold and disgusted by the disputatious theology of the schools, and they had just begun to feel cheered by a taste of the evangelical truth. But those who prefer their own glory to Christ's have plotted with so much contentiousness that I fear things may turn out the opposite. This is the conduct of men who are commonly considered to be the light of the world and the salt of the earth. Today it is a holy and pious thing to use in sermons not the evangelical truth but wicked lies, ranting and raving like a mule-skinner against the reputation of one's neighbor. And what perverse malice! Out of hatred for some people and to gain the good graces of rulers whose favor they chase after, they preach things in public which in private they condemn! They reject new books—that is, books which are seasoned with good learning, which they hate more than they do a dog or a snake. But the sort of instruction these fellows offer us in their own new books, at present I do not have the time or the desire to relate. I feel embarrassed to recall what they are not too embarrassed to put in writing.

1. Pirckheimer (1470–1530) was a German humanist and official of the city of Nürnberg. His concerns for reform and suspected authorship of the anti-Eck satire *Eccius dedolatus* caused his name to be included in the bull "Exsurge domine" which threatened Luther with excommunication. Under the influence of Erasmus and Cochläus he eventually took sides against Luther. Erasmus speaks here of the character of the traditional scholastic theologians.

TO FRANCESCO CHIEREGATO[1]

EE 1144 (9–19; 49–70)   Louvain, September 13, 1520

Believe me, if you can believe anything, nothing has been more successful in securing the favor of the masses for Luther than the stupid shouting of these monks. At the same time not one of them has refuted Luther in print, which I have constantly urged them to do. For I realized that this was the only way Luther could be quashed, if he really was the kind of person they publicly proclaimed him to be. Those who have written against him up to the present do not at all satisfy these men who thoroughly dislike him. Then there is the wicked scheming on the part of some people whereby I am made to appear more hateful even than Luther, not because I am supporting him—they know that is not the case—but because I am supporting good learning, which they have combatted for a long time, and because I have invited theologians to turn to the sources, and because I have pointed out wherein true religion lies. . . .

Such, in general, are the people here who have been howling against Luther and who, so they think, are defending the Roman See, whose authority no one will fail to support. But men of intelligence will never put up with these loudmouthed fellows. If the Pope knew them as well as we do, he would vent his anger on them more than on anyone else. If only my influence with the Pope were as strong as my sincere attachment to his authority! In that case I would have offered him a scheme that would be more helpful for him personally and more beneficial for the whole world. Shouting and threats will perhaps produce this effect: the mischief may be suppressed for a time, but soon after it will erupt again with more disastrous results. The effect of such methods will not be that fewer men will support Luther, or that men will have a better attitude

---

1. Francesco Chieregato, or Chieregati (d. 1531), was an official of the Roman Curia and papal nuncio to several countries, notably Germany in 1522/3. Erasmus comments here again on the Lutheran controversy, putting the blame for the deterioration of atmosphere on Luther's opponents.

toward the Pope, but that they will be more cautious in their dissimulation. At any rate, up to now we have seen the consequences of the threats and screaming of these monks. Some people have been so irritated as to become ardent supporters whereas formerly they had been cool in their support; others have begun to give their support whereas earlier they had not been particularly favorable.

As for myself, I shall not be in any danger. I shall never be either a teacher of error or a leader of turmoil. And yet you would hardly believe in how many ways I have been invited to become at least a little involved in the Lutheran affair. If I had wanted to arouse any hope of that, the Lutheran situation would be quite different. But far be it from Erasmus to have any such thought. Up to now I have preached peace and concord; up to now I have labored for Christ. And the end of my life is at hand. I shall not abandon my decision. I shall not lose my crown. These loudmouthed yokels, who are a disgrace to their order, I leave to Christ to judge.

TO GODESCALC ROSEMONDT[1]

EE 1153 (15–35)   Louvain, October 18, 1520

On the feast of St. Dionysius [9 October], in St. Peter's Church, in a sermon, after he [Nicholas Egmondanus] began to talk about charity, suddenly and very inappropriately he directed his words toward me, since I happened to be present. He said many things right to my face, including that I was a strong supporter of Luther, even though from the start I have consistently affirmed—and this is the truth—that I have had nothing to do with Luther except what any Christian has to do with anyone else of the same faith. I acknowledge the evangelical and apostolic teaching. But I have not so

---

1. Godescalc Rosemondt (ca. 1483–1526) was professor of theology at the University of Louvain and its rector in 1520/21. When Erasmus wrote this letter, the bull "Exsurge domine," which condemned some forty-one errors of Luther, had just been promulgated. Erasmus was one of those who initially considered the bull a forgery; the letter suggests his desire that Luther's good points be not overlooked. Erasmus defends himself here against the charge that he is a supporter of Luther and summarizes his attitude toward him.

high an opinion of any mortal man that I would be willing to accept his views in every detail. The last thing I would do would be to undertake, at my own risk, the defense of someone's cause whose books I had not read and of whom I would not know what he was going to write in the future. Since I had asserted this position even in print, it could not have been a secret from anybody. As a result of sampling a few pages of Luther's writings—and it is more accurate to say that I sampled rather than read them—I came to admire certain gifts in him; and they led me to conclude that he could be an extraordinary instrument of Christ if he were willing to use his gifts for Christ's glory. Since everywhere many things were being preached about him that were dreadful, some of them obviously false, it was my desire, if he were not a very good man, that he be corrected rather than destroyed. If that means to support Luther, then I frankly confess that I have supported him and still do, just as I imagine the Pope supports him, and likewise all of you if you are truly theologians; in fact, if you are Christians.

TO CONRAD PEUTINGER[1]

EE 1156 (11–61)   Cologne, November 9, 1520

Unless precaution be taken there may be a danger that this tragedy will have a very disastrous conclusion for the Christian religion. From trivial beginnings dreadful disagreements have often been born in the world. In my opinion, Cicero's words hold true in this case too: that "peace even on unjust terms is preferable to a perfectly just war."[2] The tragedy has already advanced further than I like; yet I still think the disorder can be remedied. At least it is more curable now than if it should proceed still further at the same rate at which it has begun. However, I should like to have disorder cured in such a way that it

1. Lived 1465–1547. Lawyer, humanist, and official in the service of his native city Augsburg. In the context of brief reflections on the nature of the Lutheran controversy, Erasmus comments here on the basic issues—esteem for the Pope and also for learning—which he does not want to see obscured.
2. Cicero, *Ad familiares* 6. 6. 5.

would be merely checked for a time, only to break out again later and reach a more critical stage. Such is usually the case when doctors administer a potion to drive away a fever without first purging the veins from which the fever arises, or when they allow a wound to heal over before the pus has been sufficiently drained off.

Some persons think that the best thing to do is to keep the whole situation sternly under control. Lefèvre does not greatly disagree with this view, except that he fears severity may not have a very happy result. He says that it is not enough to strive relentlessly toward a goal to which the will inclines. Several things deserve careful consideration. The first is that regard be had for the dignity and authority of the Pope in such a way that the evangelical truth does not suffer any loss. The Pope deservedly has the support of all men as the supreme vicar of Christ, that is, of all men who sincerely love Christ. Nor do I have any doubt that Leo's attitude is this: that then and only then would he regard himself as glorious, when he sees the teaching of his Prince flourishing everywhere. Lefèvre says that we should not merely consider what Luther deserves or what support he has, but rather what would contribute toward the peace of the world. It makes a big difference what sort of men set to work on this disorder and what remedies are employed to cure it. Some who are involving themselves with the problem are only stirring up the confusion and making it twice as bad by their perverse busyness; their concern is not so much the authority of the Pope as their own interests. Their behavior is such that they are doing no less harm to good learning and the study of languages than to Luther. It is not fair on account of Luther's cause to do harm to scholarly activity which is innocent—in fact, most sacred. Nor is it helpful to implicate a large number of men in the Luther affair without good reason. Lefèvre added that we must study the source of this turmoil. Undoubtedly it is a hatred for true scholarship, which they are now trying with malicious cunning to involve in the Luther affair, doubtless so that they can destroy both with the very same weapon, though the two causes are quite distinct. As a result many men feel hostile towards Luther's assailants for no other reason than that the fellows are employing these underground methods to attack sound learning. And some persons who are stirred with hatred at this are even supporting Luther, whereas they would never have done so otherwise. Lefèvre also pointed out how far-reaching the infection of this disease had become in just a few years. He said he knew well the disposition of the Germans, who are more easily led than forced; the situation would become dangerous if their native ferocity were irritated by the harshness of certain persons. "We have witnessed up to now," he said, "a stubborn Bohemia and neighboring countries that are not very different from it. Harshness has been the more common method up to now; we must try other remedies." He also noted that hatred for the name of Rome was deeply entrenched in the hearts of many nations; I think that is so because of what is commonly remarked about the morals of that city, and because of the perverseness of certain people who sometimes conduct the Pope's business not according to his intentions but according to their own. They act for their own interests more than for his; and yet they should not even act for the Pope's interests except insofar as his authority serves Christ and the Christian flock.

TO THOMAS MORE[1]

EE 1162 (12–84; 134–162)   Louvain, [ca. November] 1520

We met together; the Rector took his seat; I sat down at his right, Nicholas Egmondanus at his left. This arrangement was not without a purpose. The Rector was well acquainted with the character of Egmondanus, and he was convinced—wrongly so—that I was one who could be provoked. Therefore he sat between us, to break up a quarrel in case the war of words boiled over into one of claws and fists. The Rector briefly stated the problem. Then Egmondanus, looking remarkably but ridiculously serious, started out: "I have done no injury to any man in sacred discourses. If Erasmus thinks he has been offended, let him come out with it. I am ready to answer him." I asked him if he thought there was any injury more outrageous than to expose an innocent person to ridicule in a public address through

1. On the recipient see Letter 222, p. 57. The present letter, like 1153, has to do with Erasmus' defense against attacks from the University of Louvain.

lies. The fellow was quickly aroused and, dropping the mask he had assumed, turned a deep purple—you see, he was already flushed since it was afternoon—and threw the question back at me: "And why do *you* ridicule me in public with your sacred books?" "Your name has never appeared in my books." "Nor has your name ever been mentioned in my sermons," he countered. I explained that my books were not sacred, since they sometimes contained my idle whims and trifling thoughts on any subject, but that the same freedom was not permitted in sermons. "Besides," I added, "I have written much less about you than the situation allows. But you have told lies about me in public, saying that I supported Luther. I have never supported him in the sense in which the people understand your words, and you know it too." He was aroused by that remark and like a lunatic shouted, "On the contrary! You're the one who has instigated all this trouble; you're a werewolf and a crafty rascal! You can distort everything with a twist of the tail." And many other things like that he spat out rather than said—whatever his yellow bile suggested to him.

I felt my stomach becoming upset too, for there was an explosive noise, the forerunner of a somewhat intemperate speech. It was not the sound of the word "fool," but something else that smells worse than it sounds. However, I quickly controlled myself, thinking it better to spare my own health (I was not feeling very well) and also that of the Rector, as he too was under doctor's care. Besides, I considered it stupid and unbecoming to rave at a raving maniac. And so with a gentle smile I turned toward the Rector and said, "I could produce evidence of extreme abuse; I could fling back insulting language. He calls me a werewolf; I might in turn call him a fox. He calls me two-faced; I could call him a fourflusher. He says I distort everything with a twist of the tail; I could say that he fouls everything with his tongue. But such remarks are not worthy of men, and hardly even of women. Let us deal with evidence. Imagine that I. . . ." At that point be broke in with the mighty bellow of a rowdy sailor: "I do not imagine, nor do I want to imagine anything! That's for people of your ilk! You poets are always imagining and lying about everything!" By now it was easier for me to laugh than to get angry. "If you don't want to imagine it," I suggested, "then admit it." "I don't want to admit it." "Just suppose it's so," I pleaded.

"I won't suppose it!" "But assume it's so." "I won't assume it!" "Then allow it to be so." "But it isn't!" "Then what do you want me to say?" I asked. "Say: That's true."

With difficulty the Rector prevailed upon him to let me speak. "Although it may be true," I said, "that I have written some things in my books other than I should have, still I did not do what you did. To avenge your feelings you abused the authority of a sacred place and a sacred discourse, and also the credulity of the simple folk. You could have answered me in writing; you could have sued me in court. But now you are doing an injury not so much to me as to the entire University and to the whole populace and to sacred discourse, which is devoted to an altogether different type of talk." Not being ready with an answer he turned to another subject, as is his custom. "Ah," he said, "you would like to have the same authority." "What authority? the authority to preach?" He nodded assent. "But," I told him, "I not only have delivered sermons in the past, I also think I could say something better than I hear you coming out with at times." "Why don't you do it then?" "Because I think I am doing something more worth while by writing books. And yet I wouldn't censure you for your great pains if only you would instruct on matters that contribute to good morals."

Thereupon the man was reminded of the statement I had made in a letter to the Rector (which he had read) that I did not deserve such shameful treatment and that, in fact, I deserved credit for my services. "For what services do you deserve credit?" he asked me. "A large number of people admit that I have done no mean service to good learning." "Ah yes," he said, "that's what you call it; it's really bad learning." "And I have restored the text of Scripture in many passages," I added. "Quite the reverse! You have falsified many passages." "Why then did the Pope give his approbation with an official document?" I asked him. "Yes, an official document. Who ever saw that document of yours?" He was hinting that it was my own concoction. "Do you expect me to carry the document around with me, showing it to everybody, or to exhibit it in the market place? I have shown it to Briard of Ath; Dorp has seen it." "Ah yes, Dorp," he mused and would have added some insulting remark about him if the Rector had not reprimanded him with his eyes. "You too can see it if you want to," I offered. "I don't want to see anything of yours." "Then why condemn me?" I asked. "And why does the authority of the Pope carry so much weight with you when he condemns Luther, but so little when he approves my works?" . . .

He soon wandered off into another field with the assertion that he would never stop bellowing against Luther until he had finished him. I answered that, as far as I was concerned, he could go on bellowing until he split his entrails so long as he did not blather about me, and that I was not complaining about his yelling at Luther but at myself, and that he might continue along this same course if it was so dear to his heart, but he would gain nothing by it except to become the laughingstock of all good men. I had observed during his sermon that people throughout the audience were laughing. "Yes," he said, but those were all your own men." "I don't know how they could be mine. I did not even know most of them by sight." He twitted me with other charges, for instance that I had brought forward letters of eminent men who gave me some credit;[2] he intimated that those letters were my own invention and that there was no one who approved my conduct—although in general I suppress all letters of that sort. And at the same time he made it clear that nothing was to be regarded as approved unless it had been endorsed by himself. From such remarks one can conjecture the modesty of a fellow who gives himself so little credit, and likewise the straightforward and absolutely Christian spirit of a man who suspects his neighbor of every evil.

Among other things I mentioned that it should not seem strange if on occasion I made some complaints about theologians in my books, since John Standish,[3] a Franciscan and theologian and Bishop of St. Asse, had denounced me with utter impudence on three accounts in the presence of the King and Queen of England and before a large audience of nobles and scholars. He accused me first of denying the resurrection, then of making light of the sacrament of marriage, and finally of having erroneous views about the Eucharist. Such were his accusations, although in all my writings I defend nothing more firmly than the resurrection, although I have praised marriage so highly in

2. The reference is to the *Epistolae eruditorum virorum*, published in 1520. See Allen, IV, 210.
3. Erasmus erroneously gives the first name as John; it was Henry.

my published treatise[4] that theologians have regarded my excessive tribute to marriage as an error smacking of heresy, and finally, I have never written or spoken of the Eucharist except in the proper manner, that is, with the greatest reverence.

TO LORENZO CAMPEGGIO[1]

EE 1167 (135–165; 365–   Louvain, December 6, 1520
404; 427–440)

Now, as to the inner recesses of Luther's mind, which God alone can judge with certainty, I have preferred to favor, as I should, what is good rather than the bad. The world, being sick and weary of the kind of teaching that is deeply embedded in feeble little commentaries and regulations of human origin, seemed to be thirsting for the living and pure springs of water which have their origin in the evangelists and the apostles. It seemed to me that Luther was by nature qualified to fulfill this need and was also fired with a desire to do so.

So I have favored Luther; I have favored the good points I noticed in him, or which I believed to be there. Actually, I favored not him but the glory of Christ. At the same time, I also noticed things in him which made me feel somewhat uneasy and suspicious. Consequently when he, of his own accord, provoked me with a letter I seized the opportunity at once to give him some careful advice as to what I thought he should avoid. My purpose was that, once his natural qualities were corrected and purified, he might with rich results and also with great glory and profit for Christ restore for us the philosophy of the gospel which had almost become cold from neglect. Had

---

4. *Encomium Matrimonii*, written for Mountjoy and published in 1517.
1. Lived 1472–1539—papal diplomat, cardinal, legate to England in both 1518/19 and 1528/29. On the latter occasion his responsibility was to seek an acceptable solution to Henry VIII's desire for a "divorce." At the Diet of Augsburg in 1530 Campeggio was present and played a major role in the negotiations.
In this letter to a high official of the Curia, Erasmus seeks to explain and also justify his attitude toward Luther.

he succeeded in doing that, I was sure that he would have the special
support of Pope Leo himself in this undertaking. To Leo, in my
opinion, nothing is more important than the glory of Christ, whom
he temporarily represents, and the salvation of the flock entrusted to
his care. Now, please tell me if that is the kind of letter a supporter
of Luther would write if Luther wrote contrary to Christian teaching
and piety?

Shortly after there appeared in Luther's writings an element of
offensive fierceness and harshness which did not at all reflect the
gentleness of the evangelical spirit. Therefore, I advised him to
follow the example of Christ and the apostles and in all gentleness to
teach those things which pertain to true piety. That he might do this
with greater profit, I advised him not to attack the Pope, since it is
expedient that his authority be regarded as sacrosanct. Also that he
should spare the dignity of rulers, for if they are inopportunely insulted or admonished they do not improve, but rather become em-
bittered and sometimes stir up dangerous storms. As a result, the
critic loses his authority and sometimes also his life, and the advice its
effect. While it is never lawful to oppose the truth, still it is sometimes expedient to conceal it at the right time. . . .

This advice of mine, therefore, has favored Luther, but only
insofar as I wanted to prevent his being crushed undeservedly or
unjustly or amid rioting or at the cost of world-wide disturbance. In
fact, this advice clearly showed much more support for the dignity of
the Roman pontiff and for the authority of the theologians, whose
decisions should carry considerable weight, whose conduct should be
characterized by moderation, and whose behavior should be far
removed from all suspicion of stupidity, envy, greed, ambition, ill
will, flattery, and other passions which deprive us of our judgment.
Even as no one gives less support to the Roman pontiff than he who
does so imprudently or perversely, so no one does more harm to the
name of theologian than a person whose aim is to make flatterers or
tyrants out of them. Moses was not reluctant to follow the advice of
his father-in-law, Jethro. But people are indignant with me for my
loyal advice, although as far as I was concerned there was no need to
follow it. If we are eager to hear the truth, each man may be free to
express his own opinion, and the one who offers bad advice may be
pardoned, provided he is serious. But if one man is rewarded with a

mitre while another receives terrible harm, what prospect have we of knowing the truth? Of all the many universities, only two condemned some unusual statements of Luther.[2] And not even these two are in complete agreement; in fact, not even the theologians of either one are in complete agreement. We were awaiting a statement from the University of Paris, which has always been preeminent in theology even as the Roman See has been with regard to the Christian religion. Since the judgment of Paris was still awaited, should it have been a crime for me even if I had supported some of Luther's teachings? The fact is, I have never defended anything of Luther's, though I might have. I merely disapproved of the overhasty and uproarious judgment of those who displeased even Luther's opponents.

What a strange follower of Luther I am! I was the first to condemn Luther's books for the reason that they seemed to be aiming at turmoil, which I have always shunned; I was the first to oppose the publication of his works. I am virtually the only one who has not read his books; I alone never attempted to defend anything of his, not even over a glass of wine, when there is much idle chatter. I have always encouraged those who had the ability to dispute with Luther to oppose him in writing. When certain men at Louvain started to do so, I firmly approved. But would to heaven they had not been so perverse about it! The two universities issued a prejudicial statement against Luther. An alarming bull appeared bearing the name of the Pope.[3] Books were burned. There was an uproar among the people. The matter could hardly have been more odiously handled. Everyone considered the bull merciless and inconsistent with the gentleness of Pope Leo. And yet a good part of the savagery was contributed by the men involved. And meantime nobody noticed that Erasmus was restless or sadder than usual. . . .

If the corrupt morals of the Roman Curia demand an extraordinary and immediate remedy, it is certainly not for me nor for men like me to assume that assignment. I prefer the status quo in human

2. Erasmus refers to the condemnations by Cologne and Louvain, the latter being more severe.
3. The bull referred to is "Exsurge domine" of 1520, which condemned Luther.

affairs, no matter what it may be, rather than to stir up new turmoils, which very often take a different turn than is expected. Those who try to divert sea waters into new hollows are often tricked, because once the water is diverted it does not always flow according to plan, but follows its own whim as it rushes on with great disaster to neighboring areas. I have never been and shall never be a willful teacher of error, nor shall I ever be a leader or an accomplice in any turmoil. Others may desire martyrdom; I do not consider myself worthy of that honor. I realize that I am hateful to some—not for being a follower of Luther; in fact, they are angry because I am not. I am hateful to persons who are pleasing only to silly women and to illiterate and superstitious folk. Only those are really displeased with Erasmus who are not pleased with good learning and the evangelical truth: namely, men who are nurtured and enriched by the folly of the mob.

TO WILLIBALD PIRCKHEIMER[1]

EE 1268 (35–60)   Basel, March 30, 1522

As for councils, the only statement I would dare to make is that the recent Lateran Council was not really a council.[2] Besides, the schools have gradually claimed an increasing degree of authority, and they now demand that their pronouncements be regarded almost as articles of faith. And at present they are carrying on their trade under the shadow of the Pope's wing; some have made excessive claims for themselves, some have reached a point of insolence where no one can bear them. Things that have gathered strength gradually cannot quickly be uprooted. And to show open contempt for the prestige of the powerful is neither safe nor practical, in my opinion. Right now the affair is being handled on the one side by bulls, edicts, and threats, and on the other by unrestrained—not to say seditious—

1. On Pirchkheimer see Letter 1139, p. 150. Together with brief comments on the Lutheran controversy, Erasmus expresses here his tired resignation to the general turmoil.
2. The Fifth Lateran Council, which met from 1512 to 1517.

pamphlets. But if princes who are occupied with other affairs cannot turn their attention toward this situation, I am surprised that good men do not rise up to confront these terrible evils with a wise program.

However, this is not really any concern of mine. The end of my life is in sight. But even a dying man should wish Christianity well, if only we had the proper conviction that Christ is the immortal head of the whole Church. One man consults his own private interests, another is afraid of losing his possessions, still another shuns tumult and refuses to become involved. Meanwhile the dangerous conflagration spreads. I myself have been so heavily burdened with ill will through the malice of certain individuals that any attempt I might make would be destined to fail. Some theologians have felt that the revival of ancient studies, thanks to my efforts, has caused a gradual decline of their own authority, and so even before the world had heard the name of Luther they were making every possible attempt against me. Luther has handed these men the weapon by which to dispose of me, though I have always kept away from the Luther affair, except to urge him earnestly to write in a different vein if he wished to accomplish something.

TO DUKE GEORGE OF SAXONY[1]

EE 1313 (4–16)   Basel, September 3, 1522

It is not strange that you are displeased at the way the world is divided by this very dangerous dissension. Who with a Christian heart would not be displeased by it? I wish princes would give their attention to genuine concerns, so that this terrible evil could be laid

---

1. George of Saxony (1500–1539) was one of the most aggressive of Luther's opponents. The two had met at the Leipzig disputation in 1519, where the duke recoiled at Luther's implicit endorsement of Hus. See O. Vossler, "Herzog Georg der Bärtige u. seine Ablehnung Luthers," *Histor. Zeitschrift*, 184 (1957). Again commenting on Luther, Erasmus puts the blame for the controversy on the scholastic theologians of his day. Other letters to Duke George are 1526 and 1743.

to rest and never spring to life again. Perhaps it is already too late to decide which side is to blame. Luther, undeniably, had undertaken an excellent project and amid the loud applause of all the world had begun to do the work of Christ, who had been all but effaced. But if only he had handled this important business with more serious and calmer planning and with greater control over feelings and pen! If only there were not so many good things in his writings, or if he had not spoiled those good things by unbearable defects! And yet on this point some followers of Luther have sinned more seriously than Luther himself. But now both sides are acting with wild displays of hatred, and there is danger that Luther may be crushed and all those good things perish, which I should not like to see destroyed. Also there is danger that the victorious side may bring against me charges such as no lover of Christ could endure; this could turn out to the great detriment of Christ's glory and evangelical sincerity.

If it is possible for me to speak freely to a ruler who is no less prudent than learned, the world was lulled to sleep by the opinions of the scholastics, by silly little human regulations. The only things it heard of were indulgences, paying penalties, and the power of the Roman pontiff. Even if these things were valid beyond all doubt, they are not of much service for a vigorous evangelical life; they do not inspire us to a contempt of this world, they do not inflame us with a love for heavenly things. Yet these are the elements that should be inculcated most of all. We must not reject papal authority, but Christ alone must be the object of all glory. And yet some men would employ such means to exercise their power, men who do not seek the things that belong to Jesus Christ, but who like Demas, whom the Apostle Paul denounced, are lovers of this life.[2] The world had to be roused from this sleep and the spark of evangelical vigor had to be revived. But if only it had been done with the gentleness and care with which the holiest of all matters deserves to be handled! Some monks and monkish theologians became involved in this affair and by their stupid, ignorant, seditious screaming stirred up this trouble and turned a tiny evil into a tremendous disaster. At first the only thing imperiled was the profit made by dealers in indulgences.

2. II Tim. 4:10.

And just as Luther writes many things which the ears of a large number of people cannot endure, so too those fellows are making very many charges which, in the view of good and learned men, will prove detrimental to true evangelical piety. And yet those who are writing such things are not doing the work of Christ nor of the Pope, but their own. In fact, by aiming at their own private interests, they are harming the cause of the Pope and obscuring the glory of Christ. These fellows do not permit the approval even of those things in Luther which are thoroughly Christian. Yet they do not abandon any of their own positions; they even add harsher statements to their previous ones.

Since I clearly perceived that both parties under the influence of some wild fury were rushing toward a clash, I have had very little to do with this disturbance, except to make it sufficiently clear that there does not exist any compact between me and the followers of Luther and that nothing displeases me more than sedition. Furthermore, I realized that I was not equal to any such perilous business, even if I had time to read what was written by both sides, as I would have had to read everything. Also, my advancing years and my health demand a respite from the too serious a pursuit of studies. I would never be able to attack Luther bitterly in writing without appearing feeble to the opposite party. Besides, the followers of Luther are already making dire threats against me, and there is nobody whom they would rather tear to pieces than Erasmus, if he were to enter the affray. There are enough pamphlets against Luther, if that approach could be the means of destroying him. And there are others in this arena who have considerably more strength than I. Finally, I have always held the view that this tragedy could most effectively be laid to rest by silence. The same view is held by some of the cardinals and by the most intelligent men in prominent positions. A very harsh bull has been issued by the Pope.[3] It has done nothing but fan the flames. This was followed by even a harsher edict from the Emperor, who is deeply interested in this situation.[4] This fact is restraining the tongues and pens of some individuals, but it is not changing their minds.

3. The bull "Exsurge domine," issued in June 1520.
4. The Edict of Worms, May 1521.

TO JOHN CARONDELET[1]

EE 1334 (138–155; 162–174;   Basel, January 5, 1522/3
  200–234; 360–381)

It is a greater spur to us to undertake such an endeavor if the subject matter happens to be not only noble and grand, but also new and not at all trite; for the nobility of the subject, apart from making it suitable for lofty treatment, also provides an excellence of itself, while the newness adds charm. Now the ancients very sparingly philosophized about things divine; they did not dare to make pronouncements about such matters except when something had been clearly handed down in those writings whose authority is sacrosanct. The blasphemous rashness of the Ebionites and the followers of Cerinthus first forced John the Evangelist to put in writing certain mysteries about the divine nature of Christ. Later, orthodox teachers were put under even greater compulsion by the prying subtlety of the Arians and were forced to dispute fiercely and to discuss and finally to form definitions about the extension of the divine nature, and the later creation of the Son, and about His being adopted and called God, and then finally about the expressions, "identical in nature," and "similar in nature." At times Hilary, the holy man, deplores the necessity of doing this; he is well aware of all the dangers involved and how irreligious it can be to speak of things that defy human words, to pry into what is incomprehensible, and to make pronouncements on matters which are far beyond our capacity.

But pardon should be granted to the writers of old, and such is the plea of those who were driven into this situation by necessity. But as for us—how can we dare to beg for pardon, when we raise countless

1. Archbishop of Palermo and a supporter of Erasmus. The letter forms the preface to Erasmus' edition of Hilary's *Opera*. He speaks here of the true nature of theology and makes a very important distinction between matters of secondary importance which can be left undecided and those essential for salvation. The "endeavor" mentioned in the opening line is the preoccupation with the writings of ancient authors.

meddlesome, not to say blasphemous, questions about matters quite removed from our nature—and when we try to explain so many things which, without harm to salvation, could be left unknown or undecided? Will a person not participate in the life of the Father, Son, and Holy Spirit just because he cannot give a philosophical explanation of the distinction between the Father and the Son, or between those Two Persons and the Holy Spirit, or the difference between the generation of the Son by the Father and the procession of the Holy Spirit? If I believe, according to tradition, that the Three are of one nature, what need is there of laborious discussion? If I do not believe, no human explanations are going to convince me. And as a rule, such a dangerous spirit of curiosity is developed in us as a result of the study of philosophy. . . .

Although our life is so fleeting, still we continue to neglect those things without which there is no hope for any man to attain salvation. Unless I forgive my brother for having offended me, God will not forgive me for what I have done against Him. Unless I have a clean heart, I shall not see God. Thus, what I should have been wholeheartedly striving for, and what I should have been reflecting on the insisting on was this: how to cleanse my heart of jealousy, envy, hatred, pride, avarice, and lust. One will not be damned for not knowing whether the Spirit proceeds from the Father and the Son by one principle or two. But one will not escape doom if he fails in the present life to possess the fruits of the Spirit, namely, love, joy, peace, patience, kindness, goodness, long-suffering, meekness, faith, self-control, continence, chastity. These should be the aim, the objects of our efforts. Not that I think one should completely condemn either the sophisticated study of philosophy, chopped up into three parts,[2] or the investigation of things beyond this world, provided there is a happy talent for it and one engages in this without obstinacy and a reckless formulation of definitions, without the stubborn pursuit of concord or the desire to win.

2. Literally: "Divided into three parts." The reference here is to a treatise by Gregory Reisch entitled *Margarita philosophica, totius philosophie rationalis, naturalis, et moralis principia* ("The Pearl of Philosophy"), a scholastic work. Erasmus is referring to the simple profession of the Christian faith which he has discussed in the preceding paragraph (here omitted). On Reisch, see Letter 308, p. 75.

The perfection of our religion consists in peace and harmony. And this can hardly be established unless we define as few things as possible and leave each man free to form his own decisions on many questions. The reason is that there is a tremendous obscurity in so many matters, and human nature has the virtually inborn affliction of refusing to give in, as soon as it becomes evident that a point is contested. When discussion grows heated, one becomes absolutely convinced of the truth of a view which he undertook to defend without much reflection. And in this matter some men know no bounds, so much so that, after defining everything concerning things divine, they even invent some new divinity among those who are nothing more than men. Such doings have stirred up more doubts and created more violent confusion for the world than did the reckless behavior of the Arians of old. But certain professors are embarrassed when they do not have a ready answer on some point. Rather, the task of theological learning is precisely this: to explain nothing more than what has been handed down in Sacred Scripture; however, what has been handed down should be propagated in good faith. Many problems are now being set aside for referral to an ecumenical council. It would be much better to reserve them for that time when we shall see God, not indirectly and obscurely, but face to face. . . .

Such a theological profession [the previous paragraph commented on the trinitarian speculation] may not be satisfactory in our age, because under the diligence of the ancients (which was necessary) taught us more. But without this necessity we are swayed. Formerly faith consisted in life rather than the profession of creeds. Then necessity required that a creed be drawn up, but only a simple one, with apostolic sobriety. Then the wickedness of heretics led to a more exacting scrutiny of the sacred books; their obstinacy made it necessary that some doctrinal points be officially defined by the authority of synods. When faith began to be in books rather than in hearts, there were almost as many faiths as men. Creeds increased and sincerity decreased. Contention grew hot and love grew cold. The teaching of Christ, which initially knew no hairsplitting, began to depend on the support of philosophy. This was the first stage in the fall of the Church. Works increased and power was added. Then, the injection of political authority into this affair has not greatly helped the sincerity of the faith. At last the whole question was reduced to sophisticated propositions, and myriads of dogmatic pronouncements issued forth. From there it has come to terror and threats. When life leaves us, when faith is in the mouth rather than the heart, when we lack knowledge of the Sacred Scriptures, we drive men to believe what they do not believe, to love what they do not love, to understand what they do not understand. What is coerced cannot be sincere, and what is not voluntary cannot please Christ.

TO POPE ADRIAN VI[1]

EE 1352 (25–129; 158–185)   [Basel, March 22, 1523]

I wish I had the abilities you attribute to me for checking this division. I would not hesitate to heal these public ills even at the cost of my own life. There are many who surpass me in the power to write, and besides, this affair cannot be handled by the pen. My learning falls far below mediocrity, and what learning I do have is derived from ancient authors and is more adapted to the pulpit than to the battlefield. And what can be the influence of such an insignificant person as myself? Could the inducements of Erasmus carry any weight with those men who are in no way affected by the authority of many universities and many rulers, and even of the Supreme Pontiff? Whatever good will I have enjoyed has either grown so cold as to be almost nonexistent, or it has perished altogether and even turned into hatred. I, who was formerly described in innumerable letters as "the greatest hero of all," "the prince of letters," "the star of Germany," "the bright light of scholarship," "the high priest of good learning," "the champion of genuine theology," am now passed over in silence or far differently described.

I have no interest in empty titles, which are only a burden to me.

1. Adrian VI (1459–1523) had taught at Louvain, became tutor to Prince Charles (subsequently Emperor Charles V) in 1507, was made cardinal in 1517 and elected pope in January 1522. His spiritual sensitivity and concern for reform encouraged those who hoped for ecclesiastical renewal.

In this letter Erasmus seeks to interpret the nature of the Lutheran controversy in Germany and his own place in it, especially his efforts at mediation.

What wild insults may now heap on my head, with what vicious pamphlets they attack me, with what intimidations they terrorize me! Some have uttered threats of death if I so much as make a move. At the same time some are screaming that I agree with the Lutherans and write nothing against Luther, while the violent supporters of Luther loudly complain that I attack him too often and with an unbecoming bitterness. Luther deplores that very thing in his letters to his friends. Germany is a huge country and it abounds in men of outstanding ability. And yet Germany is not the only place controlled by such feelings. I would not dare to mention in writing all the places where there is sympathy for Luther and hatred for the name of the Pope, nor would I dare to describe how deeply implanted such feelings are in the hearts of the people. Besides, one can hardly believe how much stubbornness there is in men of talent—they themselves call it constancy. And a goodly number of the followers of good learning offer no opposition to such men.

I report this with grief and sorrow in my heart, Most Holy Father; and oh, if only it were groundless! I have always enjoyed a most pleasant association with the world of scholars. That, and that alone, was happiness for me. I would almost rather have died than to break off all those friendships—and, I might almost say, bring down the hatred of the whole world upon my head. And yet I have preferred that to appearing factious. That decision I have not as yet regretted. I shall not describe here the terrible tragedy, perhaps irremediable, that I might have caused had I yielded to the feelings of certain men. I would rather be cheated out of any credit for it than blurt out a secret. Nor do I expect credit for myself for having refrained from wrongdoing, no matter how much the opposite side calls it piety. If I had only remained neutral in this affair, pleading poor health and old age, I think I would have deserved gratitude. But the fact is, in my many letters and pamphlets I have given evidence of thorough opposition to the Lutheran teaching. I have completely deprived them all of any hope of my support, and have not even allowed them to use my writing under a disguised name before the masses. In public I have advised against espousing this seditious affair; in private, I have done all I could to stop some and call back others. At least I have managed to urge more discretion. I have had some success; some have expressed their thanks to me for my loyal advice. Many a time

I have openly expressed my disgust with Luther's abusive language. . . .

And yet, while taking care of this business among the Germans, in Rome I am being publicly ridiculed in wild and utterly slanderous pamphlets. In Brabant I am proclaimed a heretic, a heresiarch, a schismatic, and a falsifier, and this no longer only at dinner tables and in carriages, but in public meetings and formal lectures. Such remarks are made frequently and openly, and so they are common knowledge. If Your Holiness asks people he will find out from any one of them the names of those men. There are some on Luther's side who are promoting the Pope's cause as if they had vowed under penalty of death to destroy it in every conceivable way. And those fellows think they are supporting the cause of the Pope. They maintain that anything harmful in Luther's writings can also be found in mine. But they have never been able to cite a single passage that could prove agreement between Luther and me. One might say, they offer interpretations. True, but in an utterly distorted way. Or they are making conjectures. Yes, but with a considerable amount of malice. In the same way, I could collect a hundred passages from Paul's Epistles which are in agreement with the statements condemned in Luther's writings. What a disastrous instance of men who demand credence for themselves in a matter of faith! Such fellows undisguisedly serve their own personal feelings, and in so doing accomplish nothing except to ruin the cause of faith, destroy all authority, and provoke the hatred of the masses for the Pope.

I had written many things before I was even aware that Luther was born, and before anyone dreamed that an age like this would ever arise. I admit I did, for the most part, precipitate the whole thing. That is a real fault on my part. However, I have always submitted to the judgment of learned men and especially to that of the Church. I have asked many men to advise me whenever there was anything in my writings that needed correction. Those who at the time either said nothing or else expressed approval, now that Luther has emerged, are condemning what they approved. They misrepresent everything. Under every stone, as the saying goes, lies a scorpion. One statement excites suspicion, another causes scandal, another is disrespectful. While no censure has been pronounced against me by any university or any bishop, still some persons, on their own private authority, keep shouting that I am a heretic, a heresiarch. Is there any man, no matter how constant, who would not be driven into taking sides by such injustices? As for me, nothing has been able to make me swerve from the right path. . . .

Therefore, let Your Holiness thoughtfully decide whether such a person as myself deserves to be delivered up to the unbridled hatred of certain men, and whether such a course would be expedient in the present situation. Those in sympathy with the papal cause are endeavoring to restore heretics to orthodoxy, to recall those who have become estranged, and to brace up those who are wavering. And Your Holiness, too, is urging that such endeavors be handled in an intelligent as well as Christian way. . . . Many people have been uplifted and enriched by Luther; some have profited by being Lutherans. But my situation is utterly unhappy; after spending myself day and night in serving the good of all men, I have gained nothing except to be torn into shreds by both sides.

Your Holiness does indicate a remedy for these ills. "Come to Rome," you say, "or write against Luther as hatefully as you can. Declare war on all Lutherans." First of all, telling me to come to Rome is like telling a crab to fly. "Give me some wings," replies the crab, while I would say, "Give me back my youth and my good health." I wish this excuse of mine were not so well founded! It would be tedious to mention the reasons that have persuaded me to stay in Basel until now. I dare swear once for all that if I had perceived anything more advantageous for the Christian common-wealth I would have done it, even at the risk of my life. I have never lacked the will to accomplish, only the hope of accomplishment. However, it would be quite foolish to stir up a plague that is quiescent, if one could hope for nothing but more trouble.

Again I beseech you to allow this your sheep to talk freely and at length to its shepherd. Granted that my health allowed it, what use would I be in Rome, away from contact with the Lutherans? Even now I am actually away and have no dealings with them. As regards my spirit I face no danger from them. . . . The word would be spreading that I was cited to Rome and that I am hurrying there to have a share in the spoils. Why the burden of living there, if they have persuaded themselves that anything I write there has been corrupted by bribes? Perhaps I would write more vehemently, but that would only comfort me and not the cause. If I write modestly and politely against Luther, it will seem that I only play with him. If I imitate his violent style and belligerently incite the Lutherans, what else will I be doing but stirring up a hornet's nest? Up to this point, I believe, I have kept the friendship of learned men. Thereby, I feel, I can be of greater profit.

But you will say you have heard only complaints; you are waiting for a plan. What I have said up to now is a part of my plan: I am aware that many people want to cure this evil by severity, though I fear that the final result will one day prove that such a scheme was ill-advised. There is great danger, more than I care to see, that this affair will end up in a wild massacre. . . . If the decision is made to destroy this plague by means of prisons, whips, confiscations, banishments, censures, and deaths, then there will be no need of any plan from me. I do realize though that someone of your gentle disposition would welcome a totally different program, inasmuch as you prefer to heal rather than punish. If all men were of your temper, it would not be very difficult for them to set aside their own personal feelings, as you say, and sincerely desire the best interests of Christ's glory and the salvation of the Christian people. But if each is intent upon his own personal advantage; if theologians demand that their authority be regarded as in all respects impeccable, if monks are unwilling to surrender any of their advantages, and if princes cling fast to their every right, then it is exceedingly difficult to consult the common interests.

The first thing to do is to discover the sources from which this trouble keeps sprouting; before all else, they must be cured. And then it would be beneficial to make it clear to those who have erred through personal conviction or outside influence that they will not be punished. Even better, let an amnesty be granted for all past evils, which apparently are the result of some sort of fate. If that is the way God deals with us every day, forgetting all faults as often as the sinner shows repentance, then what prevents God's Vicar from doing the same thing? However, civil officials and rulers should keep novelties in check, which promote piety very little and discord very much. I would like to see, if possible, a rein put on the widespread practice of publishing pamphlets. Besides, let the world be offered a hope of change in certain things by which it rightly complains of

being oppressed. At the sweet name of freedom all men will breathe
a sigh of relief. In every way regard must be had for extricating their
consciences.

TO PHILIPP MELANCHTHON[1]

EE 1496 (46–107; 167–202)   Basel, September 6, 1524

You will ask me why I did not at once attack the things that
displeased me. My answer is that I was in favor of having the
freedom of the gospel restored and I had hopes that Luther, when
cautioned, would follow more prudent counsels. And so, as much as I
could, I have checked the shouting of theologians and restrained the
savagery of rulers, and I am still trying to do this. I have separated the
cause of good learning from the cause of Luther. I have seized every
opportunity to advance the interests of the gospel without causing
any commotion, or at least any serious commotion. Up to the present
I have used every opportunity to write to the Emperor and other
princes, playing the role of a Gamaliel, hoping for a happy ending to
this drama. I have written frankly to Pope Adrian about this matter.
Later, I realized that I was running the risk, not of an attack from
him, but of having him cease to protect me from my attackers. Nor
was it at all safe to trust him, no matter how complimentary he might
be. Even so, I did write quite freely to Clement also,[2] and to Cardinal Campeggio. I do not know the situation in your Church. But the
Church here certainly does have some men who, I am afraid, may
disrupt everything and drive the princes into using force against good
and bad alike. They constantly shout: Gospel, the Word of God,
Faith, Christ, Spirit! But their conduct bespeaks something quite
different. Are we going to rid ourselves of priests and prelates and

---

1. Lived 1497–1560. Protestant reformer and colleague of Luther at
Wittenberg. See C. Manschreck, *Melanchthon: The Quiet Reformer* (New
York, 1958). One might call this letter a variant of the preceding one, for here,
too, Erasmus explains his attitude toward Luther.
2. Pope Clement VII (1523–1534).

bishops only to be saddled with the savage tyranny of mangy men like Brunfels[3] or rabid ones like Farel?[4] . . .

You will say that in early times, too, the gospel had its pseudo-apostles who under the guise of piety were interested only in their belly. But meantime these fellows are being tenderly fostered by such champions of the gospel as Capito, whose cunning I could always smell, and Hedio, who supported that filthy clown [the printer Schott?] in the matter of those writings against me (for which the fellow should have been punished, but Hedio pleaded for mercy because of his wife and young children). Even now he is doing all he can to prevent the blackguard from suffering any loss of money and reputation. Oecolampadius is a little more restrained than the rest; and yet in his case too I sometimes fail to see evangelical sincerity. As for Zwingli, his conduct is utterly seditious! I shall refrain from saying anything at present about the others. They don't agree with you; they don't agree with one another. And yet, relying on their own authority, they demand that we rebel against all the orthodox Fathers and councils. You hold that it is wrong for them to reject images as something impious. But Zwingli has stirred up untold riots just over images! You hold that the religious garb is not an important point. But here several people hold that the cowl should be completely done away with. You hold that bishops and their regulations must be supported unless they lead to impiety. These men hold that they are all impious and anti-Christian. . . .

But let us have an end to that complaint. You will wonder why I published my pamphlet on freedom of the will. I was trying to hold the line against a triple attack. Theologians and those who hate good learning were leaving no stone unturned to destroy Erasmus: first of all, because I had attacked them in my writings, and secondly, because I had inveighed against that flourishing University of Louvain and had sullied the whole area with the pursuit of languages and good learning. That is what they say. They convinced all the rulers that I am bound by an oath to Luther. Accordingly, my friends, aware of my danger, gave the Pope and the princes hope that

3. Otho Brunfels (ca. 1488–1534), a humanist educator at Strassburg, afterward physician at Bern, with strong Protestant leanings.
4. Guillaume Farel (1489–1565), a Protestant reformer who in 1536 persuaded Calvin to settle in Geneva.

I would publish something against Luther. I also nourished that hope
for a time. Meanwhile these fellows, without waiting for my work,
started their assault with pamphlets. The only thing for me to do was
to publish what I had written. Otherwise I would have made enemies
of the rulers, who would have considered me guilty of cheating them.
Besides, those stormy fellows would have been screaming that they
had brought me to a standstill through fear, and while waiting for
something violent they would have raved uncontrollably. Finally,
since these men have in their possession a letter from Luther promising to refrain from attacking me with his pen if I keep quiet, I would
have given the impression that I had agreed not to publish. . . .
Therefore, if I had not published anything, I would have made it
easier for the theologians and monks . . . to convince the bishops
and rulers of what they had all along been trying to persuade them
of. Finally, I would have made these mad evangelicals even more
hostile. For I myself have handled this problem with the greatest
restraint. And yet what I put in writing is in keeping with my views,
though I would be willing to change those views, too, if convinced of
something better.

"But in the meantime," you say, "you are making those tyrants rage
all the more violently." More than anyone else I have seriously and
openly discouraged violence. Even if I were an ardent devotee of the
papist faction, I would still oppose violence, because that path only
leads to more violence. Aware of this, Julian forbade the killing of
Christians. The theologians supposed that by a few burnings at
Brussels all the rest would be made to change their ways; but that
bloodshed produced several Lutherans. Some of those fellows keep
yelling that the gospel is being stamped out whenever anybody
opposes their insanity. The efficacy of the gospel consists, not in
sinning with impunity, but in not sinning even when one could do so
with impunity.

TO GEORGE SPALATIN[1]

EE 1497   Basel, September 6, 1524

I have always made every effort so that this bitter and violent medicine of Luther which has shaken the world would produce some measure of sound health. But here I notice some men are emerging who are turning this situation to their own personal advantage. Their type is the most deleterious and unruly I have ever seen. They scorn Luther, but they plot only for their own interests. The sight of such conduct makes me feel hostile not only to their cause, but even to good learning. I always hear "the gospel," but I never see anything that resembles the gospel. They throw off the cowl, get married, and then defend their action. And meantime they go around hunting for rich fortunes that will give them security. They publish wild pamphlets anonymously, or under a pseudonym, and then insist dogmatically that this is the way to defend the gospel. What a brilliant defense! On this score I do praise Luther: he uses his own name, and he teaches the legitimacy of things which he himself does not practice. You will say, "Loudmouths mean nothing so far as the gospel is concerned." But these loudmouths are encouraged by such leaders as Capito, Hedio, Oecolampadius, and Zwingli. These men are stirring up the wrath of the rulers and they rage against me for not professing to be a follower of Luther. Shall I, at the risk of my life, profess what I do not follow, or have doubts of, or do not approve? And should I join such a faction? When I see men like that in their ranks, I would prefer to join forces with the Turks. You can be sure of this—I shall not stop giving my support to the matter of the gospel.

1. On George Spalatin see Letter 1119, p. 149. In this letter Erasmus comments on some of the by-products of the Lutheran controversy.

TO DUKE GEORGE OF SAXONY[1]

EE 1526 (13–171; 181–192)   Basel, December 12, 1524

When Luther first rang up the curtain for this drama, he won the hearty applause of the whole world; I think Your Highness was one of that number. At any rate, he did have the support of theologians who are now bitterly hostile to him; he also had the backing of several cardinals, not to mention monks. For he had taken up a very worthy cause in opposing corrupt practices in the schools and in the Church, which had deteriorated to such an extent that the situation was intolerable in the eyes of all good men. And then he opposed that class of men whose deplorable wickedness burdened all Christendom. At that time, who could have guessed that the situation would come to this? If some Daniel had predicted it, I would not have believed him. I do not think even Luther himself expected such a development. And yet, before he had published anything except his theses on papal indulgences, and while just one or two pages were circulating among his supporters, I shrank from the whole business. For in my opinion the teaching of Luther, who by waging war has become a warrior, could not cope with this problem, and besides I could see that the thing would end up in seditions and turmoil.

Although at the time I was on very close terms with those who were enthusiastic in their applause, nobody could change my mind so as to approve of this undertaking. In particular, I openly and constantly expressed to everybody my disapproval of this way of going about things. In fact when I discovered, while in Brabant, that Froben at the instigation of some scholars (including Capito) had printed some of Luther's pamphlets, I made it very clear to him that he could not be a friend of mine if he continued to contaminate his printing establishment with such tracts. Not satisfied with that, I added an appendix to my little book of *Colloquies*, then in the press

1. See Letter 1313, p. 163. In this letter Erasmus elaborates on his various attempts to mediate in the religious controversy.

at Louvain,[2] in which I clearly bore witness to my thorough opposition to the Lutheran teaching. At the same time I warned Luther privately—he had written to me first—to act with sincerity and with that moderation which befits one who professes the gospel. The Emperor was not as yet opposed to Luther's teaching. Only some monks and business agents were doing the shouting; apparently they were losing some of their profits. All the fierce violence stirred up by such men has been the principal reason why a tiny spark developed into a huge conflagration.

The more I urged Luther to moderation, the more vehemently he raged. When I sought to pacify the other party, the thanks I got was the charge that I sympathized with Luther.

You ask, "Why did you not enter the controversy after the evil had become evident?" My answer is that I felt that no one was less fitted for this affair than I; and I do not think I was mistaken in my opinion. Moreover, those who told the Emperor and other rulers that I was the best man to suppress Luther were talking glibly, for these men were, and still are, proclaiming that I am ignorant of theology.

What were they trying to do but have an unarmed Erasmus fight the wild beasts, and thus put the onus of the whole business upon him? What praise would I have received? I would merely have been the scribe of theologians who had already appropriated the glory of learning and granted me only that of eloquence. I would never have satisfied them without reveling in railing and abuse, causing tumult everywhere and raging against Luther with my pen even as they burned with hatred of him. They suggested that I had at first agreed with Luther and would now recant. They asserted, "You have written in behalf of Luther; now write against him." Truly, it was a fair proposition: first I was to lie about myself and then put my pen at the service of peevish and insane fellows who were, besides, my bitterest enemies. This they will never cease to be until they cease to hate learning. . . . Unless I defended all their positions, I would have incurred their rancor; I know that kind of men. What else was Erasmus to be, except their executioner? Is there any doubt that the result would have been the same as we now see? All who favored Luther—and there are many everywhere who do favor him—would

2. The *Colloquiorum Formulae* of 1519.

either cease to be our friends, or, as I have already learned from painful experience, would turn from friends into bitter enemies. There is no part of the world where my writings have not brought me many friendships, and I considered myself happy indeed on this account, no matter how otherwise slender my fortune. This most priceless of all possessions was not lightly to be thrown away, especially since I would have become defenseless and without friendly help, at the mercy of men who hate sound learning. I might as well offer myself to be torn in pieces by both sides.

You will comfort me by saying that I would have the protection of the Pope and the Emperor. But will they save me when they cannot themselves avoid being the target of slanderous books and accusations? As far as wealth is concerned, I have enough to feed my poor little body: bestowing honors on a man of my health and age is like putting a pack-saddle on an ox or a load on an old broken-down horse; he would fall under it. To be sure, I hear some people saying that the Catholic faith itself is at stake; but I fear the example of Uzzah, who suffered misfortune when he sought to support the toppling ark. Not everyone can put his shoulders under the tottering faith. Even Jerome, when fighting heretics, only narrowly avoided falling into heresy himself. What must I not fear, since I am not only born for other things, but also have never been trained for this arena? Besides, I had no doubt that from the multitude of theologians and bishops some would come forward willing to take up so difficult a matter and able to accomplish something. I was not mistaken in this surmise. Many and great men have stood up against Luther. Tell me what they have accomplished. Then came the terrible bull of the Pope and an even more terrible edict of the Emperor; afterward prisons, confiscation, recantations, and fagots. I cannot see any results except that the evil is spreading wider all the time. Would the pigmy Erasmus, leaping into the arena, have moved them even a little, when they pay no attention to these giants?

Apart from his extreme doctrines, Luther's books are characterized by a bitterness, joined with an arrogance, that offends me (though I must acknowledge that beside some of his followers Luther himself might seem modest). I have been little inclined to trust my own judgment when I considered how many thousands agree in their support of Luther. Although their number does not move me, there are among them many whom I know to be of good mind and possessed of great judgment, not affected by the vogue of any teaching, who have always seemed to me to be upright and pious men. I have often wondered what they saw in Luther to make them embrace his writings so eagerly and hold them so tenaciously. None of these men has quite satisfied me when a friendly discussion has arisen; therefore I sometimes feared it was my own stupidity that prevented me from clearly perceiving the things they held with such confidence and such common agreement.

There is no reason, therefore, why anyone should reproach me with delay, for I have not delayed as long as St. Hilary did before he unsheathed his pen against the Arians. His long silence was not due to covert sympathy but to religious scruples, and I too have been moved by a religious motive, though of another kind. I often sigh when I consider to what depths Christian piety had fallen. The world had been numbed by ceremonies, bad monks reigned unpunished and had caught men's consciences in snares that could not be loosed. To what trite sophistries had theology descended! There was no end to spinning out subtle definitions. I shall not mention the bishops or priests or those who practiced tyranny in the name of the pope. Accordingly, I wondered if our diseases have deserved this unpleasant physician, to cure with surgery and cauteries the evil that cannot be healed with poultices and salves. What if it is God's will to use Luther as in ancient days he used the Pharaohs, the Philistines, the Nebuchadnezzars, and the Romans? It seemed that so much success could not be possible without His favor, especially since a good part of the business was accomplished by base men of prodigious folly.

Thus I decided to commit the outcome of this tragedy to Christ, meanwhile doing only one thing—namely, to keep everyone possible from taking sides and to urge both factions to come together on fair terms, if possible, so that little by little peace might be restored. I thought my first efforts to achieve this purpose were not ill-conceived. I made the first attempt at the Diet of Worms. Soon afterward I urged the same course of action in a letter to the Emperor, to Adrian VI and Clement VII, and last of all to the papal legate, Cardinal Campeggio. The heads of the Lutheran party were approached to see if they could yield in some points, but I found them exceedingly stiff and so averse to giving up anything they had undertaken that they constantly added harsher things to the harsh things that had gone before, and the political leaders on the other side thought it best to state that the controversy should be settled by force.

Thereupon, even though my plan may have been fair and workable, I realized that my work was useless, for while it may be proper to burn a man who sets himself against established articles of faith or any other teaching that has such wide approval in the Church as to be of equal authority, it is not right to punish any and every error with fire unless it is accompanied by sedition or some other offense which the law punishes with death. The gospel ought neither to be a pretext to sin without penalty, nor to sin even though the law may allow it. Concerning the power of the pope the theologians at Paris differ at many points from those in Italy; obviously one side or the other must be in error, but neither invokes the fire against the other. Those who follow Thomas differ on many points from those who adhere to Scotus, and yet the same school tolerates both parties. I fear that such vulgar measures as recantations, prison, and burning will only increase this evil. Two men were burned at Brussels, whereupon the city began to take Luther's side. If the plague had remained confined to a few it could have been checked; now it has spread so far that even the princes are in danger. . . . I am doing the only thing left to do, and that is with a clear conscience to seek opportunities to make what contribution I can to restore public concord. Even if the best results cannot be achieved, I shall not cease to implore Christ with continual prayers for what is best. If only the dove of Christ and not the owl of Minerva would fly to us and bestow upon the excessive boldness of some people a happy outcome. This is my wholehearted striving and desire. No matter which side wins, I shall not enjoy the victory, for I shall soon leave this world; but I shall do so with a quieter mind if I see the cause of Christ victorious. Luther has offered the world a violent and bitter medicine. Whatever the remedy, it is my wish that the body of the Church, everywhere corrupted by so many ills, might regain its health.

TO JOHN CAESARIUS[1]

EE 1528 (11–26)   Basel, December 16, 1524

"I laid the egg; Luther hatched it." Indeed a surprising statement, made by those Minorites—but it does suit their fat bellies. What I laid was a hen's egg; the bird Luther hatched was altogether different. I am not surprised that such remarks come from bellies like theirs; but I am surprised at your agreeing with them. And yet you are the one who could best testify that I have always disapproved of Luther's violence for fear that the thing would end in bloody riots.

You wished I had kept absolutely silent. What do you mean? Was nothing at all to be said about superstition, or sophistry, or pseudo-bishops, or depraved monks, just so that no one could distort my words? Who could have guessed that there lurked in Germany such monstrosities as we now see emerging? "Your writings," you tell me, "seemed to tend in this direction." In what direction? Toward factiousness? I have always shrunk from it. Toward revolt? That I have never failed to loathe. I have gone all the way down to the shore's edge; do I appear inconsistent merely because I refuse to leap into the waves?

TO THE TOWN COUNCIL OF BASEL[1]

EE 1539 (47–97; 115–134;   [Basel, ca. January 1525]
137–158)

There are three main points for consideration here: the publishing of books, abstinence from meat, and the marriage of priests and monks.

1. See Letter 622, p. 112. This letter, again on Luther, contains the famous epigram about Erasmus' relationship to him.
1. This letter, a memorandum to the Basel city council, summarizes Erasmus' views on censorship and the marriage of priests.

PART ONE: *The Publishing of Books*

First of all, your concern need not be with the writings of antiquity, even if they contain error. Otherwise, not even the works of
Jerome could be issued, in fact, no book except the canonical
Scriptures. And even with them one must exercise caution with
regard to the prefaces and annotations in case something harmful
might be contained therein. According to the law of nations all civil
authorities must guard against the publishing of writings that are
libelous or of seditious intent. For if a person can be punished for
using abusive language to anyone or for spouting seditious expressions, then all the more deserving of penalty are they who scatter
abroad writings of that sort. Books which do not bear the name of the
author, the printer, and place of publication should be completely
condemned, and those who import, print, or sell such works should
be punished. And all the more deserving of punishment are those
authors who employ pseudonyms. If a work bears those three
designations but is openly libelous or seditious, the persons who print
or introduce them should be punished. This is not a new regulation,
but the law of nations.

It is very difficult to exclude all fraud in this matter. First of all,
who is going to read everything that so many people put into print?
And then, after a work has been read a person can alter the text and
make any changes he wishes, unless you keep a copy of the original.
Then the odium caused by this would fall upon the heads of those
who allowed the book to be printed. . . .

I do not know your policy with regard to Lutheran doctrines. If
you refuse permission for them to be printed, then the views of many
other men, as for instance Bugenhagen and Oecolampadius, could
not be printed either, since they contain scattered references to such
doctrines. In this way the usefulness of many would be lost. Possibly
it would be expedient to be broadminded, especially when the authors
are only discussing certain matters and are putting forth arguments,
without employing seditious or abusive language. Sedition is stirred
up most of all by untried innovations which run counter to age-old
customs and well-accepted views. Even more should innovations be
avoided if they tend to arouse turmoil rather than restore piety.

Under that heading I would put discussions of images, tonsure and garb of priests, rites of the Mass, sacred chant, and other ceremonies which are either good if properly used or at least tolerable when their endurance involves less harm than their remedy. Any inconvenience arising from such a situation can be lessened by employing other remedies. Human affairs will never be in such a happy condition that one will not have to overlook many things, no matter what changes are made. At present, some people are displeased by everything—clerical garb, sacred chant, bells, images, the tonsure, anointings, regulations, ceremonies, even the sacramental rites and laws. And there is no end to this; there is always something to replace the old complaints. While it is wrong to place too much confidence in human laws, still it is dangerous to disregard all man's laws and customs, without which the tranquility of the social order cannot endure. . . .

PART THREE: *The Marriage of Priests and Monks*

I do not think monks who throw off the cowl or priests who marry without good reason deserve your approbation. But those who in their early years were pushed into the monastic life or into the priesthood under the influence of their parents or for other reasons, I would want to have receive the assistance of higher authorities. In many cases the confinement of the cloister is an advantage, for it prevents them from committing more serious sins. There are many weak persons for whom discipline is good and freedom dangerous. But in no way should we tolerate persons who capriciously change their mode of life and even encourage others to do the same, on the assumption that it is wrong for a monk to persevere in his way of living or that priestly celibacy is in itself unholy. It is not altogether true that a person who has had a stormy life in the monastery will have a happy one if given his freedom. Nor is it probable that a priest will be satisfied with only one wife in the married state if he has had several concubines in a life of celibacy; but there is danger that an unchaste life of celibacy may be followed by a more unchaste married life. One finds it difficult to endure monks and priests who readily find fault with the laws of their bishops after they have taken holy orders in bad faith and have disgraced their high calling by a wicked life, while all along they have been nourishing their licentiousness by means of ecclesiastical stipends when they should have been confessing their sins. . . .

If you undertake the protection of such persons, this city will become the melting pot of men who are irresponsible, even criminal, and of no help for maintaining peace. If several bishops in conjunction with the magistrates, or, in case the bishops demurred, if the magistrates would in concert request permission from the Pope to pass judgment on such cases, then each case could be reviewed and the matter would have to be handled according to the merits of each case. As for the uneducated and those unworthy of the priesthood, if they were unwilling or unable to practice continence, I would permit them to marry their concubine, but they should put aside their priesthood and be considered laymen. Those who were ordained priests in good faith and whose learning could be an advantage to the Church, but who are unable to practice continence because of weakness of the flesh though otherwise men of good and sound morals, such persons I would permit to marry without depriving them of the priesthood. I feel the same way with regard to monks, namely, that each case should be considered on its own merits, and regard should be had for the best interests of those who deserve it.

So much for present problems. As for the future, precautions should be taken so that the world is not filled with so many ignorant, lazy, and bad monks and priests. Meanwhile, those who would change their state of life on their own authority or without good reason I would leave to their bishops and abbots to punish, provided they were not guilty of disturbing the social order. In other cases, I think you should continue to employ prudent moderation as you have done up to now, until the facts themselves make clear whether these doings are from God or from some other source. Meantime all breeding grounds for sedition should be carefully exterminated.

TO NOEL BEDA[1]

EE 1581 (113–145)   Basel, June 15, 1525

It certainly has always been my intention to stimulate interest in good learning and to associate it with your studies. This I have done for two reasons: first, that sound scholarship too might begin to proclaim Christ, for, as you well know, in Italy it has resounded only with paganism; secondly, that the study of languages and polite letters might contribute some advantage and insight to the program of studies commonly pursued in the schools. In this matter, I think, both sides have been seriously at fault. Those who have a deep love for scholarly learning violently attack those who pursue the opposite course. On the other hand, the latter refuse to accept excellence in ancient studies, though it could be of value to them. They do not welcome it into their fellowship, but discourteously hoot at it, condemn it, and reject it before they understand it.

As far as the dogmatic teaching in the schools is concerned, I have always shunned it as much as possible, being aware that it was not in keeping with my mediocre talents to profess to be a dogmatician in difficult matters, at my own risk and that of many others. How effective I would have been in that type of study, I do not know; in any case, my natural inclinations led me elsewhere. I have always been averse to factions, and so have been considerably more energetic in curbing those who professedly supported them than in scorning those who slandered them. As a result, if a mistake has been made or if there has been any risk, Erasmus is the only one to err or to be endangered.

With regard to the New Testament, my only aim has been to restore the true reading and, by adding light, to discuss certain passages with which I noticed many men had difficulties. Nor was

1. A theologian at the University of Paris and syndic of the theological faculty there. This letter is one of several dealing with examination of the orthodoxy of Erasmus' writings. Thus it constitutes a defense of Erasmus' literary work and theology.

there anything further from my mind than to change the Vulgate translation. In fact, I would have added the old translation to the Greek text, no matter how much it disagreed with it, had not some scholarly friends of mine, with advice that was bad rather than happy, persuaded me to this position in spite of my loud objections.[2] As for the points of admonition which I have offered in passing, I swear by God I thought I was doing something pleasing to God and necessary for Christianity. In my own mind I was acting with great moderation, so that my work could not be the cause of any dissension. At least that was my earnest endeavor. I could see that many things had collapsed, and the times were tranquil. Who would have suspected that such a disastrous storm would arise in the world?

TO CHRISTOPHER OF SCHYDLOWYETZ[1]

EE 1593 (59–68; 79–117)   Basel, August 14, 1525

The mind passes judgment on illnesses of the body. But the same cannot be done when the mind is ill, since then the faculty by which we judge is in trouble. Consequently, what remedy can you use to help a man who calls his insatiable thirst for things providence, who terms malice zeal for virtue, who gives to blind self-love the name of prudence, and who disguises the disease of maligning under the title of frankness? A person whose feet are tied down by the gout can still have sound eyes and sound ears. But any single disease of the mind makes the whole mind defective. A person troubled by gallstone may not suffer from other illnesses. But every disease of the mind carries with it a whole train of defects. . . .

Afflictions of the mind have no regard for social rank, sex, or age; they are not bound by any limits. They roam over the world with

2. Erasmus' third edition of the New Testament (1522) did reproduce the Vulgate text. It also included the trinitarian passage from I John 5.
1. This is the preface to Erasmus' *Lingua* of 1525, which deals with the potentiality of the tongue for good and evil. Christopher of Schydlowyetz was an important Polish statesman, after 1515 chancellor of Poland. This excerpt contains Erasmus' reflections on the most lamentable diseases of both body and mind.

incredible speed. They do not even yield to one another—not in the way in which plagues, quinsy, and tuberculosis take their turns in raging. But one disease of the mind provides a handle for the next. And they are not quick to leave, once they have fastened on to a person.

Now if anyone would like to know which bodily disorder ranks first, in my opinion the place would readily be given to that disease of uncertain origin which has been raging unchecked for many, many years through all quarters of the globe, though it does not as yet have a definite name. Many people call it the French pox, some the Spanish pox.[2] What plague has ever traveled with such speed through every region of Europe, Africa, and Asia? What plague implants itself more deeply in the veins and inner organs of the body? What plague clings more tenaciously or resists more obstinately the skilled treatment of physicians? What plague is more contagious or entails more bitter suffering? Vitiligo [a mild skin affliction] leaves no harmful effects except disfigurement of the skin, and it can be cured. Ringworm, it is true, covers first the face with ugly patches and scales, then the rest of the body; but there is no pain nor any danger to life, even if it does not admit of any remedy, unless one would consider death preferable. But this plague carries with it all the horrible effects found in the other types: ugly disfigurement, pain, contagion, danger to life. Nursing it is very difficult as well as very disgusting. And no matter how much it may be checked, it can quickly break out again, just like the gout.

Finally, if someone were to ask which disorder of the mind should be given foremost place for its power to harm, I would not at all hesitate to give this unpraiseworthy and inglorious glory to an unbridled tongue. This is neither a simple plague nor of recent origin; it comprises all the diseases of the mind. No age has ever been of such sound morals as not to complain of this evil. Some fevers and pestilences never completely die out, but after a respite they issue forth in a flood and their raging is even more widespread and savage, as if threatening annihilation for the human race. Similarly, we notice that this deadly disease of the tongue, being extraordinarily contagious, has gained control of the whole world; it has spread through

2. The reference is to syphilis.

the courts of princes, through the homes of the common folk, through the schools of theologians, the orders of monks, communities of priests, the ranks of the military, the huts of peasants, and with such violence that it appears bent on the complete ruin and destruction of good learning, upright morals, public peace, and the authority of Church leaders and secular rulers.

TO FRANCIS CRANEVELT[1]

EE 1655 (1–6)   Basel, December 24, 1525

Comedies after much hustle and bustle usually end with marriage. And it looks as if that is the way the tragedy of Luther is going to end. He has married a former vestal virgin. And so that you may know that the wedding had an auspicious beginning, within a few days after the nuptial song was sung, the young bride had a baby.[2] Charles will show you, if you have the time, an engraving of husband and wife.

TO ELECTOR JOHN OF SAXONY[1]

EE 1670 (9–80)   Basel, March 2, 1526

A year ago I published a *Diatribe on Free Will,* in which I took extraordinary precautions against denouncing anyone by name. I

1. A Belgian humanist (1485–1564), who from 1522 onward was a member of the Great Council at Malines, in Northern Belgium. Erasmus' letter contains a bit of contemporary news—the announcement of Luther's marriage to Catherine von Bora—and gossip.
2. Actually, Luther's first child was not born until a year after the marriage. Erasmus later retracted the allegation.
1. John of Saxony succeeded his brother Frederick as Saxon elector in the spring of 1525. Erasmus comments again on his relationship with Luther, against the background of their controversy concerning free will expressed in Erasmus' tract *Diatribe on Free Will* of 1524 and Luther's response, *The Bondage of the Will* of 1525. Luther's treatise was a bit vehement in tone, and thus Erasmus uses this letter to put the blame for the worsening relations between Catholics and Lutherans on Luther's explosive temperament.

gave the book a very modest title, calling it a discussion or confer-
ence. I do not assume the role of a judge, but of one who is
questioning and discussing, meanwhile laying aside all authority
except that of Holy Scripture. Luther could not have wanted a more
courteous opponent for debate. If his teaching is true, he had the
opportunity of establishing his position; if not, he could not be
admonished more courteously. In short, there was nothing in my
treatise that could offend anybody, no matter how irritable he might
be. And yet my courtesy stirred up a violent dislike for me among
theologians and some princes; they got the impression that I was not
combatting Luther but stood in secret collusion with him. In spite of
the fact that I refused to become involved and offered every possible
excuse not to do so, I have been pushed into this arena by most
powerful rulers; yet I swear to God that I have written nothing in
that work contrary to my sincere convictions; nor have I received a
single penny from any man to write against Luther. The volume he
sent me in return went far beyond the requirements of justice; it was
replete with sneers, witty remarks, insults, threats, accusations—so
much so that all the books he has published up to now do not contain
as much sly maligning as this single work.

I could put up with his calling me stupid, ignorant, drunkard,
addlebrained, thickskulled, or doltish. I am a human being, and such
insulting terms are human. But not content with such epithets, he
represents me as a godless Lucian for not believing in the existence of
God, and as a hog from Epicurus' herd for not believing that God is
concerned with human affairs. He makes of me a despiser of Sacred
Scripture, a destroyer of the Christian religion, an enemy of Christianity, an abominable hypocrite for being insincere in all the things
I have written out of a spirit of piety in my books, and he says that I
was merely covering up the worst form of godlessness. He made
several other remarks which no man with any self-restraint would
write of a Turk or a Mohammedan. He does all this at the instigation
of certain fickle fellows, and he does not realize what sort of mask he
is wearing. If Christianity consists in what he is teaching, then he
does not see how many thousands of men he has alienated by the insolence of his pen. For how can his teasing taunts, his silly mockery,
his barbed guffaws, his slanders, threats, and tricks, be in conformity
with such a serious and perilous business that has shattered almost

the whole world? If he had boldly and courageously destroyed my
arguments with references to Scripture, and with his own arguments,
he would have helped his cause and would have won over to his side
many men whom he is now alienating, not only in this issue but also
by his entire teaching. He proudly boasts of having the Spirit. But
who would believe that the Spirit of Christ dwells in a heart from
which proceed words that reveal such arrogance and bitterness, such
hostility, calumny, and scurrility? In spite of frequent admonitions,
he is not correcting this behavior; in fact, he is constantly becoming
worse.

For my part, I have done all I could with a sincere heart to assist
good learning and theology. Each man has his own gift from God,
and each furthers the Christian religion in a different way. But even
if Luther does not allow any person to disagree with him, well, there
are many men who do so in their published works; and they do not
argue politely, as I do, but use wild insults in raving against him.
Against such men he ought to have unsheathed the sword of his pen.
Several members of his own faction have published very impressive
articles, especially on the Eucharist, which attack his teaching. And
yet he does not allow me, who have never been a member of his
faction, to argue in a modest manner. What good can come from all
those sneering remarks, from that derisive laughter and maligning?
The only purpose it can serve is to stir up widespread sedition and
bring down the worst ill will upon the gospel and also upon good
learning, even though your Excellency may not incur any troubles as
a result of it. If it is the gospel that he is teaching, we should note
that it is not the purpose of the gospel to let us sin with greater
freedom, but to prevent us from sinning altogether, even if one could
do so with impunity. And the gospel does not undermine the authority of civil law; rather gives it firm support. Yet the law punishes any
man who groundlessly calls another a thief or a liar or a perjurer, and
inflicts death upon the authors of libelous pamphlets.

In his books, of which twelve thousand copies have already been
published, Luther states that I do not believe there is a God and that
I mock Holy Scripture; he thereby judges another man's conscience,
which God alone can do. And his disciples are imitating this
damnable example. Still, I am convinced that the law is not yet dead
in your land. If thieves and perjurers are punished, well, it is worse

than any kind of thievery to assail with deadly lies another man's reputation, which in the eyes of good men is more precious than life itself.

I am writing this, renowned Prince, not out of any desire for revenge, but because it is a matter of general public interest that Luther be forcibly reminded by law and your authority that he is not to rage with like insolence against anyone; for such conduct does no good to anybody but tends to destroy all good things.

TO DUKE GEORGE OF SAXONY[1]

EE 1743 (25–61)
Basel, September 2, 1526

There have crept into the life of Christians many vices that are no longer tolerable. Some have become so customary that they are regarded as virtues. Thus, religious-minded men are displeased by many things which they would like to see changed, if that were possible without world-wide turmoil. The Emperor, I know, shares this sentiment. But Luther is displeased by everything. However, even if nobody opposes his faction in writing, even if the Pope and the Emperor should wink at it, it will collapse all on its own, for there is such great dissension among its members. I need not mention that the morals of this crowd, which has been sired for us by this gospel, are not at all in keeping with the gospel. It still remains for prudence, with the effective backing of the authority of rulers, to restrain the seditious license of the Lutherans to prevent a more perilous conflagration from breaking out on the other side. I am talking about bad monks, also about some theologians of the same scurvy sort. What kind of men they are in your land, I do not know. But in Spain, Hungary, Poland, England, the Brabant, and especially in France, they have been the instigators, by conspiracy, of an astonishing tragedy for good learning and for myself; they think I either stirred up these interests or assisted them. They would have prevailed with their screaming and slanderous books (they rely upon

1. On George of Saxony, see Letter 1313, p. 163. In this letter Erasmus observes that the controversy precipitated by Luther has led to attacks upon sound learning too. He also comments on the reasons for his own involvement.

these supports), if the authority of princes and bishops had not checked their wild, Centaur-like rebellious uprisings. The same thing was done a short time ago by the Most Christian King in France.[2] If Your Excellency wishes to know some part of that story, you will be able to do so from the letter I have sent to Jerome Emser,[3] your servant and protégé. I did not dare to bother Your Excellency with such idle chatter, knowing that you are preoccupied with affairs of state.

I do not know how well equipped I am to fight Luther, or how much I would achieve by writing pamphlets. All I accomplished by my *Diatribe* was to confirm his teaching. But as far as my feeble powers allow, I shall not fail the cause of Catholic concord, to which I owe my very life. The second part of the *Hyperaspistes* would have been issued long ago,[4] but there sprang up a widespread conspiracy of certain individuals, whom I have just mentioned, and this forced me to drop what I had in hand and face the present evil with books and letters. . . . Even so I could have handled both affairs if in June my poor frail little body had not been attacked by such a violent illness that the doctors were unable to be of any help and did not dare to hold out hope. And so I relied upon God's support alone, and that is why I am alive today, and I shall live on as long as it seems best to Him.

TO NICHOLAS VARIUS[1]

EE 1756 (93–105)   Basel, September 26, 1526

In olden times the Corybants drove people into a frenzy with the din of timbrels and flutes.[2] That kind of noise has an amazing power

2. "Most Christian King" was an appellation of the French king.
3. One of Luther's early theological opponents.
4. *Hyperaspistes* was the title of Erasmus' reply to Luther's tract, *The Bondage of the Will*. The *Diatribe* was Erasmus' original statement on freedom of will.
1. On Nicholas Varius, a humanist and academician, see Allen, V, 527. Erasmus offers here a few brief reflections on music. His views of that art are discussed by J.-C. Margolin, *Érasme et la Musique* (Paris, 1965).
2. They were priests of a cult with origastic dances.

for arousing emotions. But the drums we use today sound even more horrible with their noisy anapaestic or pyrrhic beat. These we Christians now use in war instead of trumpets, as if it were not enough to be filled with courage, but one had also to become frenzied. Did I say war? We use them at weddings, too, and on holidays, and in churches. When they hear that wild, noisy rhythm, young girls rush out into the streets and the new bride does a dance. This is what sparks a holiday celebration; it is the height of fun when all day long throughout the streets wild confusion reigns, worse than that of the Corybants. In my opinion, this is the instrument used for celebrating holidays in hell, if they have any down there. Plato thinks the type of music enjoyed by a community is very important. What would he say if he heard such music among Christians?

TO KING JOHN III[1]

EE 1800 (155–211)   Basel, March 24, 1527

There is nothing so deeply buried in Sacred Scripture that Chrysostom cannot treat it in such a way as to make it dramatic and give it popular appeal. He digs out hidden aspects, displays them and presents them to the eye, and does so as one might hold the attention of the viewer with an exceptionally well-executed painting. The longer and the more closely one gazes at it, the more something new which had escaped the eye reveals itself, and each new discovery adds new pleasure. Truly, the divine Scriptures are like such a painting which the Spirit, an incomparable artist, has drawn for us with a heavenly brush. And if we are constantly engaged in contemplating it, we divert ourselves from the tedium of this world and continually derive some new pleasure from each new insight into eternal things. However, one cannot be a competent interpreter of this painting

1. Of Portugal. The letter forms the dedication of Erasmus' edition of *Chrysostomi Lucubrationes,* and in it he draws a verbal portrait of the orator Chrysostom and laments the absence of men of such quality in his own time. Since there was no acknowledgment of the dedication, Erasmus withdrew it when he published the works of Chrysostom in 1530.

unless he is himself a distinguished and remarkably discerning craftsman. Take for instance the way our friend Chrysostom dramatizes
the story of Lazarus and Dives. Who else could have perceived what
he points out in this tale? When the viewer, thinking he had seen
everything, is prepared to leave, Chrysostom calls him back. "Hey
there!" he calls out. "There's something else here that is particularly
worth noting." And then he points out anew one thing after another,
and does not let you leave the painting. Finally, while your mouth is
still hungry for more, he sends you away.

He frequently makes use of metaphors and comparisons, since they
are very helpful for illuminating and adding pleasure to one's style.
He is indeed remarkable in discovering such figures, but even more
remarkable an artist is his way of treating them. His method varies;
the comparison is made with something equal, or something greater,
or something less. It is amazing to see the degrees he has discovered
in minimizing and magnifying. He repeatedly touches on motives in
his audience. At times he praises them for being docile, or scolds
them for being lazy, or promises to offer them something worth
knowing if he notices that they are attentive and eager, or arouses
their interest by giving various reasons for treating a certain subject.
Occasionally he says over again what he has said on the previous day,
and quite often repeats himself within the same sermon. In this way
most eloquent Chrysostom adapted himself to the temper of the
common people, who are unlettered and thus forgetful. They do not
understand unless you explain things very clearly and without
finesse, and they do not remember anything unless you impress it
upon them by constant repetition.

I have mentioned this so that no one will condemn him for being
loquacious, since it was out of charity, which seeks to edify, that he
made these concessions to the weakness of his audience. So too did
Paul with the Thessalonians. He adapted himself to their ignorance.
With childlike simplicity he acted as a mother who feeds and looks
after her children. Nor does he hunt out brilliant sayings or exclamations, which bring shouts of applause from the audience. This style
of oratory was pleasing to Jerome and Ambrose. He does not employ
jokes, which are frequently used by Tertullian, sometimes to excess,
and even more frequently by Jerome. Instead, he holds the attention
of his listeners with an attractive and pleasant style and by delighting

them with his piety rather than with cleverness. A preacher will readily find a means of winning over his audience if he succeeds in getting people to know and love what they are learning. One can find in the Scriptures an abundance of material for charming and captivating pious hearts, without searching for bait in witty phrases from poets and mimes. If the teacher is on fire, he will easily set others aflame. If he deeply enjoys the things he preaches, he will easily inspire his listeners with that same feeling. This heart, this golden tongue which was aimed at the secular forum was diverted by Christ to the preaching of the gospel.

If only Christendom had such orators today! For all society depends especially upon such men for its instruction. The reason we understand almost nothing of the teachings of evangelical philosophy, the reason we are so insensitive to matters of charity, and the reason we are so hesitant in our faith with regard to things that should be absolutely certain, is that people can seldom hear preachers of the gospel—and even more seldom competent preachers. And yet the circumstances for preaching today are more favorable than in earlier centuries.

TO JOHN MALDONATUS[1]

EE 1805 (209–255)   Basel, March 30, 1527

The world has been awakened from its lethargy. Everywhere the croakings of the sophists have been booed. All the young men are taking up the study of languages and good learning, and actually not only young men. Theologians have been forced to return to the sources of Scripture and to the ancient doctors of the Church. The ruses of the pharisees have been detected; the preposterous opinions of the herd have been exposed to general ridicule. And yet, you will say, what turmoil there is in human affairs! But who ever saw the

---

1. A Spanish humanist and historian. In later years he considered Erasmus' writings heretical. See Allen, VI, 393. This brief excerpt expresses Erasmus' pessimistic assessment of his time with its corruption of both morals and learning.

condition of the world change for the better without great turmoil? Who has ever seen a person recover from a serious, though common, illness without being violently agitated by bitter and effective doses of medicine? Meantime, fugitive monks everywhere are marrying virgins dedicated to God; priests are living as laymen; the people are not obeying their bishops but denounce them and rebel against their rulers. Fasting is forgotten. Many show disdain for choice in the matter of food and indulge their appetites. Such people generally have no interest whatever in liberal studies, though they are warmly enthusiastic for any set of moral values except those of the gospel. What if God should send a plague of grasshoppers and locusts down upon us who so richly deserve it, so that we might be warned of our evil ways and return to the Lord? To me at least it seems that the curse which Moses in Deuteronomy invokes upon his people if they should disobey their law has almost been realized in our own time. "The Lord," he says, "will raise against you a far-off nation from the ends of the earth, like an eagle taking wing. This will be a nation whose language you do not understand, a nation grim of face, with neither respect for the old nor pity for the young. They will eat the offspring of your cattle. . . ." etc.[2] Such a nation has surged forth from the farthest reaches of Saxony and with incredible speed has spread over all the earth. Its leaders were equipped with Greek, Hebrew, and Chaldean learning; lacking in shame, they have refused to yield to bishops or universities, rulers or civil officials, the Emperor or the Pope. How much respect they have for an old man like myself is shown by the many, many libelous pamphlets they have circulated against me, especially Luther's *The Bondage of the Will,* in which the author outdid himself in bitterness after having surpassed everyone else in other respects. The rest of the prophecy has been fulfilled for us by the Peasants' Revolt.[3] For Moses' curse continues: "They will besiege you in all your towns." Surely we have experienced this. It would have been all over with this city if our prudent magistrates had not been vigorous and alert. We priests did not dare set foot outside the door.

Although these are all manifest signs that God is indignant at our

2. Deuteronomy 28:48 ff.
3. In Germany, 1524/25.

crimes, still nobody is reforming his life. Everybody is out for himself, trying to turn a public disaster to his own personal advantage. Some princes, I fear, may have in mind to touch the property of priests and monks and thus add to their own power. We also have some bishops who are anything but bishops. They are busy with establishing their own tyranny. As for theologians and monks, they are interested in titles or money or glory or revenge. The common folk are led on by the hope of freedom, so that they can do whatever they please. No matter which way the die falls, apparently the victory will not go to Christ but to men. Nor do I see what we could accomplish by an ecumenical council, if those who attend it are like the men we see acting out this tragedy. Severity thus far has only succeeded in making things worse.

TO WILLIAM WARHAM[1]

EE 1828 (20–62)   Basel, [ca. May 26], 1527

I have encouraged the interest of many men in good learning; in fact, I have encouraged and assisted theologians in their studies by my numerous works. If they contain any human shortcomings, the task of correcting those points which were rightly felt to be offensive might have been handed over to a group of men of integrity and learning whose judgment could have been followed. But those fellows are not offended by mistakes. Something else is galling them. Because the study of languages and sound scholarship are flourishing everywhere, they can see that their reputation in the eyes of men is diminishing. No wonder that all these many years they have been putting up such a vigorous battle against classical study. If they had been willing to accept it, they not only would not have obscured the greatness of other men, but would also have illumined their own. But as it is they are tormented by feelings of ill will. Throughout all the

1. See Letter 188, p. 53. Erasmus seeks to defend himself in this letter against the attacks from his scholastic detractors, noting at the same time the contribution his writings have made.

nations of the world, the pages of anything Erasmus ever published
are worn out from use, while the works of men like Sutor and Beda
are scoffed at by schoolboys.[2]

There is also another sore point. In my books I have sometimes
advised theologians to forget sophistic questions and to approach the
fonts of Scripture and read the holy doctors of the Church. I have
pointed out passages where they have made mistakes because of their
ignorance of languages and of antiquity. Likewise, I have advised
monks as to the meaning of true religion. That hit them badly. They
wanted the long-standing tyranny of theologians and monks to continue. But that was not beneficial for the Christian people. From my
books no heresy, no schism has been born. My detractors have been
stirring up turmoil by their shouting. But within a few years you will
see the scene of human events undergo a complete change; men will
embrace the moderation I have pursued in my writings. Those
obscurantists scream out against my *Colloquies,* though there is
scarcely another book more useful for uprooting silly ideas from the
minds of men. Princes must have the foresight to use their authority
to check such unruly commotions, which will otherwise end up in a
far worse disaster than has thus far been caused by the Lutherans.

My opponents have honorable pretexts for acting the way they do.
There are enough disturbances in the Church without our looking
around for new sources of turbulence; and we have abundant trouble
with those who openly profess and defend what Luther teaches without our creating difficulty for those who are fighting on our side
against Luther. Moreover, since the Emperor intends to reform certain customs in the Church, an action that would be impossible
without a large gathering of rulers, it is better to postpone any consideration of problems of that sort until that time. For the moment,
we must do all we can to strive for peace and set aside anything that
could cause dissension. Finally, if I were to spend most of my time
writing in a manner other than I should,—screams and slanders,
such conspiracies and wild pamphlets are incapable of curing human
failures. It is because of such methods that the Luther affair devel-

2. Sutor (d. 1537) lectured at the Sorbonne, then joined the Carthusian
order and distinguished himself by his rigid orthodoxy. On Beda see Letter
1581, p. 187.

oped from tiny sparks to the present conflagration that is raging over all the world.[3]

TO ROBERT ALDRIDGE[1]

EE 1858 (1–51; 147–174)   Basel, August 23, 1527

A certain fellow whom I consider not a theologian but a *tyrologus* stoned the name of Erasmus with seditious rashness from one of the most celebrated pulpits of London, namely St. Paul's Cross. He charged me with impiety and fraud because in my translation of St. John's Gospel, ch. 7, where the Church uses this reading: "The Spirit had not yet been given, because Jesus had not yet been glorified," I followed the Greek text and omitted the participle, translating thus: "There was no Spirit as yet because Jesus had not yet been glorified." In doing this, he maintained, I was placing the Catholic faith in very grave danger, because men might once again believe that the Spirit was a creature, not a being from all eternity, but one whose existence began in time. Thus spoke that babbler in thunderous tones; it was the height of insolence and of stupidity, for he addressed an audience comprising scholars and civic leaders and a very large crowd of townsfolk. . . .

I of course would gladly attribute such a godless, enormous crime to error or ignorance, except that this kind of excuse would not become, first of all a theologian, and secondly a preacher, and finally the place itself. For no one mounts into that pulpit without being forewarned or without carefully preparing a sermon worthy of such an audience. Certainly, before stepping into that pulpit, he should have looked up what I had written on this point in my *Annotations*. I note there that the Greek manuscripts are unanimous in giving the

3. Erasmus is saying that if he were to resort to slander, etc. he would only fan the controversy.
1. An English humanist (d. 1555) and intimate friend of Erasmus, later Bishop of Carlisle. Erasmus defends himself in this letter against certain charges by his detractors, specifically that of mistranslating a passage in the Gospel according to John, chap. 7.

reading I have translated, and I point out the orthodox meaning so that no one could miss it.

Now suppose what is neither true nor probable: that the word *datus* had been maliciously removed by the Greeks, since it is not found in a single manuscript. Did he want me, a translator of Greek, to add on my own initiative a word not found in the Greek text? If it had been removed, undoubtedly it would have been done by the Arians. Now, we find this subject discussed in the writings of those men who vigorously fought the Arians. . . . If any such distortion had been made by the Arians, the orthodox writers would never have remained silent about such a godless act of fraud. They would have done what they did on other occasions, namely, to expose resolutely any corruption they detected. Now, what Arian ever produced this passage in defense of his teaching? Had anyone done so, he would have been promptly booed off the stage. For the context itself explains the meaning. The words immediately preceding are: "He was speaking of the Spirit which those who believed in him were to receive," followed by the words: "for there was no Spirit as yet because Jesus had not yet been glorified." Notice that the evangelist is speaking here not of the nature of the Spirit, but of his gift and power. To say, "There was no Spirit as yet," is very much like the expression: "It was not yet day." Now there is no time without a day, but what we mean is that "there it was not yet daytime." We use very commonly the figurative expression: "There is no sun," when the sun is hidden behind the clouds and we cannot see it. So too we say, "There is no water," when the water is not deep enough to permit sailing. Thus, the evangelist says with regard to the disciples: "There was no Spirit as yet," that is to say, they had not as yet received that overflowing gift of the Spirit of which the prophet speaks. All this is explained in my annotation on this passage. It also mentions that it makes very little difference for the meaning whether *datus* is added or dropped. And not content with that, it also offers very definite proof that Augustine also had the same reading as is found in the Greek text. . . .

So that you can understand that what I am saying is true: the danger those fellows are talking about did not cause any fear for the ancients, because there was no danger. The point I am making caused all of them anxiety—Chrysostom, Theophylactus, and Augus-

tine—as is evident from their commentaries. Now if our reading had
been: "There was no Spirit as yet," and if we had understood the
words "in the disciples" (here I refer to the abundant Spirit which
overflowed like a river, according to the testimony of Joel), there
would then have been less opportunity for the Manichaeans, who
deny any authority to the books of the Old Testament, than in our
present reading: "He had not yet been given." If the translator had
added the participle for the sake of explanation, they would have
something they could plead in some way or other, on the grounds
that I had given the Church a new reading. But the truth is, those
fellows are misrepresenting the facts in this case too, although I left
the Vulgate text intact and in good faith undertook the translation of
the Greek text of the New Testament, whether that reading is correct or not. It may be that they will also be enraged at the men who
have recently done a Latin translation of the Old Testament from the
Greek, because they preferred not to follow the Latin codices but
rather the Greek manuscripts, whose text disagrees considerably with
our Latin text. But since it is known that this was due to the thoughtlessness of the scribes and not to any public authority nor to the
translator, their malicious charge is even more shameless. But if the
interpreter had translated it this way, or the participle had been
added by the consensus of the Church, then undoubtedly Augustine
and Jerome would have the same reading and the ancient codices
would be in agreement. Would to heaven this were the only instance
for which we might summon the brashness of scribes into court! It is
only too obvious how much license they took with the divine books.
Therefore let no one charge me with addition of *datus* in the translation of Didymus by Jerome, or in the Latin versions of Chrysostom,
since we see that this has constantly been done by translators or
copyists in order to stuff the Vulgate text, despite the frequent objections loudly voiced by the commentaries, whose words are of no
avail.

TO A MONK[1]

EE 1887 (9–22; 30–64)   Basel, October 15, 1527

I notice that a breed of people is emerging which my soul deeply abhors. I do not see anybody becoming better, but everybody worse, at least those I know. And so I am deeply grieved at having preached freedom of the spirit in my earlier writings. I did so in good faith, without any suspicion that such a breed would result. I was hoping for a decrease in human ceremonies, with a consequent increase in genuine piety. Now the ceremonies are discarded, but the result is not freedom of spirit but an unbridled license of the flesh. Some cities in Germany are filled with vagabonds—monks who have fled the monastery, married priests, most of them starving and naked. All they do is dance, eat, drink, and go whoring. They do not teach and do not learn. There is no moderation, no genuine goodness. Wherever such men exist, good learning and piety are in a state of collapse. I would write at greater length on this subject, if it were safe to commit it to writing. . . .

I know some men who were deluded by the mirage of freedom and left their religious communities. They changed their garb and married. Ever since they have been poor, exiles, and despicable to their family and friends, to whom they were once dear. Besides, their state is such that even those who might feel kindly toward them cannot safely help them out. What their state of conscience is, God alone knows; how delighted they are in their hearts with their type of fellowship is their concern. Now what kind of freedom is this: not to be able to say prayers, or to offer sacrifice, or to fast, or to abstain from meat? Just stop and reflect: such persons are most wretched even in this present world. If a man is young and rich, he might be able to enjoy the blessings of this life for a few years—that is, if there are any blessings here. But to do this at an unfavorable age is insanity

---

1. The recipient of this letter is unidentified. Here Erasmus speaks rather despondently about the state of society—about those who have all too readily left the monasteries—and offers a word or two as to the future.

rather than stupidity. "But one is weighed down by regulations, manifestations of ill will, and such things." Anything of that sort becomes very light, if good will is present. And in the world one would have to put up with many more woes. May God grant a better mind to fellows who are disturbing your peace of soul with such stories.

I swear, if I had just a tiny bit of strength left in my poor little body so that I could at least live on, I would rather spend my days with you than be the topmost bishop in the Emperor's palace. You do not realize your own good fortune or the wretchedness of this world. We have no council to look forward to. The dissension among princes is blocking it, and when it does come it will be too late. If it ever does convene, sixteen years will be spent on matters other than ceremonies. Therefore, my dear brother in the Lord, by our long-standing and ever constant friendship and in Christ's name, I beg you and plead with you to rid your heart completely of that impatient boredom and not to lend an ear to the pernicious stories of men who are not going to be of any help to you. Instead, they will ridicule you once they have enticed you into their trap. If you wholeheartedly scorn the illusions of this world and dedicate yourself completely to Christ and devote your time entirely to the reading of Scripture and meditation on the heavenly life, believe me, you will find an abundance of consolation, and all that little tedium you talk about will vanish like smoke. If you follow your counselor's advice and discover that my advice is not true, then complain to me.

TO JOHN GACY[1]

EE 1891 (205–228)   [Basel, *ca*. October 17, 1527]

Some people say that this Lutheran conflagration began with my writings. But they are shameless liars. Up to now nobody has been able to produce one single condemned teaching, however insignifi-

1. John Gacy, or Gachi, was a Franciscan monk and a staunch advocate of the Catholic cause. In addition to a brief response to those who accuse him of having been the real cause of the Lutheran controversy, Erasmus defends himself here against the charge that his writings disparage the monastic orders.

cant, which I hold in common with Luther. Ultimately the facts themselves show how shamefully they lied when they also said I was in collusion with Luther. (No doubt in the same way Hector was in collusion with Achilles.) You can form your own judgment on this point if you read my *Diatribe* and then Luther's response to it, which is the most hostile attack he ever made on anybody, and then the two volumes of my *Hyperaspistes,* which is an answer to Luther.

Now, I know very well that the statement is made in some quarters that my writings disparage the monastic orders. Of course I do think that Christianity would be no worse off if it did not have all these different religious habits and food regulations and titles. I think this especially because monasticism has deteriorated almost to the point where, apart from externals, the monks themselves are generally worse than other men. A good number of monasteries have no religious discipline; one can live a religious life better in almost any other place. I have never before put this in writing; and yet what difference can it make to put in writing what is common knowledge? The only thing I have been doing is to give advice as to what things form the basis of true devotion to God. I criticize certain persons who employ cajoling expressions, threats, and other illegal practices to carry away illiterate and simple folk who do not understand themselves, nor the religious life for that matter; and once these people are trapped, they cannot disentangle themselves. These men have absolutely no regard for the good of the young lads and of their own order. It would be more beneficial to have a few genuine members than a huge number no matter what they are like.

TO JOHN OF HEEMSTEDE[1]

EE 1900 (68–129)   [Basel, November 1527]

Whatever labor he [Johann Froben] undertook for me, he undertook out of love for learning. He seemed born to honor, to illumine, and to advance learning. In order to attain that goal he shirked no toil, no sleepless night. He thought it reward enough if a good author

1. A member of the Louvain Charterhouse. This letter is a eulogy on the printer Johann Froben of Basel.

was placed in a dignified way in the hands of the public. Therefore, how could I ever have robbed a man with such an attitude? Whenever he showed us and other friends the first pages of a great author, he would leap with joy, his face beaming and triumphant. It seemed as if he had already reaped in superabundance the reward for his effort and looked for no further return. I do not intend to sing the praises of Froben by casting blame on others. It is only too well known how many editions of authors have reached us even from printers in Venice and Rome which were issued in a faulty and shabby manner. But from the publishing house of Froben, in the course of a few years how many volumes marched forth to meet their public, and in what a dignified manner! For this reason, he always kept his shop free from contentious pamphlets, a source of great profit for other printers, for he did not want to stain letters and learning with ill will.

He printed two editions of Jerome. As for Augustine, he devoted himself to putting out an equally dignified edition of his works, even though several friends, including myself, tried to deter him.[2] He often remarked to his intimate friends that he hoped to live long enough to complete Augustine. He did see the completion of the first two volumes. It was a noble ambition on his part, and his was a spirit worthy of immortality. But the eternal Deity, whose designs are hidden in a mystery which we may not question nor protest, decreed otherwise.

He was advanced in years, but vigorous and sound of health. At no time during his life had he been confined to bed with illness. Six years ago he fell down a high stairway onto a brick pavement. The fall could easily have killed him, but he recovered. As often happens, his body retained some ill effects of that mishap, no matter how much he tried to conceal it. He was so noble a man that he would feel embarrassed at showing pain. A year prior to his death, he was seized by a severe pain around his right ankle. The doctors were promptly on hand to perform their services; but they only aggravated the disorder, for they disagreed in their diagnosis and therefore prescribed different remedies. Some of them suggested amputation of the foot. Eventually, a certain doctor from out of town was able to

2. Vives edited the *De Civitate Dei* and Erasmus the rest.

ease the pain at least to the extent that Froben could get some sleep and take food. At length he was strong enough to make two trips on horseback to Frankfurt. The disorder was now localized in the toes of his right foot; that was the only part of his body that he could not move; otherwise he was well. The doctor and I often advised him to appear less frequently in public, or, if he did go out, to wear clothing that would afford better protection against the cold. But he refused to listen. He thought it would be shameful to give up any of his former habits and thereby give the appearance of being sick. Then two fingers of his right hand became paralyzed, a symptom of the disease hovering over him. He concealed this fact, thinking it unmanly to make any concessions to illness. But one day, while busy with something or other high up, he suffered a full attack of the disease—so it is thought—and fell head first onto the pavement, with severe injury to his skull. Stretched out on a bed, he made no attempt to open his eyes. He gave no sign of consciousness and no indication at all of being alive, except that he moved his left hand. His whole right side was numb with the paralysis he had been concealing. He was unconscious for two days. Shortly before his death he regained consciousness. With difficulty he opened his left eye slightly, but could not move his tongue. He lived only six hours after that.

Thus was our friend Froben released from human cares. He passed to a happier life, leaving behind him deep sorrow for his wife, his children, and his friends, and a profound feeling of loss for the entire city and all who knew him. His death should cause all lovers of good learning to show their tears and mourning, to adorn his tomb with green garlands and blossoms, sprinkle it with water, and to burn incense there—if anything is gained by such kindly offices. At any rate, it will be a sign of gratitude to pray fervently for the deceased, celebrate his memory with due praises, and support the publishing house of Froben. It will not cease to operate because its owner has departed; rather, it will strive with might and main so that what he has established may ever move forward to something greater.

TO MARTIN BUCER[1]

EE 1901 (23–41; 50–99)   Basel, November 11, 1527

I want you to know that the first and most important reason that kept me from joining your communion was my conscience. If my conscience could have been convinced that God was the origin of this activity, I would have been serving in your camp long ago. My second reason is that I have noticed a large number of men in your ranks who are far removed from all evangelical sincerity. I am not reporting rumors and suspicions; I am speaking of knowledge gained from experience, in fact, gained at the cost of sorrow to myself. This information does not pertain merely to the common folk but also to men who apparently amount to something, not to mention those of noble rank. It is not for me to judge instances I do not know. The world is large and wide. I have known some who were excellent persons prior to joining your church; I do not know what they are like now. At any rate, I have learned that some have become worse, and no one has become better as far as human judgment can discern.

The third reason for not joining is the terrible dissension among your leaders.[2] I will not mention the "prophets" and the Anabaptists.[3] But what about the acrimonious pamphlets resorted to by Zwingli, Luther, and Osiander in combatting one another! I have never approved of harsh treatment on the part of rulers, but they are being goaded on to it by the conduct of certain individuals, who should have made the gospel attractive by their holiness and courtesy. . . .

I can see a savage and bloody age ahead of us, if the party which

---

1. *Ca.* 1491–1551. This former Dominican monk became an eminent Protestant theologian and the reformer of Strassburg. Erasmus seeks to explain in this letter his reasons for not joining the followers of Luther.
2. Of the "new faith."
3. The "prophets" are probably such radical Protestant reformers as Andreas Carlstadt or Ludwig Haetzer. The pamphlets mentioned below pertain to the controversy over the Lord's Supper. Andreas Osiander was the Protestant reformer of Nürnberg.

has been provoked ever catches its breath, as it is obviously now doing. You may object that in every large group of people there are going to be some bad fellows. But it should certainly be the task of the leaders to be particularly concerned about morals and not have fellowship with liars, perjurers, drunkards, and lechers. Yet I hear, and can practically see, that things are turning out quite differently. If the husband had found he had a more submissive wife, the teacher a more docile pupil, the magistrate a more tractable citizen, the employer a more faithful employee, and the buyer a more honest salesman, that would have been a high recommendation for the gospel. But the fact is, the moral behavior of some individuals is now causing apathy in those who at first supported this movement out of a love for piety and hatred for pharisaim; and now that the rulers see a lawless mob emerging, made up of vagabonds, runaways, spend-thrifts, forlorn wretches, and most of them sinful fellows, they curse it. This is true even of those who originally had high hopes for the movement.

I mention all this with deep sorrow, not only because I can foresee that a mishandled matter is going to turn out for the worse, but also because eventually I will have to bear the brunt of this. Some hostile persons are blaming my writings for the fact that scholastic theologians and monks in several places are becoming less important than they would like to be, that ceremonies are being discarded, and that the supreme authority of the pope is being slighted. These theologians and monks blame me, although the source of this evil is quite evident. They were pulling the rope too tight, and now it is breaking. They set the pope's authority almost above Christ, they measured all piety by ceremonies, they placed indefinite strictures upon confession; the monks ruled with impunity and by this time were plotting open tyranny. Eventually, as the proverb has it, the rope that was pulled tight broke. No other result was possible. I am terribly afraid that the same thing will someday happen to the rulers, if they keep pulling their own cord too tight. To repeat, since the other side started the performance of its drama, there could not have been any other conclusion than the one we see. May we not have to witness greater horrors!

The leaders of this movement had the obligation, if Christ was their aim, to refrain from vice, and in fact from every semblance of wrongdoing, and not to be in any way an obstacle to the gospel, while studiously avoiding even such conduct as is permitted but not advisable. Above all, they should have cautiously shunned every type of sedition. If they had handled this matter with sincerity and moderation, they would have had the added support of rulers and bishops, for they are not all hopeless cases. And they should not have destroyed anything unless there was a better substitute available. As things now stand, those who have given up the divine office do not pray at all. A large number who have shed their pharisaical garb are now, in other matters, worse than before. Those who scorn the regulations of bishops do not obey the commandments of God either. Those who neglect choice in the matter of food are now indulging their appetite. A great tragedy is daily unfolding before our eyes; we also hear about it from others. I never agreed to abolition of the Mass,[4] no matter how much I despised the sordid and greedy kind of priests who celebrated it. Many practices could have been altered without turmoil. These days some people dislike everything that is old—as if it were possible to form a new world overnight! Devout people will always have to put up with some things.

TO FELIX[1]

EE 1956 (24–42)   Basel, February 21, 1528

With regard to the story about the womb of the Blessed Virgin, the facts are these. I was having dinner at the home of the procurator of the Archdeacon. After the dinner grace was said by a servant of the host; it was quite long and took about as much time as a short Mass. There was a *Kyrie eleison*, then the *De Profundis*, then several *Pater Noster's*, and what not. Finally he seemed to be finished and we answered *Amen*. Since he had stopped praying, I thought there

4. In Protestant churches the Mass had been abolished; indeed, its abolition proved to be the characteristic feature of the reformers.

1. Hardly anything is known about the recipient of the letter. See Allen, VII, 335. This excerpt contains a very brief statement of Erasmus' attitude toward the Virgin Mary, arising from a comically awkward personal incident.

was nothing further to come. So I turned toward the guests and the host, intending to express my thanks to them, when unexpectedly the servant added: "And blessed be the womb of the Virgin Mary." I was embarrassed at having hinted that the grace was long enough even without that final flourish, and so I said lightly: "The one thing still lacking was the blessed womb." I did not intend the remark to be in any way contempt for the Virgin; I only meant that this prayer of thanks was a hodgepodge made up of a variety of ingredients. My devotion to the Virgin is obvious from the two prayers which I published some time ago: The *Paean* and the *Obsecratio,* and also from the new Mass which I recently published with the approval of the Archbishop of Besançon.[2] . . . The rumor of this incident got as far as Paris, as Beda informed me in a letter. And I have absolutely no doubt but that it started with those pseudo-evangelicals who are using every possible means to attack me because I refuse to go along with their insanity.

TO HERMANN OF WIED[1]

EE 1976 (26–97)   Basel, March 19, 1528

The injury done to me personally would cause me very little distress if it were counterbalanced by advantage to the general public, and especially by glory to Christ, who must be the one and only goal of all our doing. The only true prosperity and happiness possible in human affairs is that which Christ accomplishes in us. This he does when our human passions are at rest and our will is obedient to his. We have already had more than enough trouble without the relentless raging of the monarch, which has brought so much disaster to the

2. This Mass is Erasmus' *Virginis matris apud Lauretum cultae Liturgia* (1523). The other two works cited are the *Paean in genera demonstratiuo Virgini marti dicendus* and *Obsecratio ad aandem semper gloriosam,* the one a praise, the other a supplication to the Virgin, both found in volume V of the Leyden edition of Erasmus' works.

1. Archbishop of Cologne. He subsequently embraced the Protestant cause, but eventually returned to Rome. Erasmus comments here on the existing ecclesiastical turmoil and possible ways to resolve it.

world. And yet this raging continues to grow more and more violent and threatens the complete disruption of society unless some god—a *deus ex machina*—suddenly appears on the scene and gives this stormy tragedy an unexpected ending. Meanwhile, we who are caught in this wild tempest are desperate because there is almost nothing left but prayer; and so we cling to the remains of the wrecked ship, hoping that after we have been buffeted long and hard, Christ will direct us to a haven of safety. I am not casting away all hope, if only the Lord, in whose hands are the hearts of kings, will deign to change the mentality of rulers so that they consider it a far more splendid thing to subdue anger rather than the enemy, and a much safer thing to base their sovereignty on kindly service than on physical strength; and that it is a more effective means for extending their sway to have a reputation for clemency than for boldness. When things are in turmoil, a peaceful alliance cannot be suddenly arranged, though perhaps a brief truce. Meantime negotiations for repairing the state of affairs might be undertaken in a leisurely fashion. As things now stand, I am afraid we may win what is called a Cadmean victory,[2] one just as sad for the winners as for the losers.

But as I said, the only thing I can do is pray. More than once I have encouraged in the Emperor the desire for peace, and his response in his most recent letter was this: "Up to now we have vigorously done all that was possible to guarantee peace in the realm. There is no reason for anyone to doubt it. What we can accomplish for the present and what we will accomplish hereafter, that we prefer to make known by action." These words do not savor very much of peace. War carries with it an endless train of woes, which however make people distressed rather than godless. Much more serious is the damage done in the realm of ideas, because it can deprive us of soundness of mind, which is our most precious possession. And besides, the contending parties in this area are almost more stubborn than are warring monarchs. By some strange twist of fate, those who do most hard to either cause are the very ones who think they are most valiant in defending their own. Some persons are so vigorously

2. Refers to the slaying of all but five of the men who sprang from the dragon's teeth sown by Cadmus, mythical founder of Thebes: therefore, a victory won at great cost.

engaged in this tug-of-war that once the rope is strained beyond its limit, as the proverb goes, it will snap and both sides will fall on their rumps.

It is not necessary to investigate every question, much less to make pronouncements on them. It would be more advisable to treat only those matters which are particularly serviceable for evangelical doctrine. The world has its own rights and the schools have their own exercises. But the people should be given only that which is undoubtedly true and necessary for the matter of faith and conducive to pious living. Some, for instance, make confession too exacting; others are doing away with it completely, when there could be a happy medium between the two. Similarly, some have promoted the Mass with the purpose of making it more a source of money for illiterate and disgraceful priests (or rather, Mass priests) and a support for men of sinful lives. On the other hand, some want to abolish the Mass completely. Here, too, we might steer a middle course whereby we would have a Mass that is more sacred and not desecrated by abuses, but still we would have the Mass. Likewise the cult of the saints is sometimes so excessive and superstitious that it almost obscures the worship of Christ. And some go to the opposite extreme and completely condemn the cult of saints as blasphemous. Some are endeavoring to wipe out the whole monastic status, while others overstress the importance of human regulations and ceremonies, forms of address and types of habit. By following a prudent middle course in this and other matters we could uphold the authentic teachings of faith with greater certainty and effectiveness. Confession would then be more sincere and less of a worry; the Mass would be more sacred and awesome; and we would have perhaps fewer but better priests and monks.

Although this world-wide upheaval causes me great anguish, I do still have some spark of hope that divine providence will direct these disturbances to a happy ending. A very effective means for bringing it about is a prudent moderation on the part of the bishops. They should curb seditious godlessness while always having regard for true piety—that is to say, they should tear out the weeds without uprooting the wheat. This would be more easily done if we set aside our private interests and kept in mind just one aim: the glory of Christ. As it is, a large number are concerned only with their own affairs, and as a result we suffer both privately and publicly. We throw the blame on someone else, whereas this universal disaster is really the hand of God inviting all men to change their lives. If we ran to Him for refuge, He would readily turn this tempest of human affairs into a bright, sunny day.

TO ALFONSO VALDES[1]

EE 2018 (1–72)   Basel, August 1, 1528

I have learned very plainly from other men's letters[2] what you express so discreetly, as is your way: that there are some who seek to make "Terminus," the seal on my ring, an occasion for slander. They protest that the addition of the motto *Concedo nulli* [I yield to none] shows intolerable arrogance. What is this but some deadly malady, which consists in maliciously accusing everybody? . . . These fault-finders, or rather false accusers, blindly criticize what they neither see nor understand; so violent is the disease. And all the time they think themselves pillars of the Church, whereas all they do is to expose their stupidity combined with extreme malice, while their notoriety is already greater than it should be. They imagine that it is Erasmus who says *Concedo nulli*. If they read my writings they would see that there is none so humble that I rank myself above him, being more liable to yield to all than to none.

Those who know me well from close association will attribute any shortcoming to me except arrogance, and will acknowledge that I am closer to the Socratic saying, "This alone I know, that I know nothing," than to this "I yield to none." But if they imagine that I have so insolent a mind as to consider myself superior to all others, do they also think me such a fool as to announce it in a motto? If they

1. *Ca.* 1490–1532. A Spanish humanist and government official, from 1522 in the service of Charles V, whose trusted counselor he became. He was also author of a few literary works, notably a dialogue on the Sack of Rome entitled *Lactantio*. Alfonso's brother Juan was a noted "Catholic evangelical." The letter was printed at the end of Erasmus' *Interpretatio in Ps. LXXXV* and is an explanation of his use of a pagan motto.
2. These letters are lost.

had any Christian spirit they would understand those words either as not mine or as having another meaning. They see there[3] a sculptured figure, in its lower part a stone, in its upper part a youth with flying hair. Does this look at all like Erasmus? If this is not enough, they see the word "Terminus" written on the stone; if one takes this as the last word, an iambic dimeter acatalectic will result: *Concedo nulli terminus.* If one begins with this word, it will be a trochaic dimeter acatalectic, *Terminus concedo nulli.* What if I had painted a lion and added as a motto "Flee, unless you prefer to be torn to pieces!"? Would they attribute these words to me rather than the lion? What they are doing is just as silly, for I think I am more like a lion than a stone.

They will argue, "We did not notice that it was verse, and we know nothing about Terminus." Is it then to be a crime henceforth to have written verse, because they have not learned metrical theory? At least, as they knew that in mottoes of this kind one actually aims at a measure of obscurity in order to exercise the guessing powers of those who look at them, if they did not know of Terminus—about whom they could have learned from the books of Augustine[4] or Ambrose—they should have inquired of experts. In former times the boundaries of a field were marked with some sign. This was a stone projecting above the earth which the laws of the ancients ordered never to be moved. Here the Platonic saying is relevant, "remove not what thou hast not planted."[5] The law was reinforced by religious awe, to deter the ignorant multitude from removing the stone by making it believe that to violate the stone was to violate a god in it. The Romans called this god Terminus, and to him there was dedicated a shrine and a festival, the Terminalia. This god Terminus, according to the Roman historian, was the only one who refused to yield to Jupiter, because "while the birds allowed the deconsecration of all other sanctuaries, in the shrine of Terminus they were unpropitious."[6] Livy tells this story in the first book of his *History.* Again in Book 5 he narrates how "when after the taking of auguries the Capitol was being cleared, Juventas [Youth] and Terminus

3. Refers to a medal depicting Terminus.
4. St. Augustine, *Civitas Dei*, 4.29, 5.21, 7.7.
5. Plato, *Leges*, 11.1:913 C.
6. Livy, 1.55, 5.54.

would not allow themselves to be moved." This omen was welcomed with universal rejoicing, for they believed that it portended an eternal empire. The youth is useful for war, and Terminus is fixed.

Here they will exclaim, "What have you to do with a mythical god?" He came to me, I did not adopt him. When I was called to Rome, and Alexander, Archbishop of St. Andrews, was summoned home from Siena by his father, King James of Scotland, as a grateful and affectionate pupil he gave me several rings for a memento of our time together. One of these had "Terminus" engraved on the jewel. An Italian who was interested in antiquity pointed this out, which I had not known before. I seized on the omen and interpreted it as a warning that the end (*terminus*) of my existence was not far off; at that time I was in about my fortieth year. To keep this thought in mind I began to seal my letters with this sign. I added the verse, as I said before. And so from a heathen god I made myself a motto, exhorting me to correct my life. For death is truly a boundary which knows no yielding to any. But in the medal [depicting Terminus] there is added in Greek, "Consider the end of a long life." They will say, "You could have carved on it a dead man's skull." Perhaps I should have done that, if it had come my way. But this pleased me because it came to me by chance, and then because it had a double charm for me; from the allusion to an ancient and famous story, and from its obscurity, a quality specially belonging to mottoes.

TO MARTIN LYPSIUS[1]

EE 2045 (213–268)   Basel, September 5, 1528

In Spain a member of the Franciscan order who was considered learned and pious published some articles which were excerpts from my writings. One of them, which was extremely heretical, was taken from my *Enchiridion*, where I had written that the apostles possessed a true and genuine[2] theology. This fellow kept shouting in public: "Who can put up with such a writer? He says there is no true

1. See Allen, VII, 225/750. In this letter Erasmus derides the "pseudo learning" of some of his opponents from the ranks of the Franciscan order.
2. "*Germanam.*" There is a word play here on the Latin for "genuine" and "German."

theology except in Germany, although that country is practically crawling with heresies." He produced another excerpt which was no less incriminating. In the fifth canon of my *Enchiridion* I had stated that it was no great thing to be buried in the cowl of St. Francis and that the habit would have no value unless one had imitated Francis' life. And then he commented that I held the same opinion as Montanus, who said that those who had fallen into sin after baptism could not be restored to grace, as if the cowl of St. Francis were the only means of being restored to grace, or as if the cowl could give a man the right disposition. He also condemned the passage in my *Paraclesis* where I express the wish that all women should read the Gospels and the Epistles.[3] He considered that heretical, although two extant epistles of St. John are addressed to a woman. And how does he prove his charge of heresy? "That," he says, "contradicts St. Paul's command in I Timothy, ch. 2: 'During instruction a woman should be quiet and respectful, etc.'" As if a woman could not even open her mouth at home, or as if for a woman to speak at an assembly of Christians meant the very same thing as a woman reading something in quiet at home. This leader of the Franciscan tribe collected and published about thirty such items.

Not long ago a Dominican prior, regarded as a scholar among his own men, approached a physician who is extraordinarily learned in Latin and Greek and also zealous for my reputation. His intention was to wean the doctor from his attachment to me by employing deceptive language. He got no results with that method; in fact, it only encouraged the doctor to have a loftier opinion of me and to praise me more highly. Then the theologian dropped the mask of modesty and began to reveal his true sentiments. His verdict was that Erasmus' books were not worthy of being read by good men because they were replete with filthy insults. The doctor asked for an example. He answered, "Just read his recent work *On Marriage*." "What's wrong with it?" "He calls bishops buggers and also says they have four or five mistresses apiece." This got a laugh out of the doctor, who then said, "You're a sharp-eyed fellow all right. You saw something I missed, though I read it more than once." The theologian was very confident of his case and so he said, "Bring me the book

3. His *Paraclesis ad Christianae philosophiae studium* ("Plea for the study of Christian Philosophy"), first published together with his Greek New Testament in 1516.

and I'll show you." The book was brought and he pointed out the passage in which I discuss the present practice of not receiving a man into the order of priesthood who had unwittingly married a woman who was no longer a virgin, whereas one who has had relations with several prostitutes can be raised not only to the honor of the priesthood but even to four or five bishoprics. My exact words were: "One who has married a woman who is no longer a virgin without his knowing that fact is said to have shared his body; one who has had relations with several prostitutes has not shared his body, but is, so to speak, complete and whole. The Greek word for this is ιέλειος. Such a man can receive four or five bishoprics, if it so please him." The doctor with a puzzled look asked, "But where is the word bugger? Where are the five mistresses?" From the prior's words of explanation the doctor finally realized how remarkably idiotic the man was. The Spanish, like the Italians, commonly use the word *putus* to mean a sodomite or a male prostitute, just as they use *putana* to refer to a female prostitute. Now the ancients, using an expression found in early Roman law, spoke of something as being *purus putus* if it was genuine and complete. From *putus* we have the verb *putare* in the sense of cleansing. So there you have the "bugger." But where did he find the five mistresses? He thought that the word *episcope* [bishopric] was a femine form of *episcopus,* just as we use *domina* [mistress] as a femine form of *dominus* [lord]. I preferred to use the Greek word ἐπιδκοπή for bishopric, just as St. Paul did, because the word *episcopatus* is neither a Greek word nor a Latin one. The men who expose their stupidity by using such examples are the very ones who complain that I am detrimental to their authority.

TO HAIO CAMMYNGHA[1]

EE 2073 (10–35; 83–99)   Basel, November 12, 1528

It is an old and well-known adage that birds of a feather flock together. In this case there must be some strange mysterious force of nature that is drawing us together, like the power of a magnet to

1. From Friesland, a friend of Erasmus, who in this letter describes the style of life in his own household.

attract steel. However, my dear young man, it is not very easy for any and every person who lives in my household to adapt himself to my manner of life. The constant and sometimes excessive application to the pursuit of learning, as well as my age, which is becoming burdensome, but above all my health, which is a constant reminder of my mortality, all compel me to be a man who does not care for much company. Otherwise, however, I am naturally inclined to please everyone in every way possible. But if I am not deceived in my feelings toward you, if your letter has not given a false picture of your disposition, and if those men who have a thorough knowledge of your character from intimate acquaintance are telling the truth, then I shall not be reluctant to receive a person of your talent into my household; and I hope that you will be a source of honor and pleasure to our little family.

These are my thoughts on the matter. Now it would be up to your prudence to form a plan to suit the circumstances and to consider what would be most beneficial for your own interests, which I would not want to suffer in any way on my account. You will find that the relish served at my table is literary talk rather than fancy foods. Luxury is a total stranger to it; in fact, my table is not much more sumptuous than was that of Pythagoras or Diogenes, whenever they had dinner at home. You will say that you have come to a school of frugality, or that you are a guest at the common mess at Sparta. For me this is the most delightful and elegant form of living: for a man to be constantly moderate and to enjoy both peace of mind and good health, and to rise from a table where the fruitful conversation has been more pleasurable than the food, and to have his hunger satisfied without being troubled by a growling stomach and without having such a stuffed body that his mind is sluggish in case he has some studying or other serious matter to attend to. . . .

Since I understand that you find nothing so attractive as learning, if it so please you, come and be my guest and you will be as welcome as anyone could possibly be. You will come to a philosophical table and furthermore, in case you prefer this, to a medicinal table. It has given better health to some who had had poor health. At any rate, and I hope Nemesis does not hear this remark, not a single guest at my table has ever been sick. I always have very small numbers of guests. My only reason for this is so that I can ease the weariness of long, lonely hours by the interchange of conversation while eating and during the time right after eating, for I regularly spend that time relaxing, especially after dinner. I do not pursue any strenuous study then unless there is something urgent. And we never allow that period of conversation to be completely without some discussion of belles-lettres. If you decide to join our group, I will undertake that you shall not regret sharing our company. But if circumstances prompt you to decide otherwise, I want you to consider this letter as a guarantee that, no matter where you or I shall be, Erasmus is and will always be one of those who sincerely wish you every blessing; and you shall never ask any favor of me in vain, provided it is something I can do.

TO LOUIS BER[1]

EE 2136 (26–38; 117–204)   Basel, March 30, 1529

Once these stormy times are over, the Lord's clemency will grant happier days when His anger has turned to mercy. The turmoils which we today are witnessing, or rather enduring, are such, in my opinion, as no one has ever witnessed or read about or heard of from the cradle days of the Church up to the present moment. I for my part can see in this the providence of God; He is trying His chosen ones like gold in the fire and testing them to see if they truly trust and love Him. How this is affecting others, I do not know; as for myself, all these tumultuous calamities have failed to shatter me; in fact, they have given me added strength. And yet, far be it from me to attribute this to my own merits or powers; rather, I can see here the hand of the Most High revealing His power in my weakness. Having given myself up once and for all to His will, I am confident that His clemency will never fail me to the very end. . . .

What the outcome will be of these disturbances, I leave to the Lord. I am convinced that the man who has planted his foot on solid

1. Lived 1479–1554. A theologian and professor at Basel until the introduction of Protestantism there in 1529, after which he accompanied Erasmus to Freiburg. In this letter Erasmus reflects on the positive aspects of the religious troubles, and once again on his own involvement in them.

rock cannot perish. Very likely the Lord wants to use all these revolutions and disasters to punish us for our manner of life, which, if one may speak the truth, had deviated altogether too far from genuine piety. This is particularly true of those who were apparently the pillars of the Church, not only as regards the vigor of the evangelical spirit, but also from the viewpoint of the constitutions of former popes concerning the moral integrity of priests and clerics. A long list of such constitutions is given by John Gerson in one of his works. How much the morals of our own age have declined even from Gerson's day! Once upon a time the Lord employed frogs, locusts, grasshoppers, and other plagues to urge the Egyptians to repentance. However, since I rely on divine assistance no feeling of resentment nor desire for reverge shall ever drive me to the point where I would want to be either a locust or a Pharaoh. Let the Spouse punish His Bride as He wishes; for He knows what is best for her. No allurement, no savagery will ever be able to tear me away from my union with the one and only Dove. The malice of men can destroy what one has. It can destroy his reputation, it can destroy his life, but it cannot destroy his piety, a man's most precious possession, unless we willfully surrender that treasure of ours which we have received through the generosity of our Spouse. Therefore, the safest thing for us to do, in my opinion, is to entrust ourselves completely to that Physician. The artist understands his own creation; the potter understands the vessel of clay that he has fashioned. Let Him mould it and remould it; let Him break it and crush it. What has been entrusted to His hands cannot perish forever. Whether He offers us bitter absinthe by sending us sorrows or comforts us with more soothing remedies, whether He burns or cuts, our loyal and loving Physician is, beyond all doubt, accomplishing what is best for our welfare. To be sure, He alone has the power to give life even by destroying, and He alone makes that His ordinary treatment. Truly, as the old Greek proverb has it, "The slayer is benevolent."

At this point you may wish to ask me if I have ever been tempted, as a result of some superficial sensation, to join some faction. I shall not be in the least reluctant to open up my heart completely to a friend whose loyalty is so well attested and to pour out my feelings before you. There are occasions when, as I reflect upon the perverseness and obstinacy of certain individuals, I experience—and it is a human feeling—a desire for revenge. But that sense merely grazes my skin; it never penetrates the surface. It is like the prick of a pin, not a deep wound. For this feeling is promptly rejected by my deeper self. "What means this impious thought? Would you, just to take revenge on malicious men, lay impious hands upon Mother Church —the Church which gave you birth in Christ through the sacred waters of baptism, which nourished you with the word of God, which strengthens and vivifies you with all her sacraments? Just to hurt impious men, will you yourself become impious? And just to avenge a temporary wrong, will you inflict upon your soul an irreparable damage? And while trying to hurt an enemy, will you harm yourself more than any enemy could? Consider your frail body—how few years are left to you! Just when you are reaching harbor, will you deliberately fling yourself back into the deep? No vengeance should be so attractive as to prevent you from becoming better day by day. This turmoil is transient. What is eternal is alone important. Aim at that."

Such thoughts make it very easy for me to dispel the feelings which I do experience without danger from time to time. However, the result of all of this is that I realize much better what I have been told, namely, that Arius, Tertullian, Wycliffe, and others left the Church because of the hostility of the clergy and the wickedness of some monks, and that it was their personal grievances that caused general harm to the Church. I would rather forfeit my reputation and my life than stoop to such a dastardly deed. A person with such a spirit, in my opinion, will not easily slip into heresy. If only I could remedy all the disasters of the Church at the expense of my life! It was not out of a desire for revenge that I candidly answered some persons who, under the guise of zeal, made false charges against my writings. Rather, the zeal of piety aroused me to oppose the zeal of malice. To defend heresy is quite different from uprooting the calumnious charge of heresy. With regard to other kinds of insults, perhaps the gentlest approach is that of silence. But against a charge of impiety, it is impiety to hold one's tongue, if one is aware that he is without guilt. St. Paul tells us that also "with the mouth profession of faith is made unto salvation." But it is an expression of denial of faith not to speak up against a charge of heresy.

It is a well-known fact that those men first attacked me for frivolous reasons. I promoted the study of languages and proper learning to the great advantage of theology. Now they are pretending to foster that same cause, although for more than forty years they made every possible attempt to ruin it and thwart its growth. And that is the breeding place of this tragedy. I have urged theologians to put aside those petty questions which are more a matter of show than piety, and to turn to the sources of Scripture and to the early doctors of the Church. As for scholastic theology, it has not been my wish to abolish it, but that it be more authentic and more serious. In this, unless I am mistaken, I am promoting and not hurting it. I have urged monks to be what they are said to be, namely, dead to the world; to put less importance on external ceremonies and to have greater concern for true piety. Now, does that indicate a hatred for monks, or rather having their best interests at heart? I censured certain monks who take vows without thoughtful care and others who employ cunning tricks to lure callow youths into their trap. I have never given my approval to those monks who leave their order without serious reason and without papal authorization. In fact, I have consoled or encouraged many who were wavering in their vocation. I have exposed to ridicule perverted opinions, which are the principal source of harm to the Christian religion. That, I believe, helps religion and does not hurt it.

V. The Twilight Years: 1529–1536

The introduction of the Protestant faith in Basel brought about Erasmus' voluntary exile in Freiburg. He continued to write and edit, but as his De sarcienda ecclesiae unitate *("On the Restoration of the Unity of the Church") indicated, his eminent concern was the resolution of the religious controversy.*

TO THE READER[1]

EE 2203 (1–39)   Freiburg, August 7, 1529

In an earlier statement I said that I cared less for my letters than for any of my other writings, and listed the reasons for that attitude. At present I feel exactly as I did then. However, Jerome Froben has assured me that for the past two years scholars have been demanding a complete edition of my letters. Therefore I have revised what I

---

1. This is the preface to the collection of Erasmus' letters published under the title *Opus Epistolarum*. The writer comments on the character of his correspondence.

published earlier and have added a considerable amount of new material. This is the way I am, dear reader; I cannot say no to those whom I sincerely cherish.

Among the letters I had previously published were some addressed to persons whom I considered at the time to be faithful friends; those letters were written in a very friendly and flattering tone. But now I find that some of these persons have become my worst enemies; in the affairs of mortal men nothing is secure.[2] However, I have not omitted a single one of the letters, thinking that they would bring such persons dishonor rather than honor. Nor did it seem advisable to change the arrangement. The entire work being rather bulky, I did divide it into sections for convenience in reference. Some friends suggested in writing that the letters be arranged in chronological order. Even if that could have been done easily, for definite reasons it did not seem practicable. Furthermore, I decided not to arrange them according to similarity of subject, because in this type of writing the greatest attraction lies in variety. In case anyone desires that sort of thing, I have added the date at the end of each letter. Besides, I put an index at the beginning, listing the names of persons and page numbers, so as to indicate who was writing to whom and how often. There were several letters which I wanted to include, but they were not available.

Because of a frequent change of residence, I have lost many things I would like to have now. Everything has been so confused that the search for most of them has been unsuccessful. I have deemed it advisable to mention the point for this reason: if anyone should feel offended at failing to find here letters addressed to himself, while noticing that letters to other less important persons are published, I would not want him to think it was done with malice aforethought.

In this day and age I doubt if anything can be published without offending somebody. However, I have done all I could either to omit or to tone down anything that contained a considerable amount of acrimony. I have refrained from exposing names to public ridicule. I wish it had been possible to do that completely. But then that would not be publishing the letters. I have omitted solemn titles, not only superfluous ones but also those that violate Latin idiom and annoy

2. Erasmus may be thinking of such men as Oecolampadius and Hutten.

the reader. I hope no one will put a sinister interpretation on such omissions and think it was done out of contempt. Everyone knows that kings are "invincible," and "most serene," that abbots are "venerable," bishops "reverend," cardinals "most reverend," and popes "most holy and most blessed." The same applies to such appellations as "Most Invincible Majesty," "Most Reverend Lordship," "Most Gracious Eminence,"or "Reverend Father."

TO JOHN BOTZHEIM[1]

EE 2205 (20–105)   Freiburg, August 13, 1529

"But to suffer what we are suffering," you say, "is like being in exile."[2] That may be true; but it is not a harsh form of exile and probably not a lasting one. Has fortune ever smiled upon any man with such constant favor that he never encountered annoyance? If we cannot avoid troubles or drive them away, at least we can lessen much of our anxiety by enduring them with the proper attitude. This will come about if a person thoughtfully reflects that it is actually the hand of the Lord that is scourging us, though not to destroy but to correct us. We patiently endure the punishments inflicted upon us by our physical parents, even on those occasions when they are unduly angry. How much more patiently ought we to endure the hand of the Almighty, who is the father of our souls as well as of our bodies? How far we are from the ideal set by the holy Job! The Israelites suffered exile in Babylon for seventy years; yet they were restored to their Temple as soon as it seemed best to the Lord.

Of all the remedies for sorrow regularly devised by rhetoricians, none, in my opinion, is more efficacious than the thought: "It is the Lord; let Him do whatever seems best in His eyes." We have de-

1. *Ca.* 1480–1535. Jurist and humanist, from 1512 canon at Constance. A friend of Erasmus. This is almost a letter of consolation, an exposition of the nature of suffering. Toward the end it turns, however, to a favorite theme— the perversion of true religion.
2. Erasmus here quotes Botzheim on the difficulty of clearing himself of the suspicion of heresy.

served more terrible treatment. He is not less kindly when He afflicts us than when He soothes us. He alone knows what is best for us. Let Him even strike us down if He so wills. For He can only will what is best. Often He saves by striking down, and strikes down by saving. If we have received so many blessings from the hands of a most generous Father, why are we reluctant to endure the afflictions He sends us when we deserve greater punishments? He is open to our prayers; His manifestations of anger are not without appeasement; He does not send afflictions that are unbearable, but even while chastising us he is mindful of His mercy, and for each dose of bitterness He adds a proportionate amount of spiritual consolation. When that is present, neither death nor tortures worse than death can frustrate the hopes of pious souls. And when that is lacking, even the slightest troubles can prostrate us. Besides, He balances these temporary afflictions with an abundance of spiritual consolation even in this life, and in the next world He rewards us with eternal joys. Furthermore, it is within our power not only to lessen the effect of these ills, but even to shorten them. We can do this by reflecting on the poor use we have made of good opportunities and by acknowledging God's justice. And while sincerely confessing our own injustice, let us implore His mercy; and let us not devise schemes to gain revenge on others before we exact satisfaction from ourselves. If we exact it from ourselves first, then God will no longer be our prosecutor, but our protector; He will no longer strike but heal us. Let us cry out to the Lord, not to this or that ruler, nor to armies. Let us cry out to the Lord, I repeat, and He will shorten our evil days.

But, what a pity that Christian practice has deteriorated to the point where hardly anyone understands what it means to cry out to the Lord, although that is practically the very heart of Christianity. Some look to the power of cardinals and bishops; others to the military strength of princes, and others to the regiments of theologians and monks with all their intrigues. Is this not looking at things from a merely human point of view? And what in the world can we ever expect to get from it? Surely not the revival of Christian piety, but only a return to our former riches and pleasures and despotic power. And yet, the reason why the Lord has let loose upon us those shameless and savage chastisers is this: that He might arouse to sobriety those who are drunk with delights and slumbering amid earthly riches, that we might disdain the things for which we have had an evil love, and that we might turn our hearts to better things.

This brawling mob has been furnished with a large handle by some persons who have been straining the pope beyond its limit and who would rather break it than save it by loosening their hold. The Pope, being the Prince of the entire Church, possesses the highest power; therefore to him is due the highest honor. But those who have extended his powers indefinitely have at least frayed this cord, if they have not pulled it asunder. As long as papal indulgences were kept within bounds, they were respectfully received by the people. But when pardoners and monks for their own profit introduce them with an incredible amount of display and preach them with excessive zeal and make them their business with great greed—when all the churches are endlessly filled with those red cabinets and crosses and to every pillar there is attached the papal insignia with the triple tiara, and when some have even been forced to buy those indulgences —which is practically the situation, I hear, in Spain—then they come very close to breaking that rope.

So also, when they turn the invocation and cult of the saints into a superstition and extol it immoderately, then the rope is almost broken. The splendid display of images and statues was a fine thing, whether for the purpose of ornamentation or to recall the memory of those whose example could fire us to a life of piety. But when churches everywhere are filled with unbecoming pictures and we are almost slipping into idolatry in the practice of these superstitious rites, then again we provide an opportunity for that rope to break.

Also, it is a time-honored custom and a pious duty to praise God with hymns and spiritual songs. But when music is heard in churches that is more suited for parties and wedding celebrations than for divine worship, when the sacred words are lost amid the theatrical bellowing of voices, when silly ditties composed by men are sung instead of the words of Scripture, in fact, when there is nothing but the constant droning of voices in church—then too that rope is in danger of snapping. Now, what can be more sacred than the Mass? But when contemptible, illiterate priests learn perhaps three Masses and say them with as much devotion as a cobbler in making shoes, when those who approach the Lord's table live openly scandalous lives, when these mysteries are not accomplished with the proper reverence, and when something so sacred is peddled on the open market—then they all but break that rope.

TO PETER GILLES[1]

EE 2260 (312–332)   Freiburg, January 28, 1530

If you desire to hear about my condition, I can expect a bloody business in this matter unless I am deceived by the visible symptoms, or heaven, which has more power than man, can in some way bring quick relief to the severe pain. I have no special complaints to make about old age; many men in the prime of life are not capable of my literary productivity. However, for the past two years I have been nursing a stone in the bladder which is constantly growing in size and causes me chronic, though thus far tolerable, discomfort. But when it grows to such a size as to make urination impossible, then death is absolutely certain and also most painful. Would to heaven it meant dying only once! But I will have to die a thousand deaths unless a surgeon can relieve the agony. What sort of a malady is this when one regards an early death as a great blessing and views palsy or the plague with a jealous eye! With good reason did the wise men of ancient times assign to this malady the highest rank among all things that cause agony to human bodies. I suspect this was caused by some strange wine which I drank on several occasions on account of the thoughtlessness of servants, the kind that scholars usually happen to get. The hard residue from that and some undigested material caused the substances that normally accumulate in the kidneys to crystallize in the bladder. Doctors can offer no hope, and I have no intention of employing a surgeon except when death becomes preferable to life. But we belong to the Lord, my dear Peter; we must entrust ourselves completely to Him. He knows what is best for us. But why am I writing this? I should have been consoling you; instead I have been burdening you with complaints. Now read my

1. On Gilles, see Letter 476, p. 103. The present letter was included with Erasmus' translation of Xenophon' *Hiero*. It is an assessment of his health and circumstances.

verses of condolence, and my very best wishes to you and to all those most dear to you.

TO CUTHBERT TUNSTALL[1]

EE 2263 (5–30; 69–88)   Freiburg, January 31, 1530

Insofar as one can make a prediction based on the beginnings of things, this battle has long been fought with words and pamphlets, but soon the matter will be handled with halberds and cannon. If the safety of my soul were not more important than that of my body and material possessions, I would prefer to be in the place from which I fled. However, I have very little time left to live, for I am old and also nursing a stone in the bladder, which amounts to certain death. And so, far be it from me to desert the unity of the Church. What decision the ministers of the Church may make about my writings is their problem. If the Church were governed today by men like Augustine, I would be in perfect harmony with them. But I am afraid if Augustine were to write today the sort of thing he did write, or what this modern age cries out for, his reputation would be not much better than Erasmus'. Those are godly words you wrote—that fire is not quenched by fire. But it is an ungodly thing to bear the malicious charge of godlessness. Look at what Augustine wrote. I could gather hundreds of passages from his writings which today would be branded as heretical, and almost just as many from St. Paul. As for me, I shall be considered as a sheep. But even little lambs can bleat when they see men destroying the vigor of the gospel with wordly cunning. Many people do not understand what this means and many are misusing these words. If scholastic theologians and monks think that by this means they will restore peace to the Church, they are completely mistaken. Christ is the one we must resort to. In Him alone is it true that fire is not quenched by fire.

1. Lived (1474–1559), an English churchman and Bishop of London. Erasmus here speaks ominously of the future as well as the past—the causes and prospects of the religious controversy—and of the sacrament of Holy Communion.

This conflagration originated with the tyranny of the men in Rome and of evil monks, and in order to put out the flames they are pouring on oil. We see all this and it makes us grieve. But to Christ, the director of this drama, we leave the outcome. I realize that I am stuck between the devil and the deep blue sea, and I cannot see any safe position to withdraw to. All I can do is to entrust myself to the Lord. . . .

In early times men spoke of the Eucharist with reverence, before this matter came under investigation. Perhaps not even in our day has the Church clearly defined how Christ's Body is present there, whether under the accidents of bread or under real bread. Then too in apostolic times there was a Communion service conducted by the laity with the use of prayers and blessings. That bread they used to call the body of the Lord, and commendably so, since even in Scripture the same word is frequently applied to the sign as well as to the thing signified. Possibly Origen was speaking about this Communion service. In the canonical Scriptures there is no passage which definitely states that the apostles consecrated the body of the Lord as is done in the Mass today, with the exception of one passage in the First Epistle to the Corinthians, chapter 11. Yet the words in chapter 10 which led to Paul's discussion do not seem to refer to consecration by a priest. Now, if we interpret Origen's words as referring to a true consecration, there is nothing in that discussion that fails to make sense. For all the material elements, that is, the bread or the accidents of bread, are discharged into the sewer; nor does the eating of this food have any value if faith be lacking. Nor is it a godless thing to speak of the true body as being figurative or symbolical, because the body lies hidden there under figures and is invisible, and this true body which is received is a symbol of the unity between the body and the head and between the various members.

TO THE FRANCISCANS[1]

EE 2275 (35–75)   [Freiburg, February 1530]

What fools they are, a nuisance to me and also to the whole world! What will they accomplish with that constant chattering and stupid babbling? Educated men will not read them and God-fearing men will loathe them. I have not as yet come upon anyone who would prefer to read that sort of nonsense rather than my works. Yet with such pamphlets they will destroy a decrepit old man. Daggers would be a more convenient means of accomplishing their purpose, for it makes no difference what type of weapon they employ, since their intent is to murder. And yet this decrepit old man has presented you with Jerome, Cyprian, and Augustine, and now he is presenting you with Chrysostom, whose works along with those of Athanasius he has translated in great part. Employing Greek writers he has elucidated many, many passages in the New Testament. Let them read the list of his publications and they will realize how much this feeble old man has contributed to scholarship and to piety.

And what are those fellows doing? They croak and with their noisy clamor impede the work of other men, and they contribute nothing but their outrageous and stupid racket—as if the only creatures in the world were swine and asses. The Emperor once granted them the opportunity to state their accusations against me in a proper legal process, in the presence of judges of very high rank. That was the time they should have displayed their wisdom. With their contemptible pamphlets they only serve themselves up to be scoffed at by all men of learning and virtue. I too have enough strength left in me to look down upon them with scorn, even if three thousand of them should suddenly appear. Before the world of scholars and men of future generations swans will be eloquent and

1. This letter was published under the title *Epistola ad quosdam impudentissimos gracculos* ("A Letter to Those Most Impudent Ignoramuses"), and this excerpt forms part of a lengthy reply to his critics of the Franciscan order.

jackdaws will be silent. If they wish to destroy an old man, they will have to use daggers. Unless they learn how to write differently, they will gain for themselves in the eyes of outstanding men nothing but hatred and derision. You God-fearing fathers, restrain such asses. You God-fearing laymen, do not give anything to men whom you know to be insane, unless they rid their crew of such jabberers, so that with this warning they can regain their senses. For their ears are not in their heads but in their bellies. Let them use for their porridge their own dull *Dulcorationes*.[2] They can expect nothing from me; but let them see the result of wickedness.

Again I remind you that these remarks are not directed at God-fearing men; I know that there are many in that brotherhood who detest such insolent language. And afterward they keep croaking into my ears ominous threats of papal excommunication leveled against those who do harm to the Order of Friars Minor. Such an excommunication, if it has any meaning, falls especially upon the heads of those fellows who by their coarse pamphlets are bringing upon their own order the ill will of all men of learning and virtue. I have given them sufficient warning. They are constantly getting worse and worse; hereafter they will be ignored. I wish that had happened at the outset! I have no desire to exchange croaks with frogs. After showing a deep disregard for divine and human laws they can say, "One should obey God rather than men." That statement of the apostles is perfectly correct; only it is utterly inappropriate for these fellows to utter it. After all, they are not talking about the same God. The God of the apostles was the creator of heaven and earth; the god of these men is their belly.

2. Erasmus is here thinking of Carvaialus Bethicus, whose tract *Dulcoratio amarulentiarum Erasmicae responsionis*, an attack upon Erasmus, was published in Paris in 1530.

TO BALTHASAR MERCKLIN[1]

EE 2284 (89–129)   Freiburg, March 15, 1530

Many questions arise with regard to this sacrament: How does transubstantiation take place? How can the accidents subsist without a subject? How can they retain the color, smell, taste, and even the power to satisfy, inebriate, and nourish which the bread and wine had prior to their being consecrated? At what moment does the body and blood of the Lord begin to exist? When does the substance of the body and blood cease to exist and does a different substance replace it when the species undergo corruption?[2] How can a complete human body exist in such a tiny piece of bread? And there are very many other questions which can be properly and soberly discussed by men with suitable training.

In general, it is enough to believe that after consecration there is present the true body and blood of the Lord, which cannot be divided or harmed, nor is it liable to any abuse, no matter what happens to the species. If the body of the Lord when flung into the mud or into a latrine or in entering a man's stomach were thereby sullied, it would be no more sullied than when received by a man who is filthy with sin. It is the practice of the Christian religion to handle the sacramental species with all reverence. And yet just as God, who according to His nature exists in sewers as well as in heaven, cannot be harmed or defiled, neither can the glorified body of the Lord. To put it briefly, all the anxieties that trouble the human mind should be counteracted first of all by the thought of the infinite power of God, for whom nothing is impossible and nothing difficult; secondly, by

---

1. *Ca.* 1479–1531. A south-German administrator and churchman who became Bishop of Constance in 1529. It is clear, even from the few lines quoted, that Erasmus was content to let the details of the sacrament remain a mystery.

2. "Species," from its root meaning of "appearance," the Catholic term for the visible elements of the sacrament.

the thought of the inestimable qualities of the glorified body, especially that of the Lord Jesus. Therefore it remains for us to celebrate with dignity that of which we are sufficiently convinced and by our conduct to make it clear that we do believe what we believe. For who can describe in fitting language the holiness, the reverence, the awesomeness demanded by this mystery which is worthy of unceasing adoration?

Who could believe that those people are sincere in their faith who, while this mystery is being enacted, walk around in church chatting or, what is becoming the custom in some places, stand outside the church wasting time in idle conversation? At one time that used to be the place for penitents and catechumens. Some people, almost before the elevation is over, rush out to a tavern and leave the church empty. What sort of conduct is that? When people go to see some silly play, they do not leave the theater until the final curtain. But why can they not wait until the end of a heavenly mystery? Angels stand around the altar table in deep adoration; the entire heavenly host rejoices to gaze upon the One who is there present. Are you going to act as if you were watching some trivial stage play, bored or yawning or chatting or drinking?

TO JOHN RINCK[1]

EE 2285 (40–57)   Freiburg, March 17, 1530

During all these many years how many wars have we not witnessed? What shore does not bear the stain of our blood? How often have we felt the Turkish sword, which is avenging our violation of the convenant we made with God? What kind of plague have we not experienced, in the country as well as in the cities, so that flight merely meant an exchange of one peril for another? How often have we been deprived of bread, our staff of life? How many people are there in every land who eat bread rationed out by weight and are not filled! Recently in Italy, most fertile of all lands, how many died of

1. Professor of law at the University of Cologne. Erasmus offers here a comment on the ravages of war.

starvation? It may be that as yet no one has devoured the flesh of his own sons and daughters. And yet what else are we doing when we all live by tearing one another to pieces? Men with power plunder; the farmer sells his produce at four times its value; dealers raise their prices indefinitely; workmen charge all they want for their services. Everybody circumvents his neighbor by craft and trickery. We have seen magnificent churches robbed, statues broken, and priests driven out. Some time ago the beasts of the field were let loose upon us as everything was destroyed, while bands of peasants rioted with unbounded license. And we are experiencing also that curse mentioned in Deuteronomy: Men marry women but someone else sleeps with them.[2]

TO CHRISTOPHER MEXIA[1]

EE 2299 (91–108)   Freiburg, March 30, 1530

There are, as you wrote in your letter, some who say that I have made no contribution at all to scholarship and others who keep screaming that I am just a hotbed of heresy. Then explain the affection shown to me by such a large group of eminent men who, as everyone admits, are endowed with keen judgment and are wholeheartedly in support of piety! Those jackdaws who are a curse to scholarship have for the past ten years left no stone unturned in their attacks upon me in the courts of rulers, before bishops, before the Pope, and before the Emperor; in a word, before men of the highest rank and of the lowest. And they still do so today. Everywhere they have found men who would defend Erasmus; unexpected champions have arisen, often even among the lowest classes. Who are these people who are giving such support to impiety and to one who is making no contribution to scholarship? They are men of discernment, who recognize the spiteful growling that comes from the guts

2. Deuteronomy 28:30.
1. Nothing is known about this man except that he was a Spaniard, brother of Peter Mexia, the historian (see Letter 2892). Erasmus offers here a defense of his contribution to scholarship.

of these fellows. I admit that many persons outstrip me in this matter
of praise. That is no surprise, since I drew the initial ill will upon
myself when I led the way and began to clear the land for plowing. I
am sorry that there are not more persons who outstrip me. To achieve
this I have toiled and sweated. If one compares the world of thirty-six
years ago with the world today, he will realize whether any contribution has been made to learning by Erasmus.

TO JACOPO SADOLETO[1]

EE 2315 (50–86)   Freiburg, [ca. May 14, 1530]

Beyond a doubt it is upon these dogmas that the Christian religion
depends from stem to stern, as the saying goes; and they are discussed
by yourself with such clarity, expressed with such richness of
language, and emphasized with such deep feeling that the reader (if
he is not half-asleep) will readily understand that these words of
yours are not lightly spoken but spring from the innermost recesses of
your heart. Then, too, your frequent and apt use of scriptural proof
makes me believe that you are not merely a casual or listless visitor to
the inner sanctuary of heavenly philosophy.

Why should I laud that truly Ciceronian flow of speech which is
always pure and limpid, rich and charming? How often have I
prayed that heavenly wisdom could find such a spokesman as was
Cicero pleading in the law courts or expounding the philosophy of
the Greeks, someone whose genuine piety of heart would balance his
powers of eloquence. In our eyes, you have happily shown yourself to
be such a man, if ever any man can be, and we consider you as one
who will constantly prove himself. There was a special reason why
the apostles proclaimed Christ's mysteries to us in unpolished language. Obviously it was so that none of the credit which was completely owed to God would be diminished by the powers of men.

---

1. Cardinal and theologian, perhaps best known for his letter to the city of
Geneva in defense of the Catholic Church. See J. Olin, *A Reformation Debate*
(New York, 1966). This letter is in praise of the erudition and theological
prowess of the recipient.

Today the reason is different. Some men have almost buried theology under an excessive admixture of pagan philosophy and have even defiled it by their filthy language. On the other hand, you occasionally add a sprinkling from the writings of the philosophers, so as to serve piety but not to overwhelm it, to season but not spoil it, to illumine but not obscure it. You employ a very happy elegance of style, so that like an obedient maid it can be of service to religion, not displaying itself but gracing the majesty of its queen by its obedience.

How much piety is contained in those frequent apostrophes of yours, addressed sometimes to God, sometimes to the divine laws! Besides that, there is a very pleasing effect in the marvelous dexterity with which you fashion phrases; you do it so delicately that the result is not like pieces of thread sewn together. Rather, a natural flowing rhythm seems to weld into one your entire composition. But above all I was delighted with the extraordinary gift you have for purity of style, which never lapses into a rough connection, a choppy expression, an awkward phrase, a useless repetition, or a misplaced word. These are the endowments of a mind that is unclouded and not agitated by the tempests of unruly passions, endowments wherein that heavenly spirit delights to display its power.

TO PHILIPP MELANCHTHON[1]

EE 2343 (1–19)   Freiburg, July 7, 1530

No one will undo this universal chaotic tragedy except God, not even ten councils, and so I could not possibly settle it. If a person makes any reasonable proposal, he promptly hears the cry "Lutheranism!"—that is his only reward.

This is now the fourth month of my illness. First I suffered from colic, then from vomiting, and the vomiting ruined my whole stomach. This poor little body of mine does not get along very well with doctors. All the medicines they gave me did me harm. The colic

1. The negotiations between Catholics and Protestants during the Diet of Augsburg provide the setting of this letter to Melanchthon (on whom see Letter 1496, p. 174). At the same time, Erasmus comments on his illness.

Erasmus and His Age

was followed by an ulcer, or more accurately, by a hard swelling
which first extended all along the lower right groin. Then it centered
on the pit of my stomach, almost like a dragon with its teeth biting
my navel while the rest of its body was writhing and its tail stretch-
ing toward my loins; when its head was fastened tight it coiled
around to the left side of my navel, with its tail almost encircling it.
It caused constant, sometimes unbearable pain. I could not eat or
sleep or write or read or dictate or listen to anyone reading; I could
not even converse with friends. A surgeon was called and almost
murdered me with his powerful plasters. Finally I underwent surgery. After that I was reconciled with sleep as the pain was relieved.
I am still crawling around feebly, and the surgeon has not as yet
released me.

TO LORENZO CAMPEGGIO[1]

EE 2366 (6–61)   Freiburg, August 18, 1530

If the Emperor is only using threats of war to terrify the opposition, then I cannot help but praise his good judgment. But if he
seriously wants war, though I would not like to be a bird of ill omen,
my mind shudders whenever I imagine the condition of the world
once there is a call to arms. For this mischief has spread far and wide.
I admit that the power of the Emperor is supreme, but not all nations
recognize that title. The Germans do recognize it, but only on the
condition that they are in control rather than doing the obeying; for
they prefer to give commands rather than do someone else's will.
Besides, a continual series of campaigns and expeditions has greatly
impoverished the Emperor's dominions, and the flame of war has now
been fanned in Friesland, which is adjacent to us, and its ruler is
according to reports now professing Luther's gospel. The same is true
of several communities from the East to Denmark; the chain of woes

1. On Campeggio, see Letter 1167, p. 159. The present letter probably
never reached its recipient but was (against Erasmus' will) promptly printed.
Erasmus' concern here is with the political situation, the ravages of war, and
the hope for a good outcome of the existing turbulence.

extends from there all the way down to Switzerland. If the Emperor out of loyalty indicates his intention of acting completely according to the wishes of the Pope, there is danger that he will not have very many supporters. Furthermore, an invasion by the Turks is expected any day, and we would have difficulty in checking their power even if we had unity and could combine our forces. Then too, the sack of Rome made clear, as have recent events at Vienna, what it means to engage in warfare when the soldiers object to it.[2]

I have no doubt that the mind of our excellent ruler is inclined toward peace, clemency, and tranquillity; but by some mysterious fate, contrary to his mind we have one war after another. For years France has been plagued with troubles! And Italy has been even more grievously afflicted; a fresh war has broken out there again. Judging from the present course of events, I think a great part of the world is going to be involved in bloodshed. Since all wars are hazardous, there is danger that the outcome of this present turmoil may be the destruction of the entire Church, especially since the common masses are convinced that this business is being instigated by the Pope and carried out primarily by bishops and abbots. And I am very much afraid the Emperor himself will not be entirely free from danger. May heaven prevent that!

I know and execrate the shamelessness of those men who wield authority over the sects or who support them. But in the present state of affairs we must concern ourselves with the demands of world peace rather than with what those men deserve for their wickedness. Nor should we lose all hope with regard to the state of the Church. Centuries ago she was tossed about by far more severe storms under the Emperors Arcadius and Theodosius. What a condition the world was in those days! In the same community there were Arians, pagans, and orthodox believers. In Africa the Donatists and the Circumcellions raged.[3] In many areas the madness of the Manichaeans was

2. The Turks in 1529 had advanced as far as Vienna and threatened to attack. The Sack of Rome had taken place in 1527 with the conquest of that city by the troops of Emperor Charles V. The "war" in Italy must be the siege of Florence (1529–1530) by imperial troops.

3. By citing the Circumcellions, a martyr-minded and socially engaged segment of the early-fourth-century North African Donatist movement, and Marcion, a second-century theologian who sought to divorce Jesus and his teaching from the Old Testament, Erasmus refers to two heresies of the early Church.

still flourishing, as was the poison of Marcion, not to mention the invasions of the barbarians. And yet in spite of all those serious clashes the Emperor did keep control of the reins of government without bloodshed and was gradually able to restrain the monsters of heresy.

Time itself sometimes provides a remedy for incurable ills. If the sects were tolerated under definite conditions (just as, for instance, the Bohemians are being ignored), it would be, I admit, a terrible misfortune, yet less of a misfortune than war, especially such a war as this.

Such being the state of affairs, there is nowhere I would rather be than in Italy, but the fates are pulling me elsewhere. Let them draw me where they will provided they do not draw me away from union with the Dove. I am told that certain persons at the Emperor's court are not highly in favor of me. However, I am confident that Your Lordship has not undergone any change, and I pray that every happiness may be yours.

TO CHARLES BLOUNT[1]

EE 2435 (52–90)   Freiburg, March 1, 1531

May Almighty God grant that the complete works of this author [Livy] be restored to us in their integrity! There is some hope of this in light of the rumors that are flying around. In Denmark, Poland, and Germany the news is spread of the existence of some unpublished books of Livy. Since fortune has unexpectedly presented us with these remains, I do not see why we should lose all hope of the possibility of further discoveries. It is certainly my opinion that princes would be doing a worthy thing if, by offering rewards, they would attract scholars to make a thorough search for such a great treasure or even urge them to publish their findings, especially if there are men who gravely harm scholarship by suppressing and

1. This letter forms the preface to Erasmus' edition of the *Historia* of T. Livy, which he dedicated to Blount. In keeping with the nature of the letter, Erasmus discusses here the significance of Livy, including the possibility of recovering lost works of that author.

concealing something intended for the common good. It seems utterly absurd that men will undergo great expense and risk in probing the bowels of the earth almost all the way to hell merely to find a little gold or silver; yet in the case of treasures such as these, whose value is as far above that of silver and gold as the soul is superior to the body, they will completely ignore them and consider them not worth looking for. That is an attitude typical of a Midas but not proper to a prince. And since I realize that by disposition you are averse to such an outlook, I do not doubt that you will passionately embrace this bonanza. Now there are two reasons especially which preclude any doubt that Titus Livy is the true author of this section. First, the diction reflects all the distinctive features of its author; secondly, the summaries or epitomes of L. Florus correspond exactly to the contents of these books. I know that no reading is more suitable for men of high position than the works of historians, among whom Livy easily ranks first (I am speaking only of Latin writers), especially since nothing of Sallust is extant except two fragments. Also I recall what an insatiable, gluttonous appetite your father always had for history, and I am sure that you resemble him in this respect too. Therefore, I thought it would be proper if these books were to see the light of day with a special dedication to you. However, on this point, I would not want you to resemble your father too closely. For he regularly every day after dinner until almost midnight devotes himself to books, not without disgust to his wife and the women and with much grumbling from the men servants. Although he has been able to do this up to now without harming his health, I do not think it advisable for you to take the same risk, for you may not be as fortunate as he. Indeed, when your father assisted the present King in his studies when he was just a young Prince,[2] the two spent most of their time on history, and this they did with the hearty approval of the Prince's father, Henry VII, a King whose good judgment and prudence were extraordinary.

2. William Blount (Lord Mountjoy) directed the studies of Prince Henry (Henry VIII). He had met Erasmus in Paris before the turn of the century and became his principal financial supporter.

TO JACOPO SADOLETO[1]

EE 2443 (46-119; 362-432)   Freiburg, March 7, 1531

Now there are two things, as I seem to gather from your letter, in which you desire me to be either more cautious or at least more moderate: namely, in carping at practices which, though not belonging to the essence of piety, still do not militate against true religion, as for instance, the invocation of saints and the use of images; and secondly, in refuting slanders no matter who has uttered them. You suggest that I either ignore them completely or refute them in such a way as not to give the impression of humoring my temper. I shall never deny that I have sinned in both respects, and I could earnestly wish in many instances that what has been done could be undone. At least there is one thing that I can do now; I am making several corrections or modifications in my published works, being a considerably more severe critic of my own writings than St. Augustine was of his; I am encouraged from time to time by friends to imitate his example. If only you or somebody like you had given me advice at the right time! Now at last I know from my experience what little value I received in the applause of some persons and the cries of "Bravo! Bravo!" Even so there are certain kinds of slander in the face of which it would be an unholy thing to hold one's tongue—for instance, when before crowded audiences or in printed books I am publicly ridiculed as the author of godless teachings, the destroyer of papal authority, a forger of the inviolate Scriptures, and the instigator of schism. In my eyes, a man would by no means seem to be God-fearing if he could take such things in silence. Now, although I have absolutely no regard for my own reputation, what could have been less beneficial for the peace of the Church than to have a large number of people convinced of what those men were attempting to

1. On Sadoleto, see Letter 2315, p. 238. This is another instance of a response to critics, those who accused Erasmus of speaking too negatively on such matters as images and the invocation of saints, and of reacting too strongly to criticism.

perpetrate with sworn hatred? I have never engaged in bitter contention with anyone who merely found fault with my ability or who thought something was wanting in my character. I readily grant superiority of learning to any other man; as regards my character, I admit that I am nothing more than a human being. But to be tongueless when one is obviously and slanderously charged with the worst form of impiety, does that not mean admitting the charge? A gentle and calm response would not be free from the suspicion that a man does not know his own mind very well or that he is in deceitful collusion with the enemies of the Church. There might be the danger that somebody would recall that remark of Cicero: Unless you were pretending, Erasmus, you would not act in this way. However, not even in such situations have I always had a tongue or a pen. In some cases I scoffed rather than refuted, because that is what they deserved; and on no occasion did I fail to be temperate toward those who provoked me—at least so I think. For it may happen (and often does) that my judgment is deceived by emotion; I admit I am the sort of person who, when provoked, can arrive at white heat, but my anger does not stubbornly endure, and I can forget injuries just like anyone else. However, when it is a matter of a controversy in print, I usually indulge my anger a little. Perhaps you would not completely disapprove of that statement, if you had time to read the slanderous remarks of these men and then my defenses. But God forbid that you should chip off so many good hours from your very holy occupations and devote them to such an unpleasant, silly little song and dance. Furthermore, how little inclined I am by nature toward such out-and-out gladiatorial combat is clearly proved by the fact that, though I have written several apologias—indeed, up to now nothing else—I have not uttered one single bit of invective. Cato is considered a good man; yet he issued accusations more frequently than he was summoned into court.

This situation is rendered all the more shameful by the fact that, while I am like a gladiator in the arena with only a net and sickle for weapons and am facing opponents whom these men deeply desire to see destroyed as deadly enemies of piety, at the very moment when I am fighting on their behalf at great risk to my fortune and life, these people attack me in the back. This has been done one after the other by Stunica, Carranza, Latomus, Beda, Sutor, Eustatius, Clithoueus,

Vincent Theodorici and his troupe of clowns, crowds of Spanish monks, Albertus Pius, Titelmans, and Carvajal.[2] I shall say nothing about those men whose writings flit from hand to hand but have not as yet appeared in print. Nor shall I say anything of those venomous and viperous detractions that did not spare my name either in private or in public. And what great risks I am now undergoing in my combats with the authors of new teachings I cannot safely put in writing. On this point I would like to see my word carry some weight with you, even as I would want you to believe that there is nobody whom those fellows hate more or for whom they are laying more plots. If you have read my *Diatribe,* or my two *Hyperaspistes* against the violent book of Martin Luther, or my *Spongia* against Hutten, or my pamphlet against Leopold,[3] or my letter to Vulturius,[4] or my book against the clergy of Strassburg, then your good judgment will clearly perceive how much it is costing me to refuse to withdraw from union with the Roman Church. I will remain silent about those biting letters not worthy of a response. . . . I will say nothing of the threatening letters penned with poison; I will say nothing of the charges and slanders that were secretly instigated and which could have destroyed the peace of the most lofty-minded person. . . .

To come back to that Psalm which you praised. Hereafter I shall make the diligent attempt to have all my writings without exception merit your approval, something I am afraid I failed to accomplish with regard to this Psalm. At any rate, I shall never abandon hope of accomplishing this, now that I have begun to make progress under your guidance. And yet, at least in this kind of writing, I am usually more sparing in indulging my feelings, for obviously in the presence of such majestic mysteries I take the attitude of religious reverence. I very much agree with you that the reading of many interpreters can be something of a hindrance, particularly when one is handling this type of material. The results are much more felici-

2. On these men, see Allen, IX, 160.
3. "Leopold" refers to the Swiss reformer Leo Jud. The pamphlet is *De-tectio praestigiarum* ("Detection of Deception").
4. Erasmus refers here to Gerard Geldenhauer (*ca.* 1482–1542), a church-man with whom he had friendly relations until the early 1520's. Geldenhauer subsequently became a Protestant and was professor of history at Marburg from 1532. Erasmus arrives at "Vulturius" by translating (by way of popular etymology) *Geldenhauer* into Latin.

tous if, after studying the general theme, one surrenders his whole being secretly to the Spirit and at the same time turns his mind not only from moral faults but from all external and less important concerns and retires into a lofty seclusion that is peaceful and quiet and removed from all the roar of worldly passions. It is of no little importance to utter a prayer at frequent intervals, for that in a marvelous way gives fresh vigor and enthusiasm to the spirit. God immortal! How happy would we be if we could banish all disagreement of thought and feeling! Being one at heart we might seek refuge in the fertile fields of Scripture and play in its lovely meadows—if that word should be used in a matter that is not at all playful. Indeed, I am conscious of my own uncleanness and well aware that I am a very unsuitable and unmanageable instrument for the working of the Spirit in treating matters in which, according to His will, the deep mysteries of a heavenly philosophy are hidden as in some very sacred sanctuary. Therefore, it is not without trepidation that I approach this area. Almost never is this place approached with sufficient reverence except by those who abide there constantly. But your heart is serene and pure, as was first pointed out to me by Nicolaus Leonicus, who is clearly a man of high moral principles and an accomplished Platonic philosopher.[5] He pointed this out in one of his dialogues, in which he represents you discoursing on prayer in a very holy manner. If I had read the dialogue first (I would have read it if friends had sent it to me in time), my little book about praying to God would have been considerably less insipid and commonplace when it appeared in print. That work of yours gave me a rough outline of your piety; but I received a much more detailed impression of it from your brilliant commentaries on the Psalms, especially the more recent one, which I read with intense interest. I would have supervised the printing of both, if others had not anticipated me.

You would hardly believe how much I admire you for this statement of yours, with which I fully agree: "When God, who has power over all things, gives you suffering, worries, and ill health, who knows if by doing so He is granting you a greater blessing than if He were to offer you a calm, peaceful, leisurely life?" There you

5. Leonicus (1456–1531) was a humanist scholar at Padua and Venice, editor of Aristotle and Ptolemy.

seem to have a deep insight into me and to know me as well as I do myself. Amid a continual stream of disasters the only thought in which I find consolation is that this is beneficial for my salvation. God in His unutterable wisdom uses various means to purify men and make them worthy of Himself. He is like the brilliant director of a play who introduces various characters onto the stage of life and has a reward ready for all who properly play the role he has assigned. St. Paul the Hermit is distinguished for the fact that he stayed in one place and spent his whole life in obscurity. In fleeing fame, Blessed Hilary gained fame everywhere. St. Anthony divided his time between the desert and city life. None of these men suffered any adversity. What a difference there is between Jerome and Augustine, between Chrysostom and Basil, between Athanasius and Gregory the theologian? I need not mention others who were completely different in temperament and fortune, and way of life, and yet alike in piety. Now if the stage director has given me a lowly and miserable role, is it right for me to grumble at him or should I rather play the part assigned me to the best of my ability? He whose will arranges the affairs of mortal men will grant a happy ending to this drama. It is this thought that prevents me from losing all hope with regard to the disturbances in Germany; they will eventually result in some great blessing for the Church. For God knows how to turn even our woes to His own glory and to the salvation of His chosen ones. The prayer which out of your extraordinary goodness you are offering up for Germany should also be offered for many other countries in which this fever is raging no less violently, though it may be less widespread in those areas. But if this problem had been handled by men like yourself, there would now be much less suffering everywhere. The fanaticism of some who are concerned more with themselves than with Christ has aggravated this disease in the past and is continuing to do so in the present. But at a time when our play Director thinks best, all this will turn out for the good of Christendom.

TO ANTONY DALBAN[1]

EE 2472 (12–66)   Freiburg, April 1, 1531

We would have woes in abundance, even if no more were added. For some time now we have been infested by the plague, which does not come to an end. The high cost of living continues to go up. God only knows what is to follow. I myself do not like the omens. Yet it is inconvenient for this delicate little body of mine to move to a new nest where it can be perfectly safe. They say the Turks are assembling three armies: one to invade Austria, against Ferdinand; another to invade Poland, which they have long been threatening; and a third to attack Naples, and from there they will go to ask the Pope for his blessing. This is a difficult situation, but still not so bad as if all Germany and the neighboring countries should become embroiled in mutual slaughter. You will say it is a fierce disease and cannot be cured by ordinary remedies. But I loathe remedies that are more terrible than the disease itself. If the sword is the means of solving the situation, then the biggest share of calamities will fall upon the innocent, and under the guise of defending religion the world will be filled with robbers. Spain is harboring many concealed Jews and Germany contains very many who are naturally inclined toward robbery and are well practiced in it because of wars. This whole sea of filth will first engulf Germany, then the rest of the world. For they are incapable of putting down their weapons once they have them in their hands. Twice already they have given proof of this, once at Rome and once at Vienna.

The world has never had a more powerful emperor than it has now. With his religious spirit and his deep respect for the Roman See, it appears that he will do whatever the Bishop of Rome prescribes. Human affairs therefore will have a right to be considered happy if the Vicar of Christ only has thoughts that are worthy of

1. The concern of this letter is the over-all political situation—and a plea for deeper spirituality. Antony Dalban, d. 1574, a politically oriented churchman, later Archbishop of Arles and Lyons.

Christ. However, many people see a bad portent in Clement's very inclement treatment of Florence.[2] Just as children, even though unjustly treated, have no right to take revenge on their parents, so too, as many pagans have felt, it is not right to draw the sword against one's native land no matter how much merited. Themistocles and Aristides, though exiled out of ill will, were still a great support to their native city. The Lacedaemonian king who was undeservedly exiled could not venture even to complain about his native land. . . .

"The one best omen is to fight in defense of one's country," says Homer's Hector. But in the present state of affairs it seems that the one best augury is for all men to appease the divine Being. Yet this, the most important thing of all, is most of all neglected. This is an age of excellent rulers, yet how can one explain the disasters in Christendom if it be not that God is angry with our wicked deeds? When has France ever received a more terrible blow?[3] It is fortunate that fair skies have followed that storm. Who has ever seen Italy worse afflicted? I am afraid she will not recover for many years the pristine vigor she had when we visited her. And Germany is presently the embodiment of turmoil! She would be utterly wretched if the impending calamities should in fact befall her. It is easy for men to lay down regulations, for instance that there be more moderate drinking, that there be less extravagance in food and dress, that clerics wear a larger tonsure, that their garb be ankle length, that they sleep alone. But only God has the power to purify the source of all good actions, and He will do so if with sincere and complete trust we take refuge in His mercy. In response to prayer He will grant to Church leaders a spirit that will prefer Christ's glory to all worldly advantages. To rulers He will grant a mind that can rise above riches and honors, revenge and all human passions, and He will grant them a heavenly wisdom that can prevail over all earthly malice. He will grant to priests and monks a true contempt of the world and a love of

2. Erasmus refers here to the fate of Florence, native city of the Medici pope, Clement VII. In 1527 the Medici had been expelled from Florence, where a republic was established that same year. The siege of the city by imperial forces in 1529–1530 led to the end of Florentine independence; this had been anticipated by the treaty of Charles V with Clement V concluded in June 1529.

3. The reference is to the defeat of France at Pavia in 1525 at the hands of Charles V.

the Scriptures; He will grant to civil authorities and to the people a fear of Himself.

TO JULIUS PFLUG[1]

EE 2522 (20–64)   Freiburg, August 20, 1531

A deadly disease is raging, and as I see it not even an ecumenical council could remedy it; and I, who amount to nothing, am of absolutely no assistance, although you have a remarkably high opinion of me. The Pope's mind is not at all clear to me; however, I notice, since very little has been accomplished up to now by burnings, that some priests are thinking of handling the matter with the sword. Whether that would be an expedient course or not, even if the Turks should give us time for it, I have not yet decided. The disorder would be more curable if the leaders of both parties would sincerely agree to restore evangelical piety. Then the problem might be handed over to a hundred or to fifty men selected from each nation, who were commended by their holiness of life, outstanding learning, and tactful judgment. The decisions of these men could be summarized by a smaller group of select persons. The opinions of theologians would stay within the walls of the schools, and no opinions should be regarded as articles of faith. Some regulations should be abrogated; some should be changed into recommendations. However, the rulers and the people should be chiefly concerned about having such men in charge of the Lord's flock as are instructed in the Word of God and trained for teaching, for exhorting, for consoling, for reproving, and for refuting. But at present, what despots are supported by the revenues of monasteries and churches! Meanwhile the common folk float around from sect to sect, like sheep who are scattered and have lost their shepherd. And yet even here, alas, how few sheep one

1. Lived 1499–1564. An irenically oriented churchman, who participated in the Regensburg Colloquy in 1541, and became Bishop of Naumburg. In 1548 he had a major share in the drafting of the Augsburg Interim with which Emperor Charles V sought to resolve the religious controversy in Germany. This letter is a somewhat pessimistic assessment of the contemporary situation.

can see—that is, people who are wandering about without guile and not committing sin with willful malice. I am afraid that what usually happens in wars will happen to us: when both sides are sick and tired of suffering disasters, then and then only will they enter into peace negotiations. The one side is aiming at complete destruction of the ecclesiastical estate; the other side does not want it to be reformed. We all carry the world in our heart, and since we are of the earth our tastes and our language are of the earth. May the Lord implant a new heart in the members of both sides.

There are some other points, too, which it would not be safe to commit to writing—things one can more easily pray than hope for. I am exhausted not so much by my years as by my poor health and so many brawls and controversies, by so much slandering and all the disparaging remarks; for some time now I have been thinking of retiring. This request however I must make of my own soul: it is what you have prudently and lovingly urged, namely, that in keeping with Christ's wishes, and following a conscience guided by a properly directed will, I may acquiesce in the judgment of good men. The fates will find a way, and I have hopes that all these turmoils in the Church will eventually turn out, as in a drama, with a happy ending, thanks to the skill of the Supreme Director whose inscrutable design controls the affairs of men. If that should happen in my own lifetime, I shall calmly say, "Ring down the curtain." But if I do not merit this, well, "It is the Lord"—let Him do whatever His eternal will has decreed.

TO SEVERIN BONER[1]

EE 2533 (42–115)   Freiburg, September 1, 1531

Time and again I have admired your son for all the worth-while progress he has made in his studies, and this at a tender age when very few boys can read with any facility. Take my word for it; such

---

1. A Polish nobleman (1487–1549), whose son spent some time in Erasmus' home. Erasmus dedicated his edition of Terence to two of his sons. Here Erasmus, the teacher, speaks in detailed assessment of a pupil.

natural gifts promise something quite uncommon and extraordinary. His mind is quick, alert, tractable, docile, and adaptable to anything. Some persons, one might say, are born for learning. But even in practical matters of everyday life I have detected no trace of silliness in the lad, and nothing childish or out of place even in his manners. In some boys extreme bashfulness makes them dull; in other cases boldness makes them disgustingly brash; but your boy has a liveliness that is tempered by a polite respect. Although it is completely a matter of good fortune and divine favor that you should have such a son, still no little praise is owing to you for your extraordinary prudence; for you saw to it that your small boy from early infancy was formed and armed against all the chances of fortune with the finest type of education and morally good habits and furthermore with a wide-awake good sense, such as Ulysses had. . . .

How few parents would allow their sons at such an age to be torn from them and go off to some faraway land, instead of hugging and coddling them and hanging on to them until they had almost reached manhood. But in your case it was as if you had raised your boy not for yourself but for the commonwealth. Your concern has been to have him imbued right from the start with those accomplishments which would make him an honor and a benefactor to his realm. And you refused to have the best part of his life wasted in being kissed by his mother and hugged by nurses. For you appreciated the fact that we understand most thoroughly and remember most accurately the things we imbibe in those early years when we are still impressionable and, as Fabius says, adaptable to any habit. What we learn when we are older we perceive as if through a foggy mist, like things we recall seeing in a dream. It is also an indication of your extraordinary prudence that you entrusted this moist and promising clay to an eminent potter, this rich soil to an expert farmer. What good is it to be born into a good family if one lacks a proper education? It is to your praise that you searched for such an education and to your happiness that you found one. That is a blessing which sometimes even the greatest monarchs fail to receive.

Again I must ask you, distinguished sir, not to assume that I am saying this to curry favor or just to tickle a father's ears. I admit that this is a common practice. However, it is utterly alien to my character and disposition; and besides, in this case there is no need to employ fiction, and in fact no reason for doing so. I have known many molders of young men; but among the very best of them I have never seen anyone who was superior to Anselm in attentiveness, integrity, and even skill. He can induce boys to do more things merely by a nod of the head than most teachers can by using insults, by arguments or threats, or by screaming and beating. Quintilian suggested that the first precept a teacher should learn is that he should adopt toward his students the attitude of a parent.[2] It is the duty of parents to keep their children within bounds by a sense of honor and by kindliness rather than by the restraints of fear. With good reason did the ancients place great importance upon the eyes of the master and the brow, which they said was more effective than the back of the head. This above all, they said, made the horse grow fat and the farm prosper. In my opinion, however, for a father to have his eye on his son is considerably more effective than for a master to keep his eye on this particular stable or farm. Anselm performs the duty of both parent and teacher in a remarkable way, and he is never so much as a foot or a finger's breadth away from the boy; on the other hand the boy prefers his company to that of anybody else. Anselm would not constantly act in this way if he had not adopted your own attitude toward your son, nor would the boy enjoy his constant association if he did not love and respect him as a father.

Stanislaus is a very faithful servant to your son and also his companion in his studies. I do not know his background, but he is well-bred and I would very much like to see all monarchs have equally fine children. He shows extraordinary promise as a scholar. And so, I think, both of them deserve congratulations: your son John, on his good fortune in having such a suitable companion for his boyhood studies, and Stanislaus, on his good fortune in having such a kindly patron, whose generosity will make it possible for him to complete successfully his course of training in good learning.

I rejoice to see that the blessing which Plato desires for states has come to your land of Poland, where the rulers are interested in philosophy. Now, by philosophy I do not mean a system whereby one discusses the principles of things, matter, time, motion, infinity;

2. Quintilian (ca. 35–96) was a Roman rhetorician, author of the *Institutio oratoria*, proponent of a comprehensive view of education.

rather I mean that wisdom which Solomon considered more precious than all riches, and for that reason asked God to give him this in preference to all other things. Such a philosophy has the power to enable a man to regulate his life properly and to be deeply concerned for his country's interests in times of peace and war.

TO JOHN MORIN[1]

EE 2577   Freiburg, November 30, 1531

A pamphlet has been issued in Paris, published by William [Gilles] de Gourmont and bearing the false ascription of Julius Caesar Scaliger. The work is a defense of Cicero against Erasmus; it is not only libellous, but downright frenzied. It is stuffed with the most shameless lies and the worst possible scurrilous insults. It even accuses me of capital offenses, as for instance that along with my accomplices I have attempted to depose the Pope, whereas I have always continually fought to defend the Pope and the Catholic faith against the leaders of the sects. I am still carrying on that battle, not without peril to my fortunes and my life. I need not mention other accusations, such as my desire to destroy Cicero's glory or my drunkenness (those who live with me know that the fact is quite the opposite), or the charge that when I was working with Aldus I was merely a reader, though I really held the position of tutor. But it is silly of me to enumerate these things since the writing contains nothing but wild insults, the sort of thing that not even a clown would pour out on another clown. This work was published contrary to the King's edict and the authority of the theologians, but with your permission. No reason is given to justify its publication. Therefore I suspect that your name was forged; or, if you really did give permission for the printing, they convinced you of something quite

1. This man was "conservateur des privilèges royaulx" at Paris, in which capacity Erasmus addresses a request to him. He seeks redress for the publication of a slanderous book and makes a protestation of his own modesty. Scaliger, 1484–1558, a physician and author of two vehement tracts against Erasmus, was in fact responsible and later regretted it.

different from the facts. It would have been more in keeping with
the dignity of your University and its deservedly wide renown if such
a bad example had never emanated from it, to be spread abroad
among young scholars all over Christendom. I know who the author
is; he is a mitred clown. I could, without losing my dignity, retaliate
with charges that are not fictitious but true. However, I do not enjoy
mimicking a lunatic. Nor do I wish to recall the services I have
rendered to learning or to the Christian religion. But even supposing
that none of this were true and that I deserved such insolent treatment, which is worse than one would get from a mule skinner, still
one must consider what is in keeping with the reputation of your
university. As for myself, I admit that I am a lowly person, but still
the Emperor acknowledges this lowly person as his counselor, and
King Ferdinand as his tutor, which they have avowed to me several
times in writing. I would have a mitre too, except that I have preferred to serve Christ rather than men. I did not want you to be
ignorant of these facts, so that if this action was taken without your
knowledge such indiscretion would be punished. But if it was done
with your knowledge, you should realize that you were misled into a
compromising position by the fraudulent intimations of scoundrels.

TO JOHN AND STANISLAUS BONER[1]

EE 2584 (3–40)   Freiburg, December 12, 1531/2

There is nothing better for man than devotion to God, and its
seeds must be implanted in small children bit by bit right along with
their mother's milk. The next best thing for man is training in the
liberal arts. Though they are not virtues as such, the arts do prepare
the way for virtue by fashioning a gentle and tractable nature out of
rough and crude material. Besides, Aristotle's statement that young
people are not capable of learning moral philosophy is perhaps not

1. On the recipients, see Letter 2533, p. 252. This is the preface to Erasmus'
edition of the *Comoediae* of Terence. Here we have a summary of the proper
education of youth together with a note on the splendid achievements of the
present age.

altogether false. However, this is due not so much to any defect in that discipline or in human nature as to the fault of those who teach it; either they do so too late—after their pupils are already corrupted by a perverse training and taken up with evil passions—or they teach it in a boring, plodding manner, more interested in giving the impression of being sharp-witted than in improving their students. And yet, there is nothing more natural for us than virtue and learning, and if you took these away from man he would cease to be a man. Every single living creature learns most easily the thing for which it was fashioned by nature, as for instance, a horse for racing, a dog for hunting, a bird for flying, a monkey for playing. Therefore we cannot blame nature. But the important thing is the first source from which the rudiments of piety and learning are derived, and also what sort of guide is the child given, especially in those very early years when his nature is still free from any defects and, like soft wax, is plastic and readily copies any and every habit found in his model.

And so I consider you, my excellent young men, to be blessed for many reasons. First of all, you have been born in this age of a wonderfully sound revival of true piety and good learning. When I was a boy there was much superstition in religion and young lads went through great agony at school, and almost everything they learned had to be unlearned. Secondly, yours has been the good fortune to have a father who believes that his sons will not be very well off if they can inherit his wealth and rank—for which he is well known among the Polish nobility—unless he has also enriched them with genuine blessings of the soul and made them cultured gentlemen. For he does not think he has met his obligations as a father unless, after being the father of your bodies, he also molds your souls; he realizes that this is the superior aspect and most highly prized possession of man. Being a deeply religious man, he is not educating you for himself but for Christ and the good of your country. The fact that he fathered you is a natural matter; the fact that he took care that you should receive the finest education from the very moment you left the lap of your nurses—that is due to his genuine piety.

TO MARTIN BUCER[1]

EE 2615 (381–460)   [Freiburg], March 2, 1532

I should like to have your answer to this question. When there are so many men whose words and thoughts about you are very damaging, and who slash you to pieces in print and are openly attempting to ruin you, then why is it that you are so upset if my writings touch you very lightly? Against men like Eck, Faber, Clichthove, Pius, and many others you people have not a word to say.[2] For me alone do you have teeth. Now Bucer, you play the wrong note much too often. Any remark that is made in general against the pseudo-evangelicals you either promptly apply to yourself or you think it refers to the whole group. And whenever a frank remark is made, you promptly feel you are hated the way Vatinius was. You desire that the Emperor be reconciled to you. But what was the desire of the person who represented the Emperor as a seven-headed monster? What was the desire of that newfangled historian?[3] When I told some men of your camp that I was afraid the Emperor in his annoyance might mistreat some communities, with a strange contempt they laughed at my words. But we saw what happened to the people of Zürich while the Emperor was asleep. As I have said, I hear no special complaints about your city [Strassburg]. At most other places all dissenters are considered hateful. But they owe it to those hateful persons that the rulers have not as yet invaded any community. Concerning Basel, new complaints are reported daily. You frequently use emphatic expressions and oaths in your attempt to prove your sincerity to us.

1. On Martin Bucer, see Letter 1901, p. 209. In the present letter Erasmus reprimands the followers of the "new faith" both for assailing him so vehemently and also for not exhibiting any improvement in life, the most important evidence of religion. A vivid picture of the Reformation tumult and confusion appears.
2. The men mentioned—Johann Eck, Faber Stapulensis (Jacques Lefèvre), Clichthove, and Albertus Pius (Allen, VI, 200)—were Catholic theologians.
3. This may have been Sebastian Franck, who had published his *Chronica* at Strassburg the previous year.

What you should have employed was conduct worthy of the gospel and books savoring of the apostolic spirit. Whether Luther is doing this, you can judge for yourself. And yet, answering in the name of your whole faction, you say: "We desire the Emperor to be reconciled to us, not angered." I shall not mention how restrained was the conduct of certain members of your confession at Augsburg, or how respectfully they speak of the Emperor. What prince would want such a state of affairs in his realm as seems to be springing up in some communities, where those who refuse to reject their traditional religion are denied worship and the Eucharist, and where those who are convicted of having accepted that religion elsewhere are punished? Catholics cannot assemble in a church to hear a sermon or to make confession; in fact, the church doors are barred, and life in their own community is not much more pleasant for them than for Jews living in a Christian society. And what is even more difficult, they are forced by threats to join a communion form which they shrink (you will forgive me, but I am reporting what I have heard, and I have heard it many times and from many sources, from persons close to the scene). But on the other hand, in these same communities those who approve or pretend to approve the new teachings can do anything they please: they do not obey the law; they do not abide by contracts, either public or private. (To give you one out of several instances: they stoutly maintain that the treaty which the people of Basel concluded with the Swiss explicitly states that, in case any disturbance arises between the cantons of Switzerland, the people of Basel are to remain neutral and, in fact, to act as peacemakers. And yet it is public knowledge that they savagely rushed into war to lend aid to Zwingli.) In these same communities, also, priests are so treated that they freely choose exile; monks are driven out or assaulted, as is reported to have happened to the Carthusians at Basel. Promises made in contracts or official documents are not honored. One who has left town for religious reasons or out of fear cannot be a guest in his own home but is forced to go to a public inn. Monasteries are turned into barns and churches are deserted. The liberal arts and good learning are utterly dying out. I notice that scholars are being lured to join the sect, but I do not notice any one in this new sect who has a liberal education or is even interested in having one. Professorial titles are invented—but where are the students? Recently

I sent a servant to Basel. He heard a sermon in the cathedral. I asked him how many were there. He answered, "Three men and ten women." And not even these few people show any signs of genuine devotion. In general, those who give themselves over to this sect promptly conceive a fierce hatred for all who differ with them, which is not very good proof of the evangelical spirit.

To repeat what I have mentioned: I do not know of a single person who has improved as a result of this kind of gospel, that is to say, one who associates less often with prostitutes, who indulges less often in gluttony or gambling, who has become more tolerant of injury, less intent on vengeance, and less concerned with money. On the other hand, I know of several persons who have become worse. I am not passing judgment on people who are strangers to me. We merely hear the shouts: "The gospel, the gospel! The faith, the faith!" There is nothing that I pray for more than that this strange business may have a happy ending. But insofar as I can predict, basing my judgment on the initial signs, this thing is going to end up in the greatest disaster for Christendom, and not only in external matters but also in spiritual resources: What will this life be after the removal of liberal studies? And since now there is such apathy toward religion, what can we expect but paganism? And if the matter of piety in the individual communities depends upon the preacher, and if there is no one in charge of several communities; there is danger that we shall have as many sects as communities. Such a state of affairs would be utterly wretched. Even the rulers are afraid that they too may eventually suffer the same fate as has befallen bishops and abbots in several localities. And no little amount of ill will is gained for you by those who in their sinfulness or obtuseness hide under the protective name of the gospel. The preachers do not dare to give such men a tongue-lashing; they either baby them with coddling words or wink at their conduct. As a result, not even preachers are free, so long as they are afraid of being deserted by the people. Can there be any other good solution to this hazardous business except the rise of a schism? Unless perhaps you think the whole world is going to adopt your views. But I do not see how you people can have the face to expect that, since you disagree so much among yourselves.

TO BERNARD OF CLES[1]

EE 2651 (25–52)   Freiburg, May 19, 1532

I can hardly think of anything I could ask for from King Ferdinand over and above those gifts which his extraordinary goodness is freely granting me. Apart from my studies—and I enjoy almost killing myself over them—I am of no use for anything else in life. To give me a position of rank would be like piling up treasures on the back of an old worn-out nag, now that the course of my life is almost run. It would be just as absurd for a person to take on more luggage when his trip is finished. Only a little nourishment is needed for my frugality, which has always been pleasing to me and now is also necessary. Still, I would like a peaceful old age—if I am denied one that is cheerful and bright, such as I see is the fortune of many people. To ward off the feebleness of age and to restore one's health are not within the power either of the Pope or of the highest of rulers, the Emperor. Since I have the good will of both, I only wish they were at least able to shut up those who keep barking at me. But not even that is within their power.

In addition to those who openly hamper me at every turn, there are many others who are employing malicious trickery and underground methods to plot my ruin. I know there is much truth in what you in your devotedness recall for my consolation: that glory won by excellence has always been liable to envy and that this is not the only generation to produce and endure such disturbances caused by evil men. I remember how maliciously they railed at Jerome, but his extraordinary virtue either overwhelmed the envy or at least, by compensating for it, made it easy to endure. But what am I compared with men like that? If one's measure is learning and piety, I am not

1. Lived 1485–1539. An Italian statesman and ecclesiastical official, Bishop of Trent, cardinal, governor of Verona. In the context of a polite refusal of any favor from King Ferdinand of Austria, Erasmus bewails the various attacks he has had to endure.

worthy to wipe their shoes; but if it is the amount of ill will endured, then I am several miles ahead of them. Even so, I frankly admit that I owe it to the clemency of princes that I am still holding out against all these serpents.

There is nothing I could ask from King Ferdinand at present except that, no matter what tragedy is caused by my rivals, he continue to be as he always has been.

TO BONIFACE AMERBACH[1]

EE 2684 (8–12; 25–123)   Freiburg, July 6, 1532

You have lost your dear little daughter, and what is causing us even much more pain, dear friend, is that you all but died along with her, and the only cause of your illness was grief. I was late in learning of this deep affliction, and of course it was not from you that I heard it but from your doctor, who fortunately happened to come here. . . .

Since I understood very thoroughly the intensity of your feelings, I did readily expect you to feel a deep emotion; but because of the extraordinary constancy of your heart in other matters, which I knew well, I had no fears that you would fall ill and die along with her. You are a man distinguished in jurisprudence; you have won high praise for instructing others to obey the imperial law. Therefore, it would only be right that you should obey the law of nature with greater resignation. This law leads us if we are willing and drags us if we are unwilling. No matter how much your grief magnifies your loss, you surely cannot deny that it is reparable as long as you and your wife are sound of health; for you are both of an age that is still productive—in fact, you are both in the bloom, the prime of life. What if you had had a childless marriage? Since that is a common experience, a man of your foresight must have anticipated such a

1. On Amerbach see Letter 862, p. 130. In this warm and sensitive letter Erasmus reflects on the death of the daughter of his good friend Boniface Amerbach.

possibility. Any man who marries must prepare his mind for the eventualities that are common to mankind: sterility in his wife, childlessness, loneliness.

However, you are not childless now, since you have another daughter. And is it so terrible a thing that you have suffered? Have you not added a very brilliant star to the choirs of heavenly virgins? She is happy; she is leaping and dancing because she has been welcomed into eternal joy before she was ever stained by the woes of this unhappy life. But you are weeping inconsolably; indeed, you are not weeping but dying along with her. Only a sprig or tiny blossom has been plucked from the tree, but the stalk is still sound and the roots are healthy. Suppose God wanted to test you by this loss, to show you how much you depend upon Him. Suppose He replaces this daughter with a son who will inherit not only your fortune but also your precise learning along with every kind of virtue. For this is the kind of wealth that makes you far more blessed, my dear Boniface, than all your estates or money, although you are well supplied with these advantages of fortune too, which you have inherited, and they are enough not only to make you independent but they also add to your distinction. . . .

Therefore, if you patiently bear this little wound which the Lord has sent you to test your faith, I am confident that He, generous as He is, will compensate you for the loss of your baby girl with a fine boy, a boy who can succeed as heir to your full estate, which in its wealth far surpasses the riches of Croesus, a boy who will be for us the perfect image of you and who will prevent you from growing old or being forgotten. This prospect should have buoyed up your spirits, most learned sir, and you ought not to have kept your eyes fixed on what you have lost, if indeed one loses those who precede us to heaven. You should have reflected on the possibility you still have of being the father of many children. Suppose you had no children. Shall we call God to judgment for not giving what he did not promise to one who enters upon marriage? Suppose you had many fine children who were soon snatched away—what just complaint could we make against God? What He gave is a pure gift. In demanding back this gift when He so willed, He acted with full right. For He did not intend it to be a permanent gift, but only a loan.

In England I knew the mother of John Colet, a woman of rare

piety. She had by the same husband eleven sons and eleven daughters. She lost that whole family of children except for one, Colet, who was the oldest. She also lost her aged husband when she was well along in years. For she was approaching her ninetieth year, and she still looked fresh and young and full of gaity. One would judge that she had never been in mourning, never had borne any children. Eventually, if I am not mistaken, she outlived even Colet. It was not book learning but devotion to God that furnished this woman with such strength of soul. And you, a man with all your education, with your foresight and presence of mind in other matters, are you going to kill yourself over the death of a baby girl? Since we are all subject to this law by nature of our birth, and since such misfortunes meet the eye everywhere no matter where one looks, then tell me, what sort of foresight is it, when something happens that is a part of our human condition, For a man to lose all his spirit as if that were something unexpected and unnatural? Even in other matters the ancients thought it shameful to say, "I never expected it." But it would be utterly senseless in this situation to say, "I did not expect it." That would be like saying, "I did not suspect I was a human being."

I know you will say that I am late in offering you my consolation, and in fact that instead of consoling I am scolding. As to the first charge, my dear Boniface, you should blame yourself for that, for you did not want me to know your personal tragedy. As for the second, perhaps it will succeed in making you better prepared to face human misfortunes in the future. Terence's Micio expresses his amazement that anyone could so set his heart upon anything that it becomes dearer to him than he is to himself. Indeed, to be affectionate is a sign of a humane and gentle spirit. . . . But you, though without worry as to peril to yourself, and strong in the face of any mischief that could strike you, are still crushed by an illness that affected someone else; I am afraid that you will kill yourself over it. And yet what will you gain by it? Can she be recalled to life by tears? If God should demand you of yourself, either I do not know you at all or you would calmly obey. He demanded back a baby girl, and are you going to waste away with grief? You do not realize how many persons you would bereave just by your own death—God forbid that that should happen! There would be your wife, daughter, brother, sister, father-in-law, and those of us who are your friends—all completely of one mind with you and in jeopardy along with you.

Finally, you would be robbing your native land of a lovely treasure. For you are its support as much as you are its ornament, and are deservedly worth many men in its eyes. If you own welfare means little to you, at least a regard for these persons ought to inspire you with a concern for your health. Nobody could give you better consolation or better advice than you yourself, if you would apply it to yourself and tell yourself the same things you would say to someone else in a similar situation. Now please apply to yourself the words, not of that extremely affectionate person, but of that noble and sensitive philosopher whom I have always admired in you. The wise men of ancient times were right in their warning that one should not be enchanted by anything in human affairs—that is, one should not love anything excessively lest, if he lost it, immoderate grief would result. . . . Besides, God sometimes takes away something we have for the very reason that we are excessive in our love for it and imagine that it belongs to us as a permanent possession, when it was only a loan and lent to us for an uncertain period of time. As a result, the lender is free to demand back something He has just given. One might say that there is in human affairs and also in this event a kind of Nemesis.

TO THOMAS DE VIO[1]

EE 2690 (11–55)   Freiburg, July 23, 1532

What you urge I have already done in great part of my own volition.[2] I have marked and corrected several passages in which there was clearly a mistake, either my own or that of the printers. As to the moderation for which you plead, that I have exhibited to the

1. Better known as Cajetan (ca. 1470–1534), who was superior general of the Dominican order, cardinal, eminent Thomist theologian. See J. F. Groner, *Kardinal Cajetan* (Fribourg, 1951). Erasmus defends himself in this letter against the charges brought forth against his writings, including that of heresy.
2. Apparently Cajetan had asked Erasmus to revise his books.

satisfaction of all men by my response to the pronouncements of the theologians at Paris. These were recently published in the name of the entire faculty, though they were really the work of one restless fellow, whose conduct makes him scarcely tolerable to his own colleagues.[3] The name of Augustine is frequently dinned into my ears; yet I have been not a little more severe with my own work than Augustine was with his in what he calls a retraction rather than a recantation; it is really a review of all his works, so nothing would be forgotten. Although in passing he made some corrections of no great importance, he does defend certain positions, but not without some show of being evasive. I would not be reluctant to do the same with regard to all my writings, if only it be established which passages contain error or, on account of their proximity to error, could be the probable cause of offense. But what can I do with those passages which were misunderstood by my critics or distorted or maliciously twisted to give another meaning? Or with passages that referred to one person but were applied to another, or those that were intended to refer to another age but were applied to the present? There are many carping criticisms of this sort which certain persons keep yelping about, out of hatred or ill will or to gain fame. They pretend, it is true, to be zealous for the Catholic Church; still, their attack against me was never more deadly than at the time when I was putting up a vigorous battle in Germany with the sects which were then emerging. And certain individuals are so wrongheaded in their judgments that, were I to comply with them, I would have to delete from my writings things which men of learning and piety consider very good.

If I had just a grain of heresy in my heart, I would have long ago grown furious with the endless growling of those wretches and would have gone over to the camp of the heretics. The fact is, I have never attached a single disciple to myself, and any one I was able to tear away from that camp I surrendered to the Catholic Church, preferring that they be fellow disciples of the Church rather than my own. In the face of several persons I held my tongue; I was more moderate than anyone. But irrespective of the facts, though I had intended of my own volition to do what you recommend, I shall now

3. On Beda, see Letter 1581, p. 187.

do so with more alacrity, since I have the approval of an important personage for my undertaking. Contrary to your hopes, I shall never completely shut up the mouths of those who rail at me, at least not of those men whose conduct is the result of madness rather than thoughtful judgment. It would be more than enough for me if I could satisfy good men, and above all Christ.

I would like you to be convinced that your advice was most welcome, and I shall make you realize shortly that it was not offered in vain. I cannot complete this task by the time of the fall fair, but with Christ's blessing I shall have it done by next Easter. I have also decided to collect all those passages in my writings which openly attack the slanders and condemned teachings of certain individuals; then secondly, with regard to questionable passages I plan to explain or revise them so thoroughly that hereafter my works will not contain any abusive remarks directed at the name of any individual or order.

TO CHARLES UTENHOVE[1]

EE 2700 (35–72)   Freiburg, August 9, 1532

They think I am angry with St. Francis just because I have denounced those men who promise heaven to all who are buried in a Franciscan habit. Recently St. Francis appeared to me in a dream after midnight; his face was calm and friendly. He thanked me for having publicly announced the correction of those passages which he personally had always detested and he counted me as one of the friends of the order. He was not dressed in the manner in which he is represented today. The robe he wore was made of wool, but not in a variety of colors; it was dusky, as wool is when it is shorn and not yet dyed. He did not have a peaked cowl, but instead a kind of cap attached to the back of his robe, which could be pulled over his head in case of a heavy rain. We see the same sort of thing worn by some

1. Son of a councillor of Charles V. He had met Erasmus at Basel in 1528. Some of the latter's most bitter opponents came from the ranks of the Franciscan order; it is interesting, therefore, to read his comparison between the founder of the order and his subsequent followers.

Irishmen today. His cincture was not skillfully knotted; it was a plain
cord in simple peasant style. His robe did not flow all the way down
to the ground; it was nine inches or more above his ankles. He did
not wear sandals, but was completely barefoot. I could not see a
single trace of the five stigmata seen in pictures. As he walked off, he
stretched out his right hand toward me and said: "Keep fighting
valiantly; soon you will be one of mine."

I do not think there is need to trouble oneself about the type of
habit, as long as Franciscans resemble their Father in those virtues
which he considered basic to the perfection of his order. They call
them the six seraphic wings. The first is perfect obedience; the
second, evangelical poverty; the third, spotless chastity; the fourth,
deep humility; the fifth, a peace-loving simplicity; and the sixth,
seraphic charity. If only they would all carry these virtues around
with them in their hearts as they do in their pockets.[2] In that case,
men of intelligence and not just weak little females would embrace
them as angels of peace. How rare it is to find one who teaches
simply the evangelical philosophy. But what a throng of them you
can find strolling through the courts of princes and the homes of the
rich. They do no teaching; their morals are such that no dwelling
they visit is made any purer by their presence. The prudent reader
will understand what I am here leaving unsaid and stating all the
more clearly by leaving it unsaid. I wish those men would not
commit any crime that had to be covered over in silence. They show
you a bond signed by a Friar Leopold or a Friar Bernardine, and no
one knows if such a man even exists. They think it more than
sufficient just to be regarded as good men. On a long trip they will
beg for money, but any contribution is received in a handkerchief;
they will not touch money with their bare skin. Could any intelligent
person not laugh at such a sight?

2. This refers undoubtedly to the pecuniary preoccupation of the Franciscans.

TO QUIRINUS TALESIUS[1]

EE 2735 (1–17)   Freiburg, October 31, 1532

I am extraordinarily delighted, my dear Quirinus, that you have found a wife who suits your taste. That is a good omen. You seem to me to be all the luckier in that, as the epigrammatic poet says, you wish to be exactly what you are. I do pray for this: since you have found Juno favorable to you, may Ilythia also be favorable too.[2] You need have no regret at marrying a widow. That is the preference of men who marry a woman who can do the work of the house rather than for reasons of pleasure. Those who look around for a work horse want a horse that is broken in, not a wild one. And if she had children by her first husband, you won't be burdened with the worry of having married a barren woman. Thomas More has often told me that even if he married a hundred wives he would not marry a young maiden. At present he has a little old woman who is altogether too durable.[3] Had she departed this life, he could have been the husband of a very wealthy and noble lady. There is this disadvantage though; you can never become a bishop unless you first become a monk. Levinus too has gotten a wife; however, he scorned the advice of friends to his own unhappiness. That was done with more passion than reason.

1. Talesius (1505–1573), from Holland, was Erasmus' servant and at the same time his pupil. In later years he was mayor of Haarlem. This is a letter of congratulation on his being married.
2. Ilythia, a Greek goddess identified with childbirth!
3. His second wife, Alice Middleton. Thirteen years have passed since Erasmus wrote Letter 999, p. 142.

TO JOHN FABER[1]

EE 2750 (1–108)   [Freiburg, end of 1532]

With what speed the rumor has flown all the way to your country
that the distinguished Sir Thomas More has been removed from the
office of chancellor and succeeded by another nobleman, who immediately released those who had been imprisoned by More for their
contentious teachings. Both Homer and Vergil represent "rumor" as a
bird flying aloft, covered with feathery wings, to indicate that it is the
swiftest thing in all creation. But any speed possessed by a winged
creature seems to me slow and sluggish compared with the swiftness
with which this rumor has quickly spread over all the world. It was
almost like the speed of lightning when it flashes into every quarter
of the globe. Although this story is being buzzed abroad and is
everywhere the topic of the day, and though I have not received any
letter from Britain (Thomas More's letter which I am forwarding to
you was held up several months in Saxony), still I was absolutely
certain that this was just pure gossip. I have known very well the
character of this most humane ruler and the constancy with which he
cherishes friends once he decides to take them to his heart and the
reluctance with which he removes anyone from his favor, even when
he detects some human error in them. Also I have known very well
Thomas More's sincerity, his skill in handling both important and
unimportant matters, and his extraordinarily prudent vigilance,
which never indulges in secret conniving. In fact, to my way of
thinking, the king's benevolent attitude toward More was made more
obvious when he released him from an office that was most honorable, but also burdensome and perilous, than when he conferred that
high position upon him. When the king, in spite of More's protests,
piled this heavy load upon his back, he showed that he loved

---

1. John Faber, or Heigerlin (1478–1541), an Austrian humanist and
churchman, was later Bishop of Vienna. In this letter Erasmus summarizes the
achievements of Sir Thomas More as an officer of state. The occasion was
More's "retirement" from the office of chancellor.

his country and was consulting his own best interests and those of his realm; when, at More's request, he removed that load, he showed his love for More. In the former instance, he merited praise and universal acclaim for his loyalty and farsightedness in entrusting a most difficult post to the man best qualified in the realm for bearing so heavy a burden. In the latter instance, he gained high praise for his humanity, because, on his own decision and out of regard for the common good, he yielded to the request of a friend who was asking for the kind of leisurely retirement which Cassiodorus once obtained from his ruler. And I have no doubt that More had very solid reasons for pleading with the king to grant him that release. Otherwise, he would never have been so presumptuous as to ask for a discharge so soon, nor would the king have been so compliant as to grant his request for any excuse whatsoever.

The king realized full well that the condition of his entire domain depended in great part upon the integrity, the learning, and the wisdom of the chancellor. In England, the position of chancellor is not, as it is in some countries, merely that of a secretary. In dignity it ranks next to the crown. For that reason, when the chancellor appears in public, there is borne on his right a golden scepter mounted by a golden imperial crown, and on his left a book. The one symbolizes supreme power under the king, the other, knowledge of the law. For he is chief justice of the whole British dominion, and he is, so to speak, the right eye and right hand of the king and of the royal council. A very prudent ruler would never entrust such a lofty responsibility to one who had not been tested. Hardly anyone else had a deeper insight into or a warmer appreciation for the rare and almost divine endowments of More's nature. In fact, even the Cardinal of York,[2] no matter what his own misfortune, was no fool; and when he realized that he himself had no hope of returning to his former power, he declared that there was no man in all that island who was equal to this heavy duty except More. And this vote for More was not the result of favor or good will. For all through the cardinal's life, he was hardly fair to More; he feared rather than loved him. And the judgment of the people was no different. And so he entered upon his office with the warmest congratulations of all the

2. Cardinal Wolsey.

realm, such as no man had ever received before him; and when he resigned, it was with the deep sorrow of all wise and good men. For he resigned after earning the most wonderful praise: that no predecessor had administered that office with more skill or with greater justice. And you know how hypercritical the people usually are of the conduct of the top civil officials, especially during their first years. However, I could easily convince you of what I am saying by producing letters from the most eminent men who extended their congratulations with unbounded enthusiasm to the king, to the realm, to More himself, and even to me when More accepted that high office; and then I could show you letters written later by those same men deploring the fact that the state had lost such a justice and, to use the Homeric word, such a counselor.

I have no doubt but that the king has replaced More by some distinguished person. However, he is an utter stranger to me. As far as family rank was concerned, Thomas More, having a philosophical cast of mind, never had any ambitions, nor did he boast of it. He was born in London, and among the English to be born and educated in that most famous of all cities is regarded as bestowing some nobility upon a person. His father was by no means unknown; he was a doctor of British law, and in England this profession possesses very high distinction; it is said that a large part of the gentry of that island come from that profession. Young More followed in his father's footsteps, and though the father was highly illustrious in his own right, still his son overshadowed him. However, one who overshadows in this fashion, truly casts a favorable light upon his forefathers.

I shall pass over the titles of honor with which each man was decorated; they were due not to favor that was solicited or bought, but to the free decision of the king—unless perhaps we think that true nobility is won only by repeated exploits in war, whereas no honor is due to one who has rendered distinguished service to the government during times of peace through wise decisions rather than by weapons of war. The more military preparedness a state has, the less it needs the use of arms. But kings and kingdoms always, in times of war as well as in times of peace, need the services of men who are eminent for learning, good judgment, and jurisprudence. We hear the words of Sacred Scripture: "By me monarchs rule." However, that is the voice, not of the military, but of wisdom which is responsible for preventing war, and when war cannot be avoided wisdom sees to it that it brings the least possible damage to the commonwealth. It is a greater blessing to avoid war than to carry it on bravely. Peace cannot long endure, or if it does, it engenders bad morals in men unless it be directed by the decisions of prudent men. . . . Will he not win fame who for many years has provided his native land with a just judge and a loyal counselor? The ancient emperors thought he should; they conferred the highest honors on their legal aids, who were eminent for their knowledge of the law. In fact, they even decreed that teachers of grammar and of logic, and professors of law who over the course of twenty years had given evidence of learning and integrity, should be decorated with the same honorary insignia as were the imperial deputy governors. . . . Today, however, men are recognized as nobles only if they are bluebloods, but not if they are given (I would not blame people for saying "sold") the insignia of nobility by the ruler. Rank can be conferred by the decree of a prince upon those who have served the state well. Therefore in my opinion there is a twofold nobility, since in this case the authority of the ruler acknowledges the presence of virtue, which is the parent of all true nobility. If one does not happen to come from an old noble family, then it is a more excellent thing to have merited nobility than to have received it from one's forefathers.

TO EUSTACE CHAPUYS[1]

EE 2798 (26–48)   Freiburg, April 23, 1533

I do not know what sort of picture you formed of me from my writings that caused you to develop such a strong affection, when I know that everything I am and do is less than mediocre. However, the less merit I can see in myself, the more indebted I feel to you for your regard for me. Over and above that, there is certainly nothing in Erasmus that you could consider worth looking at. You would see not

1. This man (d. 1556) was the imperial ambassador to England between 1529 and 1544. A brief self-assessment by Erasmus.

a human being but a mass of wrinkled skin, and one who is utterly wretched, unless we could convince ourselves that once this hide is sloughed off there will emerge a fresh creature with the gleam of youth. Evidently you also realize the waves that toss me about and the winds that buffet me. But a harbor is coming into sight, not far away, which with Christ's blessing will put an end to all my woes. I have a bad name; I am being slashed to pieces by tongues and most of all by those men for whom I have done the greatest service. One might say that is my bad luck. And yet the publishers say that no one else's name is quite so much in demand. I might suspect them of flattery except that they are constantly begging me for material, and if nothing else at least a brief preface.

To give you another instance of what I mean, the world today is overrun by vagabonds, men who have simply left their communities or have fled for some reason. Since these fellows are about as destitute as an empty pea pod, they have to resort to various tricks to acquire money for food and travel; the belly, you know, is remarkably inventive. Some of them know my friends from my writings. So they go to them and pass themselves off for servants and students of mine, even though they have never seen me. By this deceptive means they swindle them out of huge sums of money. And when they become afraid that their deception will be discovered, they move on to other pastures. I thought you should know about this so that you would not trust anyone unless he is explicitly recommended in a letter from me.

TO VIGLIUS ZUICHEMUS[1]

EE 2810 (12–25)   [Freiburg], May 14, 1533

I am grieved that the situation in England is advancing toward serious trouble. And affairs are not much more tranquil among the Dutch. The Pope has told the king of England that he is to

1. Wigle ab Aytta (1507–1577) of Zwichem (Friesland), a distinguished jurist and statesman in the Netherlands, was a filial friend of Erasmus, who at one time designated him his heir. The letter is Erasmus' assessment of the political situation in the spring of 1533, noting especially the English state of affairs with respect to the "divorce" of Henry VIII.

continue living in marriage with the queen until a pronouncement has been made on the case in Rome. But everybody understands that this dispute will never be settled during the lifetime of the spouses. It is eight years now that this matter has been discussed, and the king, not without reason, feels a heavy weight on his conscience. Two hundred doctors have proved from Scripture and reasoning that the first marriage could not have been contracted according to either human or divine law. But if the Pope declares it was not a valid marriage he will, first of all, offend the Emperor and secondly will condemn the Roman See, which granted an unlawful dispensation. Such cases, which contribute a considerable amount of money to Rome and cause our ecclesiastical princes to become servile, usually drag on and on. Perhaps there is some other passion burning in the heart of the king, which he does not want to have published.

TO JOHN VLATTEN[1]

EE 2845 (1–38)   Freiburg, July 25, 1533

It is very difficult, when human affairs are so utterly confused, to give effective advice, and for me it is not at all safe to do so. If I were to give any impulse to a reform movement, superstitious theologians, who have now been stirring up riots in Paris, would immediately scream that Erasmus is the father of a new sect to be called "the Moderates." However, if that advice of mine turned out to be effective, the credit should go to the skill of an excellent ruler rather than to my prudence. I do not reject the generous offer of the ruler, although I have done nothing to deserve it. He will not have to bear the burden of paying the pension for a very long time, for this caterpillar is planning to become a butterfly.

As to the Lord's Prayer, there is no controversy. Even Luther has written about it with pious affection. . . . I have made a careful explanation of the Apostles' Creed and of the Ten Commandments.

1. A humanist and statesman mainly in the service of the Duke of Cleves (d. 1562). The letter is a brief summary of continuing phases of the controversy of the Reformation.

The book came out at the spring fair. I shall send you a copy by this
carrier if I can get one; I do not have any left here. Jerome said he
sold every single copy at Frankfurt within three hours.

I have read the ordinance of the Duke.[2] If only the people would
choose to follow his godly warnings rather than pay attention to
vagabonds, who are interested only in their own advancement, not in
that of Jesus Christ, and who desire security and power at the expense of the people.

How many opinions have arisen concerning the sacrament of the
Eucharist? Some fellow recently at Frankfurt began to spread abroad
a new teaching, one that would completely do away with the sacrament. However, as I am told, he was thrown into prison; he deserves
a worse punishment. That sacrament, the unique delight of pious
hearts, has been altered almost to the point of revulsion by the ridiculous opinions of sinister characters. If they have doubts about it, as
they obviously do, how much more beneficial it would be to per-
servere in what the Catholic Church has handed down to us and
what the practice of many, many centuries has approved. I am
working just now on a pamphlet entitled *The Harmony of the
Church Against Schisms and Heresies*,[3] which will appear in time
for the next book fair. I have been feeling very feeble all summer
long; my strength has not yet returned. My prayer is that Christ may
graciously deign to assist the excellent Duke in his pious project, and
I hope that I may help it as much as I desire to. The first concern
should be to impose silence or a curb upon seditious preachers. When
that is done, any valid complaints made by the people can be corrected gradually and without rioting.

2. The reference is to the Church Order of Duke John of Cleves, promulgated in 1532. Erasmus was consulted. See O. R. Redlich, *Jülich-Bergische
Kirchenpolitik* (Bonn, 1907), which reprints the Church Order. In Protestant
territories the ruler assumed the right to order, by statute, the external affairs of
the Church.
3. The work is the *Liber de Sarcienda Ecclesiae concordia*, ("Book Concerning the Restoration of Concord in the Church").

TO DAMIAN A GOES[1]

EE 2846 (39–76)   Freiburg, July 25, 1533

You mentioned in your letter that the story has been bandied about Louvain that I am on the side of those who approve the King's divorce [Henry VIII of England]. And you ask what response should be given to those who are saying that. What other reply could you make, excellent Damian, except to quote the Psalm: "Their teeth are spears and arrows; their tongue a sharp sword"? I am certain you did not hear the story from any serious-minded person but from some gossip, some wild loudmouthed babbler. Today the world is crawling with that pestilential type of individual. Nobody has ever heard me utter a single syllable in approval or disapproval of this act. I have said openly and frankly that I felt extremely disturbed that a ruler who was otherwise most fortunate should have become entangled in this labyrinth. It has always been my desire that he and the Emperor be in perfect harmony, because I realized that this was of utmost importance for universal peace. It would have been not merely thoughtless but idiotic on my part to volunteer a pronouncement on so difficult a matter when all the learned English bishops and even the apostolic legate, Lorenzo Campeggio, an expert in both civil and canon law, were reluctant to express their opinion. With good reason do I love the King, since I have always found him kindly and gracious. Yet ever since this business began the only kindness I have received from him has been his good will. As for his wife, there are many reasons why I have loved her and still love her, and in this I believe I am in the company of all good men; I do not think the King has any personal hatred for her. As for my ruler, the Emperor, of

1. This correspondent (1501–1574) was a distinguished official in the service of the Portuguese king and a humanist scholar in his own right. See E. F. Hirsch, "Damiao de Gois," *Internat. Archives of the History of Ideas* 19 (1967).

In this letter Erasmus comments on a concrete political situation—the "divorce" of Henry VIII of England—and in particular refutes the charge that he approved of it.

whom I am a sworn counselor, he has done distinguished service to me and to my scholarly work, and if I should refuse to admit that I am completely indebted to him, I would be either extremely stupid or extraordinarily ungrateful. Therefore, how could I be so perverse as to involve myself freely in such an odious business, when if I had been asked or pressed to do so I would have resisted tooth and nail?

No prince has sought my opinion of this subject, although two years ago two nobles from the Emperor's court visited me. We had one or two conferences in which they urged me to express my views on the case. I answered—and it was the truth—that I had never given my attention to this question, which I realized had been for many years the subject of debate among the most outstanding men of influence and learning. I added that it would be a very easy thing to declare what I personally would like to see, but to make a pronouncement on what divine and human law permit or forbid would require a lengthy study and also an acquaintance with the circumstances of the case. The two nobles openly admitted to me that they were in no way acting on mandate from the Emperor; they then left.

TO JUSTUS DECIUS[1]

EE 2874 (48–71)   Freiburg, November 1, 1533

To get back to my eulogizers. Their cunning tricks might remain concealed, except that some of these fellows are extremely brazen in their attempts to fleece my friends. They extort great sums of money from the wealthy and from princes with the intention of putting me under obligation and forcing me to express my thanks in the name of men whom I either do not know, or else know that they are good-for-nothing. There have been many such incidents. Some ten years ago in Basel a young fellow was arrested in a fight because, when ordered to stop, he refused to sheath his sword. In Basel this is an offense,

1. Justus Ludovicus Decius (*ca.* 1484–1545) of Alsace, a supporter of Erasmus, was in the service of the Polish court. In this letter Erasmus reports an insignificant incident that nevertheless tellingly reflects his personal experience.

though not a capital one. He was jailed. I didn't even know the man by sight. I guess he once worked in the printshop. Some friends urged me strongly to request pardon for him by interceding with the legate of the king of England,[2] who happened to be in town at the time and was a man of sterling character. On the previous day the ambassador had come to pay his respects to me because he had heard that my health was not at all strong for the work I was engaged in. The urgent demands of my friends prevailed, and I was induced for the sake of that worthless clown to go out to visit the king's representative—while I represented that damned fool. In the evening I met with the legate, who was extremely busy, and briefly explained the case. The next day the belligerent fellow was released. The city council thought that this act of kindness should cost me a considerable amount: I had to voice my gratitude for this favor in a very carefully worded speech. How did that fellow, once he was freed, express his thanks to me? On the very same day he was released, he went to the printer's house, got drunk, and flew into such a wild rage against Erasmus that he bared his sword and threatened to kill me if I were there. The next day, when asked if he really meant what he had said, he pleaded intoxication.

TO THOMAS BOLEYN, EARL OF WILTSHIRE[1]

EE 2884   Freiburg, December 1, 1533

You are inviting me to the very colophon of Christian philosophy, most distinguished sir (though more distinguished for your pursuit of piety than for the trappings of fortune), when you encourage me to add to my previous work just a brief explanation of how each person should prepare for death. For this is the last act of human life—as of

2. Probably Richard Pace. See Allen, X, 310.
1. *Ca.* 1477–1539. English courtier and father of Ann Boleyn. The letter forms the preface to Erasmus' De preparatione ad mortem ("On the Preparation for Dying"), published at Basel the following year. He comments on the Christian view of death. (This was some three years before the imprisonment, trial, and execution of the recipient's daughter.)

a play—and upon it depends the eternal happiness of a man or his eternal destruction. This is the final conflict with the enemy; after it the soldier of Christ can look forward to everlasting triumph if he conquers or everlasting disgrace if he is defeated. I had been for some time now quite taken up with this subject when your words of encouragement acted as a spur to me, though I was already running. Still, at that time I was philosophizing all to myself. But your piety desires that the fruit of this work should through our efforts be shared among many others. May the graciousness of the Lord grant to your very holy wishes and to my endeavors a happy result. At any rate, I shall not oppose the will of Him who, I think, inspired you to request this service of me.

TO PETER AND CHRISTOPHER MEXIA[1]

EE 2892 (27–63; 91–101; 128–147) Freiburg, December 24, 1533

I am still holding fast to my earlier position whereby I maintained that it was more advisable to follow the example of that well-known Delayer who preferred to triumph by refraining from action rather than by engaging in battle.[2] This is especially so since it is neither a single combat where one man is pitted against another nor an affair of one man dealing with two opponents (though we read that Hercules avowed that he was no match for two men); rather, it is a case of a single individual having to oppose an endless throng of spiders and wasps, countless battalions of frogs and magpies, heaps of grasshoppers, and swarms of starlings and jackdaws. And even if these creatures did not have stings and beaks and claws, they could with their chattering alone drive a man out of his mind, no matter how imperturbable he was. How often have I challenged their obvious brazen slanders? And yet, as if nothing had happened, they keep chirping the same old lies about me right up to the present

1. Of these brothers (see Letter 2299, p. 237), the former was the author of several histories including one of Charles V. This letter is an *apologia* from Erasmus' own pen for his religious writing.
2. The reference is to Vergil, Aeneid. 6, 846.

moment, even in print: Erasmus considers confession an arbitrary matter, he condemns all ceremonies, he mocks the cult of saints and the rites of the Catholic Church, he rejects the fasting of Christians, he condemns abstinence in the matter of food, he relaxes priestly celibacy, he destroys monastic vows and observances, he condemns human regulations. In short, he paved the way for Luther. And those who feign modesty to make their slanders the more believable declare that I am a good man and that I had no intention in writing these things of causing all this turmoil. They even praise me highly for a radical change of viewpoint in my present writings.

Why, this is the black juice of the cuttlefish, this is sheer venom! They can use that kind of color to protect other men. I do not want that sort of defense. I have frankly admitted in the past and I say again that if I had known beforehand that such an age as this would arise, I would not have written many things, or would have expressed them differently; also some things which I did I would not have done. A man with foresight, they say, can divine the future; yes, but not the whole future. I do admit that I have been, to some degree, simple-minded and thoughtless. But all that stuff they keep yelping about cannot be found in my writings, except of course by a malicious interpreter. And in my *Declarations,* which my enemies consider to be a recantation under a polite title, there is nothing that differs from the views I held when I first wrote those things or from the manner in which I then expressed them.[3] Again, I except the spiteful reader, for whom nothing can ever be voiced with sufficient caution. I intended my annotations or commentaries for an audience of scholarly and virtuous men. I did not look upon myself as writing out legal bonds or bank notes. . . .

I admit that I have been guilty of many defects. However, if I clearly understand what envy is, I must say that, thanks be to Christ, I have never felt myself attacked by that passion. I think a person is envious when he burns at the happiness of another person, even though that happiness is not causing him any personal inconvenience. But if a person feels sad that an enemy is being elevated to a post of honor because that enemy will then be in a better position to hurt him, that is fear rather than envy. Now, I have even felt happy

---

3. *Declarationes ad censuras Lutetiae Vulgatas* (Basel, 1532).

when a former mortal enemy of mine was raised to some very high office[4] because, as often happens, the attainment of a post of honor puts an end to strife, either because that person now condemns his opponent or because he is too busy to fight. . . .

Amid all the din of contention and abusive language, I can readily find consolation in those words of St. Paul: "The Lord chastises those he loves and punishes all those that he acknowledges as his sons."[5] I am happy to apply to myself that truly Christian saying of St. Augustine: "Lord, here cut, here burn, but spare me in eternity."[6] It is something great to become an image of Christ even in this manner. He, in His lifetime, though a Lamb purer than purity itself, had to hear many charges from the lips of the Pharisees: drunkard, impostor, possessed by the devil, blasphemer. And think of all the mockery He had to suffer: the soldiers spat on Him, they struck Him with a reed, they crowned Him with thorns, they hit Him with their fists and they slapped Him. Then why should I, who deserve worse punishment, object to being whipped and spat upon and struck by the abusive language of insolent men and, by means of this merciful remedy, being cleansed? Moreover, my soul is consoled by that statement made by holy men and approved by equally holy men: The judgments of God are very different from the judgments of men. Now, if those fellows are firmly determined not to rest until they have driven me to the cross, then I shall pray to the Lord to grant me patience, and to them a better mind. Meantime, I have decided not to engage in any more hostilities with such creatures, nor to have any close relationship with them. Otherwise, I desire to enjoy the peace of Christ with all men. And I shall endeavor to attain that goal, at least insofar as I can. I hope that such too will be the disposition of all those who are battling on my behalf.

4. Perhaps Girolamo Aleander.
5. Hebrews 12:6.
6. I have been unable to trace this reference.

TO POPE PAUL III[1]

EE 2988 (51–91)   Freiburg, January 23, 1535

Far be it from me to be so blindly rash as to attempt to give advice to you whose wisdom provides for the whole world. Nonetheless, just as even an experienced captain of a ship, when caught in a violent storm, will accept advice from anybody, so too your outstanding humanity will accept in good part this solicitude of ours. One point above all, I think, will have no little influence on settling this business: if the Supreme Pontiff, the universal father of all rulers and nations, will not attach himself exclusively to any one faction but will be impartial toward all; for every person who is most devoted to a true spirit of religion will be most in favor of unity. In this manner the Pope will preserve his authority intact before all men and will stir up less ill will for himself. Secondly, rulers and princes should in harmony direct their efforts toward this goal. Although this is a duty which all men owe to Christ, the King of Kings, to whom they have all taken the same oath of allegiance, it is especially important for rulers and princes. For, unless this license is bridled, princes are in danger of eventually ceasing to be what they desire to be. It would be expedient to check whatever dissensions exist between men in power by declaring a six or seven years' truce. Meanwhile, these men must join forces and restrain those who continue to stir up rebellions and cause this mischief to become worse and to spread more and more. The definition of dogmas should be reserved for a council. However, I do not think it necessary for the council to pronounce on any and every opinion but only on those crucial points on which the Christian teaching hinges. There are some points to which the Apostle Paul wishes each person to assent according to his own understanding; and then there are some matters about which he writes: "If there is some

1. Paul III (1534–1549) is perhaps best known for his determined (and successful) effort to convene an ecumenical council at Trent. A very brief comment from Erasmus' pen on how the religious controversy might yet be resolved.

point on which you see things differently, God will make it clear to you."[2] Just as a variety of ceremonies does not disrupt the harmony of the Church, so too there are points of view on which it is possible to disagree and still preserve Christian peace intact. It would also be profitable if hope were held out to the leaders of the various sects that they could obtain any fair demand that they would make. Furthermore, since this pestilence seems fatal, it would be a profitable thing if, in accordance with the decision of the council, those who woke up and repented were promised an amnesty for past offenses. However, I think the most important point of all is that everybody should put aside his own private interests and keep in mind only this objective: the glory of Christ and the progress of the Christian religion. If that is done, God Himself will bless every action of those who seek the kingdom of God and His justice, and those very advantages which are the object of one's personal desires will be added to them, and in greater abundance. On the other hand, though this noisome infection has, unfortunately, spread much too far, we must not despair of a happy issue. The vast majority of men, especially of those who hold high office and are eminent for learning, are still untouched by the contagion; also, very many of those who had been infected by its foul breath have long since been weary of what they now have and long for what they leave behind.

TO CHRISTOPHER OF STADION[1]

EE 3036 (117–143)   Basel, August 6, 1535

As far as the outlook for this work is concerned, if it should fail to receive the approval of scholars, perhaps the result will be that someone more learned will feel challenged by this precedent and achieve what we tried to achieve, and instead of confusion will produce an absolutely perfect work. And, as a final outcome, the Lord will send a greater number of genuine laborers into his harvest.

2. Phil. 3:15.
1. Christopher of Stadion (1478–1543), from 1517 Bishop of Augsburg, shared belief in Erasmus' program of ecclesiastical reform. Erasmus reflects on the need for practical consequences of any thought or theory: a tree must bear fruit.

There is an amusing old proverb that says: Many men will spur on the oxen, but few will do the plowing. Similarly, you can easily get men who will address the people, but it will not be so easy to find one to dispense the Word of God sincerely, earnestly, and conscientiously. It is by God's gift that the sowing done by loyal ministers turns out well. The world, it seems, has for some time now been in travail to bring forth Christ; if He be truly fashioned in our souls, then by many signs the authentic roots of our hearts will reveal themselves. For the gospel is not just words, no more than a sacred grove is just firewood, as Horace observed. Whenever the seed of a productive word is received by good soil, it produces manifold fruit. And like a seed that thrusts forth fresh green blades, it reveals by various external signs the genuineness of the heart within: the people are more obedient to government officials, they adhere more to law, are more devoted to peace and more averse to war. Between married couples there is greater harmony, more thorough fidelity, and a deeper loathing for adultery. The husband becomes more gentle toward his wife, the wife more respectful toward her husband. Children submit to their parents with more reverence, slaves obey their masters more from the heart, and servants are more eager to lend a helping hand. Workers and employees are more faithful in performing their service. Businessmen do not do to another what they do not want done to themselves. In short, all men become more disposed toward good service, slower to seek revenge or to injure, less greedy, and more temperate. If these things are not evident in a person's behavior, but the opposite is the case, then there is danger that the good seed has not yet taken root in his heart.

TO BARTHOLOMEW LATOMUS[1]

EE 3048 (37–97)   Basel, August 24, 1535

If I should count the number of years, I have lived a long time. If I should calculate how much of that time I have spent wrestling with fevers, the stone, and gout, then I have not lived very long. But it is

---

1. *Ca.* 1498–1570, Greek and Latin scholar, professor at Paris, afterward counselor of the Archbishop of Trier.

right for us to bear patiently whatever the Lord sends us; for no one can oppose His will and He alone knows what is best for us.

You offer me words of comfort by speaking of my fame and the immortality which will be mine with future generations. That is the kindly service of a loving will. However, that glory means nothing to me, and I am not anxious about the applause of posterity. The only concern that is close to my heart is that I may leave this world with the blessing of Christ.

Several French nobles came here for refuge, fearing the wintry blasts. They have been recalled. "The lion roars," says the prophet, "and who can help being afraid?"[2] A similar terror, but for a different reason, has seized the hearts of the English. Some monks have suffered capital punishment, one of them a Bridgettine monk who was dragged on the hurdle, then hanged, and finally drawn and quartered. There is a persistent rumor here, probably true, that when the King discovered that the Bishop of Rochester[3] had been appointed to the college of cardinals by Paul III, he speedily had him led out of prison and beheaded. In this fashion did the King bestow upon him the red hat. It is all too true that Thomas More has been in prison for some time, and his money confiscated and forfeited to the royal treasury. There has also been a rumor that he was put to death, but I have no certain information on that. I wish he had never become involved in this perilous business and had left a theological matter to theologians. My other friends who occasionally used to honor me with letters and gifts are now too fearful to write or send anything; neither do they receive anything from anybody—as if under every stone lay a sleeping scorpion.

The Pope seems to be seriously planning a council. But I do not see how it can convene with all this dissension between rulers and regions. All of North Germany has been shockingly infected by the Anabaptists; in South Germany they are in hiding. They come pouring into this city in droves. Some are heading for Italy. The Emperor is laying siege to La Goulette.[4] In my opinion, there is more to fear from the Anabaptists. I do not think that France is completely free from that plague. But they keep their mouths shut there out of fear of being cudgeled. You know that Münster, the capital of

2. Amos 3:8.
3. John Fisher (see Letter 540).
4. In North Africa, part of Emperor Charles' campaign against the Turks.

Westphalia, has been captured. In the city of Amsterdam there is dangerous rioting. You are aware also, I think, that your fellow countryman, Viandalus,[5] died of the plague at Tournay. He was a truly learned man, married twice and the father of several children.

My work on preaching is appearing in print.[6] May it be with good omen! I must say, I have never found this subject pleasing. That's a witty remark you made about girls, that sometimes in having pleasure they receive what it will be very painful for them to give back, and you want me to have fun more often like that. But it also sometimes happens to girls that what they receive while having pleasure they have to get rid of by a miscarriage or die in the very act of delivery. I was afraid the latter would happen, but in fact it was the former. I have no intention of having that sort of fun again.

Now here is something about my situation for your amusement. With the encouragement of the distinguished theologian, Louis Ber,[7] I had written to Paul III. Before he opened my letter, he spoke of me in most honorific terms. And when he decided to admit some scholars to the rank of cardinal for the coming council, the name of Erasmus was among those proposed. But the following impediments were presented: my health, which would prevent me from discharging the duties, and my slender fortune. They say there is a decree of that venerable college which excludes from its ranks anyone whose annual income falls below three thousand ducats. And now they are trying to load me down with preferments so that I'll have the proper income to receive the red hat. As they say, a saffron court robe for a cat. I have a friend in Rome who is especially behind this. I have warned him in several letters, to no avail, that I am not interested at all in benefices or pensions, that I am just living from day to day, expecting death at any moment, at times even desiring it, so severe are my sufferings. It is hardly safe for me to put my foot outside my bedroom; and the most stupid small things upset me. This thin, fragile little body cannot stand a breeze unless it is soft and warm.

5. Melchior Viandalus, to whom in 1534 Erasmus dedicated his paraphrase on Psalm 3. See Allen, IV, 590.

6. The reference is to the *Ecclesiastae . . . sive de ratione concionandi* ["Ecclesiastes: On the Art of Preaching"] (Basel, 1535). Apparently Erasmus thought the witticism about girls an appropriate reflection on his attitude toward the work.

7. A humanist (1479–1554) who studied theology at the Sorbonne and was professor of theology at Basel, whence he moved to Freiburg in 1529.

TO PETER TOMICZKI[1]

EE 3049 (58–74; 160–164)   Basel, August 31, 1535

If the new year has restored you to your former vigor, then there is reason for us to give thanks to Christ. But as for myself, until May 15 it treated me most unkindly, so much so that out of weariness with being in almost constant pain I sought a change of climate (that is usually the last sacred resort of doctors when the patient's case is hopeless). I thought I might thereby find some relief from suffering, or at least by death reach the end of my troubles. I was brought to Basel in a covered carriage such as women use. I had enjoyed the hospitality of this renowned and attractive city for several years. In fact, a special room had been constructed for me to live in there, in hope of my return, a room that they knew would be convenient for me. . . . When I left this city some seven years earlier it was somewhat turbulent, but now I found it very calm and an orderly place to live. I am still hounded by the hostile judgments of men and by the minds of so many who are unjustly prone to suspect evil. Even so, I think that with my age and my experience and my learning, however little it be, I have reached a point where it is safe for me to live anywhere. . . .

What happened in England to the Bishop of Rochester and to Thomas More, the holiest and best pair of men England ever had, you will find out from a section of the letter which I am forwarding to you. In More I feel as if I had died myself; there was but one soul between us, as Pythagoras says. But such is the ebb and flow of human affairs.

1. *Ca.* 1465–1535. A Polish churchman and statesman, and vice-chancellor of Poland. The letter indicates Erasmus' far-reaching ties and is a brief summary of recent events.

TO GILBERT COGNATUS[1]

EE 3095 (22–34)   Basel, February 12, 1536

This winter has dealt meanly with me. Early in November it greeted me nastily with the first frost. I had not yet regained my strength when a violent windstorm put me flat on my back. And I had just begun to recover very nicely from that experience, with not a trace of pain left, no more running nose, and my stomach gradually getting stronger, when, of all things, so-and-so dropped in for a visit right after lunch. He kept me sitting at the fire for three hours as he argued about dogmas of the faith. The strain of listening to him, together with sitting close to the fire—both were very unhealthy for me—gave me a complete relapse. He was not going to call a halt until nightfall. But I interrupted him and bade him good-by. Soon after, I had a throbbing ache in the back of my head, a loud ringing in both ears, and an upset stomach. Now those terrible pains have gone, but I still stay in bed most of the time, except for three hours around lunchtime and again around dinnertime.

FROM JOHN HERWAGEN TO BEATUS RHEANUS[1]

EE 3135 (10–21)   Basel, July 17, 1536

I am sending you a copy of the works of L. Annaeus Seneca which we have printed. For lack of good manuscripts it is impossible to restore the text of Seneca to its original splendor. But though the text

1. This man (1506–1572) served Erasmus for three years as "famulus" or household servant. A few months before his death Erasmus comments on his frail physical state.
1. John Herwagen (ca. 1497 to ca. 1557) was a printer at Basel. Rhenanus (1485–1547) was a scholar and historian there. With this letter Herwagen informs his friend of the passing of the great humanist Erasmus. See G. Ritter, *Erasmus und der deutsche Humanistenkreis am Oberrhein* (Freiburg, 1937).

hobbles along, you can study it carefully enough to be able, with your keen judgment, to undo whatever monstrosities have crept in through our fault or were introduced earlier, and at the same time to consider whether any passages could be fashioned more elegantly and beautifully. . . .

The day after I reached Basel—I had arrived in the evening—Erasmus of Rotterdam exchanged life for death. It was July 11, close to twelve o'clock midnight. His death was due to various ailments, of which you know; the immediate cause was dysentery. The funeral was attended by every scholar, by one of the two mayors, and by a large number of members of the town council. The place selected for his burial in the cathedral had previously been consecrated to the Blessed Virgin. There a short eulogy was delivered by Myconius,[2] which reviewed briefly a large number of Erasmus' laudable achievements. Next Tuesday (the day chosen by the city government) according to our custom, his funeral celebration will be held. On August 23 with God's blessing, we shall sing the nuptial song in honor of our beloved Erasmus. You will, I hope, join us in honoring him.

2. Oswald Myconius (1488–1552) teacher and reformer in Basel.

The Life of Erasmus

BIBLIOGRAPHY

We begin with two historiographical studies that examine the image of Erasmus from the sixteenth to the eighteenth centuries. A. Flitner, *Erasmus im Urteil seiner Nachwelt. Das literarische Erasmus-Bild von Beatus Rhenanus bis zu Jean Le Clerc* (Tübingen, 1952), and W. Kaegi, "Erasmus im achtzehnten Jahrhundert," *Gedenkschrift zum 400. Todestage des Erasmus von Rotterdam* (Basel, 1936), 205–227. A brief survey of recent Erasmus literature is offered by E.-W. Kohls, *Die Theologie des Erasmus* (Basel, 1966), 1–18. The supplement volume (*Das Schrifttum der Jahre 1940–60*) of K. Schottenloher, *Bibliographie zur deutschen Geschichte im Zeitalter der Glaubensspaltung* (Stuttgart, 1962), lists recent publications.

Of biographical studies the most eminent is that of Johan Huizinga, *Erasmus of Rotterdam*, first published in 1924, now available under the title *Erasmus and the Age of the Reformation* (New York, 1957). Of equal stature is P. Smith, *Erasmus: A Study of His Life, Ideals, and Place in History* (New York, 1923, reprinted 1962). A competent, but brief sketch is M. M. Phillips, *Erasmus and the*

Northern Renaissance (New York, 1950). A recent biography is by R. H. Bainton, *Erasmus of Christendom* (New York, 1968). Of the studies of Erasmus' thought the following should be noted: W. Dilthey, *Gesammelte Schriften*. Band 2. (Stuttgart, 1957), 1 ff.; P. Wernle, *Die Renaissance des Christentums im 16. Jahrhundert* (Tübingen, 1904); A. Renaudet, *Érasme, sa pensée religieuse et son action d'après sa correspondence, 1518-1521* (Paris, 1921); W. Köhler, "Erasmus von Rotterdam als religiöse Persönlichkeit" in *Voordrachten gehouden ter herdenking van den sterfag van Erasmus* ('s-Gravenhage, 1936), 213 ff.; M. Bataillon, *Érasme et l'Espagne* (Paris, 1937); C. Augustijn, *Erasmus en de Reformatie* (Amsterdam, 1962); L. W. Spitz, *The Religious Rennaissance of the German Humanists* (Cambridge, 1963); A. Renaudet, *Études Érasmiennes (1521-1592)* (Paris, 1939); J. Lortz, "Erasmus-kirchengeschichtlich," in *Aus Theologie und Philosophie: Festschrift für Fritz Gillmann* (Düsseldorf, 1950), 271-326; K. H. Oelrich, *Der späte Erasmus und die Reformation* (Münster, 1961); A. Renaudet, *Érasme et l'Italie* (Geneva, 1954); L. Bouyer, *Autour d'Érasme: Études sur le Christianisme des humanistes catholiques* (Paris, 1955). The best over-all study of Erasmus' thought is that of E.-W. Kohls, noted above, but see the critical review in *Archiv f. Reformationsgesch.* 58 (1967), 250 ff.

Basic bibliographical tools for Erasmus studies are V. Haeghen's *Bibliotheca Erasmiana*, first published in 1893, now reprinted (Nieuwkoop, 1961) and the more recent J.-C. Margolin, *Douze Années de Bibliographie Érasmienne (1950-1961)* (Paris, 1963).

Of recent publications we note the reprint of the *Erasmi Opera Omnia* (London, 1962); W. K. Ferguson, ed., *Erasmi Opuscula* (The Hague, 1933); A. and H. Holborn, eds., *Desiderius Erasmus Roterodamus: Ausgewählte Werke* (München, 1933); C. R. Thompson, ed., *Inquisitio de Fide* (New Haven, 1950).

The following editions of Erasmus' letters may be noted: J. Förstemann and O. Günther, eds., *Briefe des Erasmus* (Leipzig, 1904); K. L. Enthoven, ed., *Briefe an Desiderius Erasmus von Rotterdam* (Strassburg, 1906); P. Smith, ed., *Luther's Correspondence and Other Contemporary Letters*, 2 vols. (Philadelphia, 1913-1918); W. Köhler, ed., *Erasmus von Rotterdam: Briefe*, Erweiterte Neuausgabe von A. Flitner (Bremen, 1956); D. F. S. Thomson, ed., *Erasmus and Cambridge: The Cambridge Letters of Erasmus* (Toronto, 1963); J. C. Olin, ed., *Christian Humanism and the Reformation: Desiderius Erasmus, Selected Writings* (New York, 1965).

Finally, of course, there are the *Opus Epistolarum*, P. S. Allen, H. M. Allen, and H. W. Gerrod, eds., 12 vols. (Oxford, 1906–1958) and *The Epistles of Erasmus*, F. M. Nichols, ed., 3 vols. (London, 1901–1918), as well as W. T. H. Jackson, *Essential Works of Erasmus* (New York, 1965). Of a comprehensive French translation of the letters, the first volume has appeared, M. Delcourt, ed.; *La Correspondence d'Érasme*. Vol. I: 1484–1514 (Bruxelles, 1967).

INDEX

70 71 72 73   12 11 10 9 8 7 6 5 4 3 2 1